PUBLICATIONS OF THE INSTITUTE OF HIGHER EDUCATION

Copies of these reports may be obtained from the
Bureau of Publications, Teachers College, Columbia University

LIBERAL EDUCATION

and

MUSIC

WILLIS J. WAGER

Professor of Humanities and
Chairman, Department of General Studies
School of Fine and Applied Arts
Boston University

AND

EARL J. McGRATH

Executive Officer
Institute of Higher Education

PUBLISHED FOR THE

INSTITUTE OF HIGHER EDUCATION

BY THE

BUREAU OF PUBLICATIONS

TEACHERS COLLEGE, COLUMBIA UNIVERSITY

FOREWORD

THIS MONOGRAPH IS ONE IN A SERIES, NOW NUMBERING FOURTEEN, WHICH report studies of certain aspects of professional education and of liberal education and their interrelationships. In particular this statement concerns undergraduate programs in the various fields of music. Dr. Willis Wager, Professor of Humanities of Boston University, did the research and made the institutional visits on which the findings are based. The interpretations of the material and recommendations for action by members of the profession and others concerned with higher education in music have also been Professor Wager's responsibility.

The Executive Officer of the Institute of Higher Education wishes to express his gratitude to the Carnegie Corporation of New York for providing the funds for this and the other companion inquiries. Too many persons supplied ideas and information helpful in the study to be identified and thanked individually, but the Institute also owes them a large debt of gratitude.

The criticisms and proposals contained in this document speak for themselves, but perhaps the observations of a sympathetic observer outside the field of music may lend some additional validity to the findings. Some members of the profession hold the view that no one except a professional musician can or should criticize education in this important branch of learning. The author of this foreword considers this opinion unrealistic and unduly self-protective. One who knows something of the theory and practice of music and who has for some years studied the varied facets of American higher education ought to be able to make critical comments on the current scene in music education, especially when these observations spring from a desire to strengthen and enhance the position of music in the entire structure of higher education.

To such a person the implications of this inquiry seem to be:

1. Considering schools of music as a group, the present requirements for various undergraduate degrees have not been clearly conceived. Some

other types of professional schools also exhibit ambiguities in their programs and a lack of sense of direction, but generally to a lesser extent than in music. The evidence suggests that each school of music ought to review its own purposes in the light of the status, current and potential, of music in American culture and the types of educational programs required to prepare young people for the various levels and branches of the profession. Instructional programs should then be designed realistically in terms of the types of students each school can hope to attract.

2. This local exercise ought to be paralleled by a more comprehensive study at the national level. The appropriate accrediting associations in the field of music might very well take the leadership in this effort. The membership of such a study group ought, however, to include others, such as professors who have no administrative responsibilities, state education authorities, and distinguished practicing musicians who have no connection with an educational institution. It ought to be possible, as indeed it was in earlier years, for the national leaders in music to devise a generally acceptable set of objectives for undergraduate programs. Thus a rational basis would be provided for determining what should or should not be included in the various divisions of the music curriculum.

3. The facts in this report reveal that with notable exceptions undergraduates in schools of music generally receive less instruction outside their own field than any other group of professional students. As Dr. Wager states, "The nonprofessional requirements in music schools are pitifully low." There are reasons for this situation, but they lose much of their validity in the light of the needs of contemporary life. The fact that some reputable schools of music find it possible to devote a considerable share of the undergraduate years to nonprofessional subjects without damage to their students' professional accomplishments ought to argue for a wider adoption of broader curricula. Under the requirements of the NASM as of 1962, individual schools will be able to reduce the nonprofessional subjects still further by placing in the nonprofessional area certain courses which are really instruction in music. Hence, unless the NASM delays the application of its new standards until this matter can be given further study, some students will be receiving an even narrower professional education than was hitherto possible.

4. It may well be that normally students in a four-year curriculum will not be able to master the broad range of knowledge and skills required for competence as a professional musician and for informed citizenship. The schools of music may have to face a choice already made by some other professional schools, that is, either to extend the undergraduate course to five years as schools of pharmacy have uniformly done; or to move a considerable portion of the present specialized subject matter into a graduate program as some engineering schools are doing. In any event

this report suggests that the whole question of what is necessary and desirable in an undergraduate degree program in music requires the most objective and serious appraisal.

5. Professional ethics would suggest that the accrediting associations in music ought to require approved institutions to meet the minimum standards set by these associations. At present some institutions patently fall below the nonprofessional requirements set by national accrediting bodies. This may be additional evidence that in undergraduate music curricula schools cannot accomplish all that may be ideally desirable. If so, the undergraduate program ought to be realistically adjusted by official action rather than by institutional deviations from the accepted standard.

The facts in this study suggest that the year 1962 will probably be another turning point in the history of the professional study of music in the United States. In the future will undergraduate curricula produce persons who possess not only initial professional competence, but also at least an elementary understanding of the other facets of contemporary life? This is the issue which now faces the members of the profession. The history of education in music reviewed in this inquiry reveals that though there have been periods of drift, there have also been times when the leaders in music have piloted their educational enterprise toward more secure moorings. This can be done again today if the national associations and the constituent schools of music seize the initiative at once and re-examine undergraduate courses of study in music with objectivity, with rigor, and with determination.

Professor Wager's analysis and recommendations provide the guide lines for much needed reconstruction for the profession of music.

EARL J. McGRATH
Executive Officer

CONTENTS

LIBERAL EDUCATION

AND MUSIC

In the footnotes, the abbreviation *PMTNA* has been used for the proceedings of the Music Teachers National Association, at one time published annually under the title *Studies in Musical Education, History, and Aesthetics, Papers and Proceedings of the Music Teachers' National Association*. The abbreviation *PMENC* has been used for the proceedings of the Music Educators National Conference (formerly the Music Supervisors National Conference), and *YMENC* for the yearbook of that organization. *NASM Bulletin* means, of course, *The Bulletin of the National Association of Schools of Music*. Also used in the footnotes is the abbreviation *MQ* for *The Musical Quarterly*.

Chapter 1

PROFESSIONAL EDUCATION FOR THE SECOND HALF OF THE TWENTIETH CENTURY*

THE EVENTS OF THE PAST SEVERAL YEARS HAVE SHARPLY FOCUSED ATtention on the purposes and the functions of American higher education. Stimulated by the advances in science and technology in other parts of the world, educators and laymen have become particularly concerned with the merits of professional and technological education on the one hand and liberal studies on the other, and even more with the relationships which should obtain between them.

The questions involved are ancient. In the fourth century B.C., Aristotle, commenting on the educational principles and practices of his time, said: ". . . the existing practice [of education] is perplexing; no one knows on what principle it should proceed—should the useful in life, or should virtue, or should higher knowledge, be the aim of our training; all three opinions have been entertained. Again, about the means there is no agreement."[1] Ever since those ancient days partisans of two main types of education—often called "professional" and "liberal"—have defended their respective merits. The debate continues today with renewed vigor, and for a number of reasons it is timely.

First, the general public is agitated by Russian advances in the fields of science and technology. Many Americans are raising questions about the reasons for what they rightly or wrongly consider to be the superiority of the Russians in the type of education basic to their startling achievements in the sciences. Although the issues involved in these questions extend far beyond the boundaries of higher education, some of the more urgent problems as seen by many educators and thoughtful laymen are related to the functions and programs of colleges and universities.

Those who advocate an intensification of education in the professional

* By Earl J. McGrath. The ideas in this chapter have been considerably elaborated and expanded in *Liberal Education in the Professions,* by Earl J. McGrath (New York: Bureau of Publications, Teachers College, Columbia University, 1959).
[1] Aristotle, *Politics* (New York: The Modern Library, 1943), p. 321.

and semiprofessional vocations and in the fields of scholarship concerned with science have the onerous responsibility of describing how preparation for the other broad activities of life is to be adequately provided. Those, on the contrary, who stress the social and personal values of liberal education must realistically face the increasing need in the modern world for persons with advanced training in an occupational field—and show how this is to be furnished in increasing measure. The significance of occupational education can be appreciated only when it is realized that there are now twenty-two hundred occupations requiring highly trained manpower, and that ten to twenty more are created annually. As valuable as liberal arts education may be, it is not all that is needed by those employed in the specialized vocations. It is necessary and reasonable, therefore, to reconsider the full complement of educational services these workers must have if they are to be vocationally efficient and civically competent.

Second, for several decades the proportion of all college students attending professional units in colleges and universities has steadily mounted. Many of the present schools, such as those in business administration and journalism, were inconspicuous, if not completely missing, in the total enterprise of higher education at the turn of the century. There were, for example, only three schools of business before 1900 and these enrolled a mere handful of students. Now tens of thousands of students attend several hundred such institutions. The growth of the college and university divisions devoted to the various forms of education directly related to an occupation is evident from the enrollments in these institutions. Dael Wolfle has shown that in 1901, of all the first degrees granted, the aggregate of those in business, agriculture, education, and engineering was only 4.1 per cent of the total awarded by all types of institutions.[2] By 1951–53, however, the figure had risen to 46.4 per cent, or almost half the first degrees awarded. If these students are to receive any education other than that which prepares them for their occupational activities, this general education must in some manner or other be made an integral part of the professional program. There are many issues in this merging of two sets of educational objectives which deserve thoughtful analysis on the basis of which systematic planning can take place.

Third, although the series of questions involved in establishing the proper proportions and relationships between the professional and the liberal education of college-going youth most obviously apply to the universities, those queries must also be answered by the faculties of liberal arts colleges. These older units in our system of higher education, like their sister institutions, have in the past several decades inaugurated a wide variety of professional and semiprofessional curricula. Another study con-

[2] Dael Wolfle, *America's Resources of Specialized Talent* (New York: Harper & Brothers, 1954), p. 292.

ducted by the Institute of Higher Education[3] has revealed that some independent liberal arts colleges offer more than twenty vocationally oriented programs leading to one or another bachelor's degree, and that virtually all such institutions provide some instruction of this type. Moreover, the specialization in the various conventional liberal arts departments has now become so intense that to all intents and purposes these programs are no less vocational than their counterparts in schools of engineering, business administration, and education. If, therefore, the graduates of the liberal arts colleges are to leave these institutions adequately prepared to live intelligently and effectively in the larger sphere of life outside their occupation, the same questions which are matters of consideration in the separate professional schools must be raised concerning the relationship between general and specialized education in the liberal arts colleges.

Fourth, there is increasing concern among our citizens about the rising cost of higher education in money and in time. Medical education is the prime example of the steady lengthening of the course of formal study and the consequent increase of the financial burden on the student and his family. As late as 1900 young men could enter a medical school with no more than a secondary schooling and complete the medical course in two academic years considerably shorter than they are at present. Now the average for premedical and medical education is eight years, to which are added varying but usually long periods of internship or residency.

In some schools of education, nursing, pharmacy, and commerce, and in other professional fields as well, formal education has been extended to five or six years. Serious social problems are involved in the steady extension of pre-employment education. There are curtailments of earning capacity, maladjustments in personal and family life, and an often unrecognized selection of individuals whose parents are in the social and economic groups which can afford the large capital investment required to complete a long professional course of study. This investigation is only tangentially concerned with these latter matters. It is, however, directly concerned with the related question as to whether a more carefully considered plan for the total education of the individual, involving a clarification of the purposes and character of both liberal and professional education, could not keep the scope of higher education within more reasonable and defensible bounds.

Finally, the opportunities for adult education now provided by almost all institutions of higher education, and the opportunities for continuing education of high quality within commerce and industry, make necessary a re-examination of the amount and kind of higher education a prospective

---

[3] Earl J. McGrath and Charles H. Russell, *Are Liberal Arts Colleges Becoming Professional Schools?* (New York: Bureau of Publications, Teachers College, Columbia University, 1958).

practitioner needs before he enters upon his intended life work. Considering the wealth of postgraduate educational opportunities now available, all baccalaureate curricula, both those in professional schools and in liberal arts colleges, require critical reappraisal aimed at determining as objectively as possible which educational functions can most properly be performed before graduation and which can most profitably be conducted after the individual actually assumes his vocational responsibilities. A review of these matters again requires a reconsideration of the relationships between the various types of instruction now offered in undergraduate programs which too often operate under the fallacious assumption that the student's education does and necessarily must conclude on the day of graduation.

These, then, are the chief reasons for the present study of the curricula of selected undergraduate professional units in colleges and universities. Before undertaking the detailed analyses of various institutional policies and practices which constitute the major purpose of this study, it was necessary to explore the meaning and purpose of liberal and professional studies and to establish a working basis for properly interrelating these two educational functions in an integrated whole.

In considering a desirable pre-employment higher education for vocational competence, one must begin with the assumption that such education is necessary and desirable in the United States today. To some this suggestion may appear obvious and fruitless. Yet many educators and laymen question the whole concept of undergraduate education as preparation for earning a living except insofar as general, nonvocational instruction may be considered to provide that preparation. They would be satisfied with, or even prefer, either no training other than that provided on the job, or a formal vocational education beginning at the postbaccalaureate level. Such a concept is unrealistic because of the over-all purposes of higher education in our democratic society with its increasingly complicated economic structure and its mounting demands for higher education for individuals of ever more varied abilities, interests, and vocational objectives.

If the existence of undergraduate professional schools is justified, there can be no question that they must prepare students for their prospective work in a particular family of occupations. If the baccalaureate curriculum in commerce, for example, is not related to the activities of business enterprise, its existence per se cannot be justified. Some of those who have analyzed the need for education for business, and for other vocations as well, have advocated programs of studies so general that the *raison d'être* of a school of commerce is denied by the very breadth and the remoteness from business activities of the studies they recommend. Such proposals really deny the need for specialized education, or at least reserve it for graduate study or on-the-job training.

Even if such views were defensible in the abstract, they are unrealistic.

The undergraduate professional units of our colleges and universities are firmly established in the academic structure and in the minds of our people. They are here to stay. They will be augmented by others in the years ahead. Enrollment trends in institutions of higher education show that undergraduates in professional schools increasingly outnumber those in liberal arts colleges. Hence, the meaningful question to be asked about the professional schools is how their offerings can be patterned to meet the needs of youth who have at least a tentative vocational objective but whose education must be so designed as to prepare them to act as intelligently in the broader contexts of life as in their own work.

A review of the emerging characteristics of the American economy and the history of higher education supplies convincing evidence that the number and the variety of baccalaureate programs with a specific occupational orientation will inevitably increase. It is important, therefore, that steps be taken now to justify the assumption that undergraduate professional schools will have both vocational and general objectives, and that these aims will be clearly reflected in the structure and the content of the curriculum. The compelling responsibility of those who determine the character and substance of undergraduate professional education is to design curricula which prepare the individual concurrently for a specialized calling and for the other varied activities of life. At first sight these broad purposes might appear to be visionary and unattainable within the normal four- or five-year period. If, however, only clearly comprehended and essential purposes control curriculum planning, and if all instruction which does not manifestly contribute toward the attainment of these twin objectives is cut away, a defensible program can be designed. The success of such an effort will, however, be dependent upon the acceptance of the basic principle that the professional course of study ought to be a whole in which traditional liberal arts instruction and the technical courses related to a particular occupation are joined to provide the full and relevant higher education appropriate to the needs of our times.

Before considering the matters of fact and theory which are germane to a discussion of the structure and content of professional undergraduate education, it should be observed that in an earlier day much of the education in this country in all professional callings was narrowly technical. Most curricula in that day and indeed up to very recent times emphasized handbook information and rule-of-thumb procedures while neglecting basic theory and generalized knowledge useful in the infinitely varied circumstances of everyday practice. This kind of training was in fact *illiberal* in terms of any modern definition of either liberal or professional education. But this exclusive purpose of earlier professional programs—to make the individual technically competent—has now been largely replaced in theory if not in practice by the conception that all specialties must rest on a solid basis of theoretical knowledge and be practiced with the imaginative employment of general intellectual skills.

The most advanced views today assume that, if it is to be fully effective in preparing graduates for the complicated demands of contemporary life, professional education must have not a single goal but rather three comprehensive objectives. First, because of its very nature, it must obviously inculcate the corpus of knowledge, the complement of skills, and the traits of personality and character which constitute the distinctive features of a particular craft. It is these characteristics which give the profession its cohesiveness and identity. The celebrated psychologist William James, who, in his monumental *Principles of Psychology,* analyzed the attributes which differentiate one occupation from others, observed that "Already at the age of twenty-five you see the professional mannerism settling down on the young commercial traveler, on the young doctor, on the young minister, on the counselor-at-law." At one time, cultivating these distinguishing qualities of an occupational group was the sole purpose of its entire preparatory educational program. Today, however, at least the more forward-looking institutions consider two other aims as hardly less significant than that of equipping the student to perform effectively the duties of his chosen work.

A second purpose, and one of rising importance, is concerned with the general education which all those who attend an institution of higher education must have if they are to understand, and to live competently in, an increasingly complex democratic society. President John Hannah of Michigan State University expressed this newer conception when he told representatives of the land-grant colleges that "It is not enough that our young people be outstanding technicians. The first and never-forgotten objective must be that every product of our educational system must be given that training that will enable him to be an effective citizen, appreciating his opportunities and fully willing to assume his responsibilities in a great democracy."[4] Intelligent living today requires a knowledge of matters of domestic and international affairs infinitely more complicated and shifting than those of even a generation ago. Moreover, recent advances in the physical and biological sciences impinge so directly on the life of the average citizen that he cannot live capably today in ignorance of these arresting penetrations of the unknown regions of the physical world. The rapid growth of reliable knowledge in the physical and the social sciences requires that the purposes of higher education for a vocation be extended beyond the bounds of technical knowledge or expertness in his own field.

Furthermore, an educational institution can hardly absolve itself of a third responsibility—that of assisting the student in gaining self-understand-

[4] John A. Hannah, "The Place of the Land-Grant College in the Public Educational System of the Future," *Proceedings of the Fifty-Eighth Annual Convention of the Association of Land-Grant Colleges and Universities,* Vol. 58 (1944), p. 76.

ing, a moral grounding, and a consistent view of the world. In the words of the Committee on Aims and Scope of Engineering Education, the humanities and the social sciences have a responsibility to assist the student in the "development of moral, ethical, and social welfare and to a sound professional attitude."[5] Though a graduate may be ever so competent a practitioner and citizen, without knowledge of his own nature and a reasoned philosophy of life, he will fail to realize his full potential. Throughout his adult life the kaleidoscopic world around him will remain a meaningless flux of unrelated events. Recognizing the need for this philosophical orientation, many leaders in professional education appraise it as highly as professional skill and civic competence. In fact, one leader lists these three dominant purposes of journalism education in the following order: "(1) It should fit the student for being an effective citizen. (2) It should fit him for living a useful, full, satisfying life. (3) It should provide basic preparation for work in journalism."[6]

If these three comprehensive objectives of professional education are to be achieved, a judicious readjustment must be made in the balance of instruction directly related to the student's prospective occupation and instruction in the disciplines traditionally termed "the liberal arts and sciences." Before considering what types of readjustments are necessary, however, consideration must be given to the purposes of liberal arts education in order to determine to what extent and by what means they can be served in the curricula of professional schools.

What are the major purposes of liberal education in contemporary American society? Though it would doubtless be difficult, if not impossible, to arrive at a generally acceptable definition of liberal education, perhaps a measure of agreement can be reached through a description of the types of abilities and personality traits which liberal education might be expected to engender in those who have been subject to its influence.

First, it would probably be generally agreed that those who have had a liberal education should have acquired a broad knowledge of the various major areas of learning—the natural sciences, the social sciences, and the humanities, including the fine arts. Though it is doubtless true, as Whitehead observed, that "A merely well-informed man is the most useless bore on God's earth," it is no less true that today the ignorant are a menace to themselves and to their fellow citizens. No person can now live fully and effectively, according to Ortega y Gasset, without at least a modest knowledge of "the culture, the vital system of ideas, which the age has attained"—and Ortega meant the age in which the individual is living.

[5] Society for the Promotion of Engineering Education, Committee on Aims and Scope of Engineering Education, "Report," *Journal of Engineering Education,* Vol. 30 (March 1940), p. 564.

[6] Leslie G. Moeller, "Goals of Professional Education for Journalism," *The Quill,* Vol. 40 (August 1952), pp. 6 ff.

Yet it must be apparent to anyone who moves among "educated" people that some who leave our institutions of higher education today are unacquainted with the living ideas of their time. Haltingly they feel their way in darkness through many of the common avenues of life because their path is unilluminated by even the most elementary knowledge of many aspects of their own being or of the physical and social universe which surrounds them. That many who have spent four or more years in an institution of higher education are innocent of much of the reliable knowledge of their time is attested by the experiences of the author of a best-seller on the social implications of atomic energy. In discussions with college audiences he observed that on many matters of fundamental significance they were no better informed and hardly more curious than the man in the street.

In view of the enormous mass and accelerating rate of growth of knowledge, students cannot fairly be expected to encompass any large portion of it in four, or even in forty, years. They can, however, properly be expected to gain an acquaintance with the basic facts and principles of the various disciplines. A student who completes a professional education of four or more years with however distinguished a record in engineering, pharmacy, education, or agriculture, but with little or no knowledge of English literature, history, philosophy, or economics, is not liberally educated. He will be prepared to think and act effectively neither in his chosen occupation nor in the many life situations which are the common lot of all.

The mere possession of facts, however, does not guarantee the efficient, the incisive, and the imaginative use of the mind. Cardinal Newman, in his monumental analysis of the nature of liberal education, *The Idea of a University,* has said:

> Knowledge then is the indispensable condition of expansion of mind and the instrument of attaining to it; this cannot be denied, it is ever to be insisted on; I begin with it as a first principle; however, the very truth of it carries men too far . . . the end of a Liberal Education is not mere knowledge.[7]

Second, then, liberal education ought to cultivate those skills and habits of reasoning which constitute intellectual competence, the capacity to think logically and clearly, the ability to organize one's thoughts on the varied subjects with which the citizen today must unavoidably concern himself. In a sentence, these faculties might collectively be described as the capacity to order and interpret a complex set of circumstances in the physical, social, or artistic world, and to bring one's full intellectual resources skillfully to bear on the solution of a problem.

Just as the student must have some knowledge of many fields, so also,

---

[7] John Henry Newman, *The Idea of a University* (New York: Longmans, Green and Co., 1955), p. 115.

in order to gain competence in using the diverse forms of reasoning, he must have experience with intellectual processes other than those conventionally employed in his major academic field of interest. The various disciplines do, of course, employ some intellectual processes in common—the logical deduction of conclusions from valid premises, for example—whether the matter under consideration involves the facts of science, history, or art. Yet they also use intellectual methodologies in part peculiar to themselves. The chemist or physicist will only be satisfied with knowledge in which the probability of error is reduced to negligible proportions, while the historian or the sociologist, dealing as he does with human acts and events, must be satisfied with a much greater range of error of both fact and judgment. The student of art enjoys much greater freedom of subjective evaluation and interpretation than either the physical or the social scientist, but the intellectual processes by which he deals with reality are no less important than those employed by other disciplines.

The most distinctive and yet the most widely used processes of reasoning are doubtless the deductive method of formal logic and the inductive method of science. Those who are to be liberally educated can gain familiarity with these mental processes and skill in their use most readily by the study of mathematics and the sciences. No person can live intelligently today unless he understands the methods of reasoning with which scientists have so dramatically explored the unknown regions of the universe, from the boundless oceans of cosmic space to the infinitesimal region of the atom's nucleus. The intellectual procedures used in the conception of a hypothesis, the arrangement of an experiment to test it, the drawing of conclusions from the facts thus established—all these skills every citizen needs to acquire if he is to reason validly and objectively about physical phenomena. Moreover, properly taught, these habits of thought can be broadly applied in analyses of the complex social world with which all human beings are surrounded. Since the sciences differ in their use of these procedures with a wide variety of physical problems, the broadest range of acquaintance with these subjects will accomplish the fullest understanding and skill in the use of their methods.

Other branches of learning, the humanistic disciplines for example, use somewhat different intellectual operations in their interpretation of the world and the activities of men. Though they naturally employ the laws of logic in constructing a reasoned view of reality, their distinctive characteristic is their concern with values, with the ends of life, with the destiny of man. Those who teach history, literature, foreign languages, philosophy, and the arts cannot confine themselves to a consideration of the characteristics and behavior of exactly measurable phenomena. They must introduce the student to the reflection of creative minds on the nature of man and his world and their conclusions which are usually couched in much less precise terms than those of the scientist. The concern of teachers of these subjects must be with man, not as a physico-chemical complex within a mechanistically determined system, but rather as a being of purposes, values, loves, hates, and ideals—and sometimes as a seer or prophet with divine inspiration. In literature, the student should vicariously enjoy many of the richest experiences of life, gaining insight into human motivation and behavior attainable in no other way except through personal experience.

Still another area of human intellectual endeavor uses somewhat different approaches in its interpretation of reality. The social sciences—economics, sociology, and political science, for example—insofar as possible follow scientific procedure by constructing hypotheses, setting up experimental controls, and making accurate observations. These disciplines also use other investigative procedures, including statistical method, historical analysis, and case studies. Unlike the natural scientist, however, the scholar concerned with social phenomena often cannot arrange experiments which others can repeat. On the contrary, he must sometimes accept data of unprovable authenticity or of incomplete representativeness and, reasoning cautiously, arrive at tentative conclusions. Much of his material does not lend itself to the exact measurement used by the physical scientist. In the words of Taussig, one of this country's most celebrated economists, the social scientist is concerned with the "wavering and incalculable behavior" of man. The educated person must be skilled in these processes of tentative and precise reasoning about phenomena of inexact measurement. Most human actions must be based on evidence which, though not fully conclusive, is the best available at the time. One of the chief aims of higher education should be to cultivate habits which will prevent human beings from acting blindly, with no facts, and also from procrastinating indefinitely because the last shred of evidence is not in.

The liberally educated mind possesses another set of intellectual abilities, those involving the effective use of the various symbols and media of expression and communication. In the formulation of concepts and in the orderly development of a reasoned view of life, the meanings of words are the building blocks; the logical relationships among these verbal expressions, the cement which holds them together. No aspect of higher education has been more severely criticized than the teaching of the skills of communication. Yet instruction in this subject is highly valued by those who realize its importance in all phases of adult life. Several years ago this statement was well documented in a study of over thirteen thousand degree-holding employees of the General Electric Company. These graduates were divided into two groups, those who had attended engineering schools and those who were graduates from nonengineering curricula, mainly liberal arts colleges. When asked to appraise the various subjects they had pursued in undergraduate days in terms of their career value, the nonengineers placed English communication, both oral and written, at the top of the list, and this subject was placed second only to mathematics by the engineering graduates.[8] The symbols of mathematics and of the arts, though not as widely and as frequently used by the ordinary citizen as words, are nevertheless essential elements in the lives of cultured men and women.

Equipped with essential knowledge and the skills of intellectual workmanship, the college graduate may nevertheless have failed to reach another important goal, perhaps the *sine qua non* of liberal education. Though richly informed, and capable of clear and cogent reasoning, he may yet be intolerant, unwise, intellectually stagnant, and inept in the arts of human association. The *third* major objective of liberal education is, therefore, concerned with attitudes, ideals, and traits of personality and character. These qualities, harder to describe and to measure than the other outcomes of liberal education, are yet the hallmark of the liberally educated person. As has been said, they are the qualities that remain after all the facts which were learned have been forgotten.

The liberally educated person embraces certain values. He has at least a provisionally formed and examined philosophy of life, a *Weltanschauung,* a religion around which he organizes the varied purposes and activities of his existence. These values of the liberally educated man represent not only the ideas and causes for which he would live, but more importantly those for which if necessary he would die. They give stability to his being. They serve to keep the ship of life steady on course as it is buffeted by the unpredictable forces of man and of nature. Without them the lives of men have no direction, for, as Socrates said, "If a man does not know to what port he is sailing, no wind is favorable."

Knowing his limitations, the liberally educated man has respect for the rights and views of others. He is humble, not only before the capricious and uncontrollable forces of nature, but also in the presence of his own ignorance. And most important of all, he continually seeks wisdom through the extension of his knowledge and reflection on its meanings. Realizing how much he does not know, he is driven by an unrelenting curiosity, an unquenchable thirst for deeper knowledge and fuller understanding. Unless professional education inspires the desire to learn, to extend the scope of one's knowledge, to increase one's insights into the nature of things, it has condemned its recipients to eventual ignorance and mental stagnation. For the explosive increase of knowledge is the most arresting fact in today's world of learning, and swiftly accelerating change the most characteristic feature of modern life.

[8] "What They Think of Their Higher Education, A Report of a Survey of the Opinions of 13,586 College Graduates, Employees of the General Electric Company," *Educational Relations Bulletin* (January 1957).

Even if higher education were able to supply each student with all the knowledge needed to understand the world in which he currently lives, and even if it could sharpen the intellectual skills to a fine point, it would have failed if it had not added to these achievements the inculcation of the irresistible desire to learn and to know. For as knowledge grows and the world changes, all who wish to live intelligently must continue to grow and to change through learning. Unless education initiates a chain reaction in which each advance in understanding sets off the desire for greater growth in wisdom, those who leave our campuses will soon reach a state of permanent intellectual rest. They will lose touch with the ongoing world.

The purposes and character of professional education require a similarly intensive and critical analysis. Since, however, the remainder of this volume is concerned with a review of the attitudes of faculty members and administrative officers, and of the practices in selected institutions with respect to this matter, only general guide lines for the development of a professional curriculum will be suggested at this point.

The dominant principle to be applied in determining the character and content of an undergraduate professional program has to do with the degree of specialization the curriculum may be expected to provide. The substance of a professional course of study, and the manner in which it is organized and presented, must be decided in terms of the vast bulk of modern knowledge, its rate of growth and change, the time available to the average student for pre-employment training, and especially the proper purposes of initial education in a vocation. As these various factors which irresistibly shape professional education are analyzed, the dominant principle in curriculum construction is thrown into high relief. It becomes axiomatic that the student can be, and in principle should be, given only enough basic specialized instruction related to a vocational field to qualify him for initial gainful employment. W. Earl Armstrong sets forth this controlling idea in relation to teacher education, for example, when he says:

> It is not assumed that the pre-service curriculum should attempt to provide all of the insights and skills that the teacher will need in order to be a fully competent person. Rather, the function of the pre-service curriculum as here assumed is to provide the best possible preparation for the teacher to *begin* to teach. A pre-service curriculum based on this assumption will of necessity leave all aspects of the teacher's education incomplete. That is to say, the general education of the teacher will need further strengthening, the area or areas of subject-matter concentration will need either further broadening or deepening, and further additions will need to be made to the professional insights and skills of the teacher.[9]

If the several values in a professional curriculum are to be kept in proper balance, the student cannot be prepared as an expert in any specific

<hr>

[9] W. Earl Armstrong, "The Teacher Education Curriculum," *The Journal of Teacher Education*, Vol. 8, No. 3 (September 1957), p. 232.

job. Undergraduate instruction can be expected to do no more than acquaint him with the vocabulary and the basic principles of a broad field such as pharmacy, engineering, or nursing, and cultivate the intellectual skills by means of which new knowledge can be acquired and applied to the infinitely varying problems of day-to-day practice. This conception of the scope of a professional school's purposes has been well expressed by Dean Helen Nahm of the School of Nursing at the University of California:

> I think our major problem in a professional school . . . is that we must, in a period of time which seems reasonable to students and their parents, prepare both a liberally educated person and a person with competencies essential for beginning practice in a professional field.

Cogent reasons support the view that an undergraduate professional curriculum should embrace only those learning experiences necessary to orient the student broadly in his chosen occupation without aiming to cultivate a high degree of competence in any of its specialized branches.

The store of detailed knowledge in any professional field is enormous, and it expands prodigiously. This accelerating growth of fact and theory, the invariable characteristic of every intellectual realm, explains why no one can become or remain a genuine expert in a specialized branch of learning except by long years of study and by continually renewed acquaintance with evolving fact, principle, technique, and practice. It is for this reason that even those who, for example, graduate from a school of business administration with distinction and with the beginning of a specialization in management or retailing are nevertheless given positions relatively low in the structure of a business enterprise.

Second, highly specialized undergraduate instruction fails to reach its reputed goal because each set of circumstances in professional life has its own peculiar structure. To a degree it involves concepts and techniques which vary from those of all other situations. Consequently, the principles of accounting, orchestration, *materia medica,* or educational psychology must be adapted to the special circumstances and needs of a particular situation. The beginner who takes up his duties in any profession prepared to apply a specific body of detailed facts or procedures to new sets of circumstances will find his bag of tricks hopelessly inadequate. Unfortunately, he will only then belatedly realize that in concentrating excessively on a narrow specialty he has failed to gain the flexibility of mind and personality required to understand and to deal effectively with a host of important matters both professional and otherwise. Inevitably he will lack breadth in both general and professional knowledge and in the intellectual skills essential to their profitable use in the varied patterns of professional exigencies.

In the making of a professional curriculum, another guiding principle is related to the technical courses themselves. Those who have considered the matter most studiously are convinced that *even professional instruction* should stress broad principles, key ideas, and overarching generalizations rather than detailed facts or techniques. Here it is profitable to raise questions concerning what kind of education is of most worth, and how much can be accomplished in the time available.

The curricula of forward-looking engineering schools, for example, provide convincing illustrations of successful efforts to place greater emphasis on principles than on techniques, thus making possible the enlargement of the general education component and a broader orientation in the vocational field itself. Even in the engineering subjects many schools have adopted a core program of professional subject matter as the common basis of the specialties such as civil, chemical, electrical, and mechanical engineering. The enlargement of these common components has been possible only through the dropping of some specialized instruction which in earlier years pre-empted a considerable portion of the four-year curriculum. This shift in emphasis has increased the student's knowledge of theoretical engineering and of the liberal arts disciplines, thus enhancing both his occupational and his civic competence.

Another principle to be applied in designing a professional course of study relates to the cultivation of attitudes and motivations which are not the sole concern of any subject-matter field, but rather the responsibility of all. Proposals for the reconstruction of professional curricula will succeed or fail largely to the extent that students are helped to recognize undergraduate education as only the beginning rather than the end of a long process of personal growth. Unless the experiences of the college years are viewed in this light the student is likely to misconceive the aims of higher education. Not uncommonly, faculty members and curriculum makers encourage students' misconceptions of the purposes and the potential of undergraduate education. A subconscious feeling, subtly transferred to those under instruction, that they must "learn it now or never" is the origin of the common compulsion to include every last bit of information, to explore every remote corner of the subject, in a single course. Under the influence of this point of view all curricula have become swollen with masses of dispensable facts, and the atmosphere of the classroom has become one of hurried absorption of facts rather than of reflective analysis and the orderly expansion of mind.

A curriculum with the proper objectives ought to provide the basic experiences needed by the neophyte to begin his practice with a sufficient body of knowledge to give him confidence in his own ability and to make possible further professional growth through individual study, practice, and additional part-time instruction in so-called "refresher" courses. He ought to have the flexibility of mind to pursue and to accept additions to knowledge and innovations in procedures as they appear. He ought also to have a vision of the wider significance of his work in the whole social context of his time. More than this an undergraduate program cannot and need not be expected to accomplish.

The achievement of these two sets of purposes for a responsible and full life as a private citizen and as a member of an occupational group is an ambitious undertaking. Yet, under proper conditions it is not an unrealistic goal. Our national and personal welfare demand that it be reached within the next decade; our needs for highly skilled workers and for informed and active citizens are patently urgent.

If these aims are to be realized, however, certain of the presently controlling ideas and practices in American higher education require reassessment. Many of the graduates of institutions of higher education will not reach these goals if it is assumed that only those disciplines commonly classified under the caption "liberal arts" have these desiderata as their aims. On the contrary, much of the instruction in professional curricula such as engineering, business administration, education, and nursing must be expected (as it already lives up to the expectation) to cultivate the qualities of mind and character often considered the exclusive province of the liberal arts.

No one has better described the possibility of achieving the ends of liberal education through the study of specialized subjects than President Virgil M. Hancher of the State University of Iowa, who at a meeting of the Association of Land-Grant Colleges and Universities in 1953 said:

> We forget that it is possible to become liberally educated by the teaching and study of professional or specialized subjects in a liberal manner. . . .
> While in general I would support the proposition that there are some things which every liberally educated man should know, I fear that we have been led into error sometimes by believing that the study of certain subject matter inevitably results in a liberal education. This is a doubtful proposition. It is nearer to the truth to say that there is no subject matter, worthy of a place in the curriculum of a modern Land-Grant College or state university, which cannot be taught either as a professional specialty or as a liberal subject.[10]

It is obvious that courses in engineering or pharmacy, if properly taught, acquaint the student with a wide range of scientific facts and cultivate the intellectual skills of the scientist. They also instill a respect for truth, a humbleness of spirit, a desire to learn, and the habit of philosophical reflection about the place of man in a limitless cosmos. The same can be said for instruction in other professional programs, though the emphasis on particular subject matter and skills would obviously vary with the field concerned.

Engineering can be used to illustrate how a rounded education can be

[10] Virgil M. Hancher, "Liberal Education in Professional Curricula," *Proceedings of the Sixty-Seventh Annual Convention of the American Association of Land-Grant Colleges and State Universities*, Vol. 67 (1953), p. 45.

provided for the student in a professional course of study. The first objective of liberal education, acquainting the student with the fundamental facts and principles in the three main areas of knowledge, can be accomplished by supplementing the basic courses in science with instruction in the social sciences, the humanities, and the skills of communication. The requirements in the social sciences and the humanities ought to be met by the pursuit of courses especially designed to bring the student into touch with the leading principles and the key ideas in a broad range of subjects not included in courses in engineering and basic science.

In the social sciences, for example, such subjects might include history, political science, sociology, and economics. Courses should be unlike conventional elementary courses in that no attempt should be made to cover all the detailed knowledge necessary for advanced study. Instead, selected special topics ought to be studied intensively, so that the study would emphasize relationships between the constituent disciplines, and inculcate skill in the use of the methods of thought employed in dealing with social problems. Thus the second objective of cultivating intellectual skills in the social sciences would be accomplished. Comparable instruction in literature, languages, philosophy, and the arts should acquaint the student with the content and methods of the humanities. Since scientific subjects are necessarily basic to specialized engineering courses, it could be assumed that all students would have gained a considerable knowledge of science and skill in the use of its methods.

The third objective of liberal education, that of cultivating the attitudes and the traits of character which signalize the liberally educated mind, must necessarily be the responsibility of all teachers of all subjects. Any subject can be taught so as to increase the student's respect for truth and for the worth of the individual, his appreciation of his own smallness in our vast universe, and his love of wisdom and desire to learn. For this reason, as Hancher holds, courses of study cannot on the basis of content or method alone be classified as liberal or not liberal. Instruction in a professional school which aims to achieve these objectives may certainly be classified as liberal, and courses in colleges of liberal arts which do not have these aims can surely not be described as liberal.

The graduate of such a program in engineering would possess not only the knowledge of his world at large and the aptitude to use his intellectual resources in expanding his learning. He would be capable of seeing his own occupational activities in the larger social context of his time. Similar curricular arrangements are feasible in all other professional schools. The general principle of curriculum construction involved is that the two major areas of knowledge not basic to the professional subject matter be adequately represented by appropriate general instruction. In business administration, for example, these would be the humanities and the natural sciences; in agriculture, the social sciences and the humanities; in music, the natural and the social sciences; and so on for all the other professions.

Whether these broad purposes of liberal education will really be achieved will depend on the teachers. A course in finance, for example, taught with emphasis on general economic principles, with consideration for the historical development and the present importance of financial institutions in Western society, and with constant reference to the interrelationship of money and banking with the facts of sociology, anthropology, political science, and psychology, not to mention ethics and art, will have many of the values of liberal education, whatever its uses may be in educating a student for employment in the world of commerce. Conversely, a course in Greek literature with an emphasis on dates, literary style, linguistic analysis, and the esoteric subject matter of the teacher's research on some peculiar characteristic of Greek grammar, may produce few of the desirable results of liberal study. The teacher and the preparation he receives for his responsibilities in the classroom are, always have been, and always will be the decisive factor in liberal or, for that matter, any other kind of education. The present inadequacies in American higher education, particularly in its failure to preserve the heritage of liberal culture, have their origin in the attitudes, purposes, and skills of the teachers. Many teachers—whether in professional schools or liberal arts colleges—in their preoccupation with the cultivation of specialized knowledge and the techniques of their own chosen narrow field of intellectual activity, have lost sight of the more inclusive purposes of higher undergraduate education.

Professional schools which adopt a broader set of objectives and make the requisite changes in their practices to bring them into conformity with these principles will provide more fully that generous education required by this generation to live more intelligently in the complex contemporary world. They will contribute more fully to the enrichment and strengthening of this democratic society in which high production is of undeniable importance in peace and in war, but of no more pressing urgency or greater significance than informed citizenship and self-knowledge. As institutions generally adopt the pattern already in effect among the most enterprising, the ideal of education for high professional competence, for informed and active citizenship, and for a rich and integrated personal life will be within reach of all undergraduates in professional schools. It is to the realization of these ideals that these institutions might well dedicate themselves in this period when our people, with an eye to the ultimate destiny of our nation, are reassessing all of American education.

Chapter 2

HISTORICAL ACCOUNT OF HIGHER EDUCATION
IN MUSIC

UNLIKE THE OTHER PROFESSIONS INCLUDED IN THIS STUDY OF LIBERAL ED-ucation in undergraduate professional schools, music—at least in name—was one of the seven liberal arts in the medieval university, belonging (with arithmetic, geometry, and astronomy) to what we might today call the upper-division courses of the undergraduate curriculum. Perhaps everyone who has been granted the degree "Bachelor of Arts" has asked himself what arts are meant by these words; a moment's thought will remind him that they are the seven liberal arts. The bachelor's degree was the medieval teacher's certificate, and it is lucky for most A.B.'s that they are not called upon to perform their certified function. During the first centuries of the European universities' existence, the seven liberal arts represented what was regarded as necessary for a university-educated member of the clergy, and their actual "use" was in the perpetuation of the educational system.

Turning the matter around, however, and asking what liberal studies the would-be professional musician pursued in the medieval university, one runs up against the fact that the split between liberal and professional study had not yet occurred. The very concept of "liberty" implied in the word "liberal" did not have the glamor for medieval as for later man. More meaningful, perhaps, to a medieval musician would have been the question of the relative claims of devotion and of learning—a conflict more or less resolved in the early Middle Ages but perhaps never to be eliminated com-pletely.[1] What we would call a composer or performer, in the Middle Ages, was always primarily a member of a community that existed for a wider purpose than a purely musical one and that imposed definite rules and re-

[1] "Many American universities represent a consolidation of diverse historical concepts in music instruction—the practical and theoretical or speculative aspects—*musica practica* and *musica speculativa* . . . contained to a higher degree in the in-stitutions of higher education in the United States than in any other country in his-tory. . . ." Virginia Ruth Mountney, "The History of the Bachelor's Degree in the Field of Music in the United States" (unpublished D.M.A. dissertation, Boston Uni-versity, 1961), p. 2.

18

quirements not only on his musical but also on his nonmusical activities.[2] Thus music was only part of his life, which was directed toward more comprehensive ends—his life in the religious community or at the court, and ultimately in eternity. This is not to say that there were no outstanding musicians in those days. An easy way to rationalize the situation would be to say that they were only amateurs—but that is not quite true either.

We might forget the whole early history of education in music were it not for the fact that certain aspects of these earlier institutions continue on, both in letter and in spirit. The Moravians in Pennsylvania who, according to Elson, "undoubtedly had the first regular music schools of this country,"[3] were a definite throwback to the medieval pattern. Certain aspects of the Puritan attitude were, too. When, finally, "colleges" of music were established, the very word "college" was a revival of the medieval term for a religious community, although a medieval musician, suddenly called back to life in the nineteenth century, would no doubt have been at a loss to understand what a college "of music" might be. Many matters which were sharp and clear in the earlier period became blurred by subsequent adaptations, particularly of a religious to a secular system. The greater antiquity of music as a subject of what we would call liberal study perhaps justifies our starting earlier in our account of its development.

EUROPEAN PATTERNS

What the ancient Greeks called *mousiké* was a much broader concept than our "music," embracing also poetry and dance, and being more an ethical, political, and religious category. From Plato and Aristotle we get an idea of how important *mousiké* was in the fourth century B.C., and how some aspects of it were dealt with in higher education—informally and speculatively at the Academy, after the model of Socrates and his followers; more formally at the Lyceum. Both these institutions were tiny, but, of course, widely influential. Roman education perpetuated many Greek traditions, though directed somewhat more toward fitting the student to play an administrative role in governmental affairs. Music there retained its important position in all higher education. In the first century A.D., for instance, Quintilian in his *Oratorical Institute* gave considerable attention to music because the would-be public speaker could learn from it how to work on the emotions of his audience, and as a lawyer he might have to handle cases involving musical details, such as a man accused of manslaughter "because he had played a tune in the Phrygian mode as an ac-

[2] Frank L. Harrison, *Music in Medieval Britain* (London: Routledge and Kegan Paul, 1958), p. 1.
[3] Louis C. Elson, *The History of American Music* (New York: The Macmillan Company, 1904), p. 340.

companiment to a sacrifice, with the result that the person officiating went
mad and flung himself over a precipice."[4]

Ancient Greece and Rome bequeathed a well-defined tradition of integrated studies in which music had an important place. Also bequeathed
were some almost legendary concepts, no less fruitful because of their
vagueness. When the first conservatory of music in the United States was
yet in the planning stage (that is, the conservatory first projected and still
functioning today—Peabody, in Baltimore), the spokesman for the trustees
proclaimed: "It is reviving the thought and practice of classic Greece, and
carries us back to the Republic of Plato and the Academy of Athens."[5]
The fact that this statement was not strictly accurate did not prevent the
impulse behind it from being fruitful, just as the desire of the Camerata
in Florence to revive Greek tragedy was not unproductive—not of ancient
drama but of a new form, opera. Similarly, the wish to perpetuate or revive
—at least in name—other aspects of the ancient European tradition in
higher education has been fruitful of new forms on American soil. The
retention of old names, however, has often given rise to ambiguities, particularly when the actuality beneath has been quite different from that which
had prevailed in the earlier period.

As for the Middle Ages, there were, of course, differences between
what would be studied as *musica* at, say, thirteenth-century Oxford and
what might be studied as "music" today. The matters dealt with were much
more philosophical than those usually stressed at the present time, and
there was a close interrelationship between what was studied under *musica*
and what was studied under the other members of the *quadrivium*. "Like
its allied disciplines," Cone has written, "it was a study of measurement,
of proportion; and conversely the medieval scholars sought in mathematics
and astronomy the harmonious relationships they found in music."[6] There
was thus a certain integration of studies in the medieval curriculum that
went back, by way of Aristotle, to the Pythagorean speculations on number.
This truly theoretical and somewhat verbalistic approach is, of course, no
longer the main content of music as it is studied today in American institutions of higher education; in all fairness, however, one must recognize that
theory occupies a very important place in the study of music in undergraduate professional schools, and that even in the most practical situation of
training for musical performance, matters of measurement, proportion, and
relationship are quite crucial, even if they are dealt with in a more empirical

---

[4] Quoted in Nan Cooke Carpenter, *Music in the Medieval and Renaissance Universities* (Norman, Oklahoma: University of Oklahoma Press, 1958), p. 9.

[5] *The Peabody Institute of the City of Baltimore: The Founder's Letters and the
Papers Relating to Its Dedication and Its History* (Baltimore, Maryland: Boyle, 1868),
p. 15.

[6] Edward T. Cone, "Musical Theory as a Humanistic Discipline," *The Juilliard
Review*, Vol. 5 (1957/8), p. 4.

way than they were in the thirteenth century. Also one must recognize that a distinct phenomenon of the twentieth century, musicology in America, has placed a form of music study squarely back in the academic world with the full sanction of the German university tradition, although, to be sure, with a historical rather than a mathematical slant.

In the Middle Ages, some of the Continental universities perhaps stressed *musica* more than the English did. The University of Salamanca, according to Rashdall, "appears to be the first which gave both degrees and practical instruction in music."[7] Having been established in 1215 by royal authority so that native students would not have to go abroad for study (a purpose which is to reappear 750 years later when conservatories, under middle-class auspices, were being founded in America), the University of Salamanca had an endowed chair of music as early as 1254, and, in 1355, two *"magistri* in music."[8] The closer relationship between American and English procedures, however, justifies our concentrating on England.

During the fifteenth century, not only did music figure in the general education of the would-be Bachelor of Arts, but also the specifically professional degree of Bachelor of Music was conferred—by Cambridge University on Henry Abyngton in 1463, by Oxford University on Robert Wydow probably in 1499, and many others. In fact, a very impressive proportion of Tudor composers held Bachelor of Music degrees from Oxford or Cambridge, as for example, Morley, Dowland, Farnaby. Other important Tudor composers, such as Aston, Tallis, and Edwards, held Bachelor of Arts degrees. Apparently the line between the training for the more specific or more general bachelor's degree was not very strictly drawn. In fact, the requirements for music degrees at Oxford seem to have been quite flexible until the promulgation of the statutes of 1636, established by Laud under the authority of Charles I, when music was officially recognized as a separate faculty at Oxford, "on a par with the faculties of theology, law, and medicine—the only member of the liberal arts to be so distinguished—privileged to award its own degrees,"[9] a state of things that had apparently been on the way at both Oxford and Cambridge since the mid-fifteenth century.

This "Bachelor of Music" degree was a survival of an earlier move to give degrees in the separate arts of the trivium and quadrivium: A "Bachelor of Grammar" degree, for instance, was at one time given.[10] The Bachelor of Music degree, however, was, by virtue of the higher status of music in the curriculum, by no means an inferior or merely partial degree. Rather,

[7] Hastings Rashdall, *The Universities of Europe in the Middle Ages* (Oxford: Clarendon Press, 1936), Vol. 2, p. 81.

[8] Carpenter, *op. cit.*, pp. 93 f.

[9] *Ibid.*, p. 186; *cf.* p. 197.

[10] C. F. Abdy Williams, *A Short Historical Account of the Degrees in Music at Oxford and Cambridge* (London: Novello, 1894), pp. 11–14.

it was an indication of further specialization, having some aspects of the master's degree as granted in America today. In the fifteenth and sixteenth centuries, if one had a B.Mus., he had the right to lecture on Boethius' *De Musica* at Oxford and on *scientia musicalis* in general at Cambridge; the acquiring of the degree entailed many years of actual study and practice of music, and the writing and performance of a large composition. Many of the recipients of the B.Mus. had previously taken their B.A., and even M.A.; and from various records of academic activities of this period it is clear that the bachelors of music, medicine, and law formed an echelon in the academic hierarchy above that of the ordinary bachelors of arts. Still today, at Oxford, the B.Mus. candidate must already have his B.A. or have passed a "Final Group" examination in Classics, French, German, or English Literature. When the Bachelor of Music degree was introduced into America in the 1870's, it was also an advanced degree, the A.B. (or its equivalent by examination) being required before it was granted.

On the basis of its early history, many aspects of the Bachelor of Music degree become clear. In England, the degree lost significance during the seventeenth and eighteenth centuries as it could be taken without residence; in the late nineteenth century, however, its requirements were stiffened.[11] In America, the degree began to be confused with some of the new bachelor's degrees, like B.S. and Ph.B., introduced on the analogy of the A.B. and in response to pressures from studies that had invaded the liberal arts field. The result was that by the early twentieth century the Bachelor of Music degree had begun to mean very different things in different institutions. To a great extent, the meaning that it had had during its earlier years in England and America had been taken over by the master's degree, which in late-nineteenth-century America had been given a specialized course-content. As a result, there arose the danger, as Hanson has put it, "that the basic degree in music might be entirely wiped out of the academic scene";[12] and, partly to prevent this happening, the National Association of Schools of Music was organized in 1924. No doubt more deliberately than Laud had done back in 1636, the NASM established standards for the degree, more in terms of making it equal rather than superior to the A.B. There are problems here involved that will have to be considered in more detail later, but for purposes of a general historical orientation to these problems it may for the present suffice to note that the American situation in which music degrees are given by universities is not an innovation but rather a return, under its own terms, to the state that prevailed in the early centuries of the British universities' existence. What needs to be explained

[11] Edward J. Dent, "Music in University Education," *MQ*, Vol. 3 (1917), pp. 605–619.
[12] Howard Hanson, "Professional Music Education in the United States," *Musical Courier*, Vol. 151 (1955), p. 63.

is not so much how music got into the liberal arts field as how it got crowded out of it by various changes in the university curriculum that took place in the late Middle Ages, Renaissance, and Reformation.

The concentration on Aristotle that occurred in the late Middle Ages injected into the curriculum a number of fundamentally philosophical studies—ethics, politics, physics, and metaphysics—that had not been given place in the original seven. The Humanistic ideal of the Renaissance entailed the educated man's knowing Latin not merely as a "tool subject" but as something in its own right. He should be familiar with the Classical Latin of Cicero and Virgil, and men like Erasmus began to demonstrate the desirability and possibility of knowing Greek, too, as well as Hebrew. The Reformation ideal, finally, was that a liberal education should include some theology. A figure like Milton represents the peculiar breadth of the seventeenth-century educated man, and both by precept and example he continues to be an inspiration in discussions of education today.

So far as music was concerned, however, the proliferation of studies in the curriculum that had taken place by the early seventeenth century and the shift of the university's base of operations from the ecclesiastical to the secular world were fatal to the study of music as a liberal art, and, vice versa, to the study of the liberal arts by the musician. When Harvard was established in 1636 (the very year in which the Caroline Code was promulgated by Laud), all the seven liberal arts from the Middle Ages were represented in the curriculum—except music. The Aristotelian, Humanistic, and Reformation tendencies account for other courses which had crowded it out. For the ensuing two centuries, music had to be satisfied with a marginal existence in the academic world, regarded more as a genteel ornament than a discipline. Strangely enough, this neglect, as McGrath has pointed out,[13] was shared also by logic and dialectic, which had originally been the very bedrock on which the academic structure had been built.

Particularly in the academic world, the way an institution happens to be established often has very far-reaching and subtle consequences. Throughout its over three centuries of academic leadership, Harvard has continued to exhibit an attitude toward music as an academic study quite consonant with the principles on which it was established. Unlike most large American institutions of higher learning, it does not recognize "applied music" as a study worthy of academic credit; its famous choral and instrumental organizations are entirely extracurricular; and justification of the Harvard attitude toward any study of music other than theoretical or historical has occasioned the appearance in print of numerous explanations of amazing intellectual subtlety.

[13] Earl J. McGrath, *Liberal Education in the Professions* (New York: Bureau of Publications, Teachers College, Columbia University, 1959), p. 11.

This attitude is all the more surprising when viewed in the light of the very strong pressures exerted on Harvard to modify its position. When in 1862 John K. Paine, organist and music director there, offered to give a series of lectures on musical forms, without compensation, the board reluctantly gave permission on condition that the course not count at all toward a degree. Harmony and counterpoint were added on the same basis, but it was not until 1873 that college credit was granted for these courses and Paine was paid for teaching them. This was, of course, during Charles W. Eliot's presidency, when there was high administrative support for specialization and the offering of individual choice among courses as a royal road to liberal education,[14] and one cannot help wondering how laboratory science can be given credit and applied music not. Davison, over thirty years professor of music at Harvard, and apologist for the system there, wrote:

> It is sometimes urged that there is an analogy between the type of ability required in the manipulation of apparatus used in the physical laboratory in preparation for entrance examinations, and the merely mechanical business of playing the pianoforte, for example. This is hardly true, for ability to handle skillfully laboratory instruments presupposes the use of logic and original thinking in the experiments which are to follow, whereas playing the pianoforte may be a purely physical matter in which the intellect plays a relatively small part.[15]

The well-known composer and Harvard professor Randall Thompson has formulated the point a little more succinctly: that in a laboratory science understanding is being furthered, while in applied music ability is being trained.[16] Although this distinction is no doubt clear to one who already feels its cogency, it seems merely a verbalism to one who does not. Regardless of the philosophical basis for the situation at Harvard (which, in view of its long history, is easier to understand on historical than on purely logical grounds), the relationship between the Department of Music and the University is much like that of any other department—for example, that between the Department of English and the University. Viewed historically, the fact that the sciences were on the march into the field of

[14] Charles H. Russell, "Charles W. Eliot and Education," *Journal of Higher Education,* Vol. 28 (November 1957), pp. 437–439.

[15] Archibald T. Davison, *Music Education in America: What Is Wrong with It? What Shall We Do About It?* (New York: Harper and Brothers, 1926), p. 103. To the would-be music teacher the answer given in this book to the second question posed in its subtitle is: Complete an A.B. and then take music education in the Graduate School of Education. Thus, the recognition of any study of music other than theoretical and historical is carefully excluded from undergraduate academic status.

[16] Randall Thompson, *College Music: An Investigation for the Association of American Colleges* (New York: The Macmillan Company, 1935), p. 85. In using this report, one should not overlook the dissenting opinion of eight members of the sponsoring committee, pp. 98–105, 119–121, and 137.

"liberal education" during Eliot's presidency no doubt has something to do with the fact that credit is granted for work in the science laboratory and not for work in the music practice or rehearsal rooms.

The opposite point of view with regard to the appropriateness of "applied music" to the liberal college curriculum is widely held. The head of the Music Teachers National Association in 1900, Arthur L. Manchester, wrote:

> . . . it is practical music that conforms more closely to true educational ideals. The theoretical study of music supplies a fund of facts about music and, to those who are exceptionally endowed, opens the way for specialization as composers and theorists, but these subjects, as taught in our colleges, do not touch the daily life of the majority of students nor do they prepare the mass of the student body for living. They are practically vocational in trend. On the other hand, practical music, being actual participation of the student in musical re-creation, induces activity of those faculties through which the fullest measure of education is secured and preparation for future living is attained. The proper cultivation of practical music develops a quickness of perception, an acuteness of visual and auditory analysis, a rapidity of coordinated action and a keen power of observing and comprehending beauty and symmetry which are educational factors of undeniable value.[17]

Just to follow out this issue since it has been raised, one might note that when the subject of music came up in the deliberations of the committee charged with formulating the Harvard Report on General Education, no particular place could be found for music: "A training in the musical skills is hardly within the province of general education. . . . We believe that one or more courses in music should be designed and given for the purposes of general education, but we are not qualified to suggest which types of courses would be suitable for these purposes."[18] In response to the actualities of the situation, Harvard has made it possible for students to take "Basic Piano" as a noncredit course, much as English A was set up for students deficient in writing skills or as some sort of remedial work is provided in many fields by most colleges.[19]

One must, of course, recognize that this attitude toward music in higher education has been subjected to special consideration here not merely because of its embodiment in the oldest institution of higher education in this country, but rather because it is typical of the older New England colleges and of many institutions throughout the country which used them as

[17] Arthur L. Manchester, "Practical Music and the College Curriculum," *MQ*, Vol. 7 (1921), p. 252.

[18] *General Education in a Free Society: Report of the Harvard Committee*, with an introduction by James Bryant Conant (Cambridge: Harvard University Press, 1945), p. 213.

[19] Archibald T. Davison, "The Humanistic Approach to the Teaching of Music," *PMTNA*, Vol. 43 (1951), p. 79.

models. Also, it does have historical justification, in that the Bachelor of
Music was what we would consider a graduate degree, in the same sense
as the Bachelor of Laws. The older New England colleges were the lower
levels of an elaborate academic structure (as we glimpse it, for instance,
in the Caroline Code). This partial state of things became traditional, and
developed its own adherents and defenders who found virtues in what may
originally have been its inadequacies. Music, having been crowded out of
the regular seventeenth- and eighteenth-century college curriculum by more
verbalistic studies, had to develop under other auspices—the church and
the community—and make its re-entry into the academic world as if it
were a stranger. During the twentieth century, however, it has made itself
at home there in an unprecedented way—as we shall see.

The problem here involved is not merely a matter of curricular structure in the abstract, nor of whether music is to be included in the training
of the average university-educated individual. The underlying attitude
works both ways, and there is also involved the question of whether the
would-be musician or music teacher can hope to pursue his higher education with a feasible combination of his vocational and generally human objectives. Music is somewhat different from the other professions included
in the present series of monographs in that it requires—or, at least, most
musicians believe that it requires—a great deal of regular practice, which
must be begun fairly early in life and continued without extensive interruption if the person wishes to pursue it as anything but an avocation.[20] If it
were financially feasible to postpone serious professional study until one
had an A.B. degree, or to carry on musical studies privately in complete
isolation from the regular college studies, it is not clear that this would be
the best procedure for the aspiring musician.

Unquestionably, many individuals have done just that. An interesting
essay on some three hundred college graduates who, early in the present
century, were engaged in pursuits connected with music—composition,
authorship, musical journalism, criticism, conducting, teaching, performing,
and public school music—was published in 1915 by Winton Baltzell. Most
of these men came from colleges like Amherst, Bates, and Harvard,
where presumably their studies were simply the normal liberal arts curriculum of the time. "Compared with the number of college men who were
working in lines connected with music, say a score of years ago," Baltzell
observed, "the increase is marked"; and he concluded: "There is a career in
music to-day for the man who includes its study in his college course, an

---

[20] It has widely been assumed that a year or so interruption of technical study is
catastrophic to an intended musical career. Though the idea sounds plausible, it
should perhaps be investigated. It would be ironical if it turned out that an appreciable
number of great musicians had had precisely such experiences of leaving music for a
comparatively brief period and coming back to it.

honorable career, a useful career, one in which the rewards are probably as certain and as ample as the average in other lines of professional activity."[21]

Also some writers have emphasized the idea that even the would-be concert pianist did not need such sheer *quantity* of muscular exercise at the keyboard. The director of music at the University of Iowa, Philip Greeley Clapp, for instance, maintained that "two hours of intelligent and concentrated practice upon musically significant material with the emphasis upon musical values rather than upon theoretical technical attainments, are worth more than from four to ten hours spent upon technical grind." He cited opinions of great pianists—Bauer, Gabrilowitsch, Leschetizky—who deprecated over-practice. "To sum up, then:" Clapp concluded, "The young musician should not be deprived of a liberal education."[22]

On the other hand, Frank Damrosch, founder of the Institute of Musical Art in New York City and long-time dean of Juilliard School of Music, stressed the conservatory point of view: A serious music student needs to spend four or five hours at his instrument and two hours on theory every day. "How can he add eighteen hours of college attendance a week plus the necessary home work to this already heavy schedule?"

> It may be suggested that he attend college first, get his degree, and then begin the serious study of music. The late Franz Kneisel, one of the greatest teachers of the violin that ever lived, held that in order to attain perfect control of the instrument the technical training of the ear, hands and arms must be done between the eighth and eighteenth years, followed by further intensive studies in repertoire, ensemble, etc. In other words, while the general education must not be neglected, it must not absorb so much of the time and strength of the future musician as to interfere with his musical studies.[23]

These two equally positive statements by no means exhaust the authoritative testimony on both sides of the issue, but they may serve to underline the fairly obvious fact that music involves an emphasis on sheer drill that is different in kind from that involved in law, medicine, or journalism. Some authorities consider more, some less, necessary. But at least a certain amount has to take place: Music study cannot be completely carried out in the intellectual realm, as the study of philosophy or literature can, and as perhaps some of the older Eastern colleges would wish it might be before it would be readmitted to a place at the academic table alongside the disciplines that they consider appropriate there.

Besides—particularly in the nineteenth century—there was the pres-

[21] Winton James Baltzell, "The American College Man in Music," *MQ*, Vol. 1 (1915), p. 632.
[22] Philip Greeley Clapp, "Music as a Subject of Concentration in the Liberal Arts College," *PMTNA*, Vol. 25 (1931), pp. 42–43, 47.
[23] Frank Damrosch, "A College Degree in the Education of the Musician," *PMTNA*, Vol. 21 (1927), p. 82.

sure of sheer quantity of demand for music teachers and for some kind of musical activity that would be meaningful to the people of the growing nation. This need, almost of itself, forced into existence agencies for training musicians, with or without, at first, the benefit of the traditional institutions of higher education. The situation was somewhat the same as that in medicine: The demand for doctors forced the term of training down from seven years to a year or less.[24]

In Europe, an elaborate system of conservatories had grown up to supply musical needs. Originally these had been orphanages, under religious auspices, to "conserve" the lives of children committed to their care. The first was the Conservatorio Santa María di Loreto, established at Naples in 1537. Another notable early conservatory, for girls, was an extension of the hospital San Salvadore degl'Incurabile, which had been founded in 1517 at Venice. The problem faced by these institutions was to train their wards in some profession that would assure them of a livelihood; and with the craze for music—particularly opera—that swept Italy in the seventeenth century, making Italy the musical powerhouse for all Europe, these foundlings' homes gradually came to focus their activities more and more on musical training. There was a kind of sheer professionalism involved here that is difficult for us to understand, separated from it as we are by the eighteenth and nineteenth centuries with their emphasis on nature and the inalienable rights of the human individual, particularly the child. An art that was unlike nature (as we understand the word) was the ideal. Anyone who hoped to make his way as a soloist had to master an elaborate style of performance, completely over and above the written notes of the music. Promising boy-singers were castrated to prevent their voices from changing, apparently without compunction. The musical world for which the conservatories groomed their charges was a hard and hectic one, and the attitude of a pupil at a seventeenth-century *conservatorio* had a do-or-die quality about it quite different from that of a late-nineteenth-century American girl who perhaps wished to fill in a few years between high school and marriage with a little study of the piano or the voice.

In eighteenth-century Paris there were, under state control, one school for training military bands and another for singers. In the nineteenth century, some of the European conservatories—particularly that in Paris under Cherubini and that in Leipzig under Mendelssohn—experienced notable improvement. By the end of the nineteenth century there was, according to Damrosch,[25] scarcely a town of twenty thousand inhabitants without a music school, whether highly endowed like the Hochschule at

[24] Kevin P. Bunnell, "Liberal Education in American Medicine," *Journal of Medical Education*, Vol. 33, No. 4 (April 1958), pp. 319–340.

[25] Frank Damrosch, "The American Conservatory, Its Aims and Possibilities," *PMTNA*, Vol. 1 (1906), p. 14.

Berlin or independent like the "free schools" in Paris and Brussels. In this whole Continental system of music schools, however, the approach was largely that of a trade school, with both students and teachers interested mainly in performance, their aim, as observed by Kinkeldey, "not to provide a general cultural musical equipment, but to turn out men and women who are competent professional composers, performing artists, or music teachers."[26]

Obviously, the kind of state and church support that had called the European conservatory system into existence was not to be found in America. During the seventeenth and eighteenth centuries, moreover, the colleges and universities considered music as an extracurricular activity, much in the spirit of Lord Chesterfield writing to his son at Venice in 1749:

> There are liberal and illiberal pleasures as well as liberal and illiberal arts. . . . As you are now in a musical country, where singing, fiddling, and piping, are not only the common topics of conversation, but almost the principal objects of attention, I cannot help cautioning you against giving in to those (I will call them illiberal) pleasures (though music is commonly reckoned one of the liberal arts) to the degree that most of your countrymen do, when they travel in Italy. If you love music, hear it; go to operas, concerts, and pay fiddlers to play to you; but I insist upon your neither piping nor fiddling yourself. It puts a gentleman in a very frivolous, contemptible light; brings him into a great deal of bad company; and takes up a great deal of time, which might be much better employed. Few things would mortify me more, than to see you bearing a part in a concert, with a fiddle under your chin, or a pipe in your mouth.[27]

Colleges and universities, so far as their curricula were concerned, were expanding their offerings in the fields of Latin and Greek under the impetus of a strongly classical trend in all the arts toward the end of the eighteenth century; then, in the early nineteenth, the study of English and other modern languages and literatures came in; and, in the mid-nineteenth, the natural sciences, to be followed by the social sciences.

AMERICAN DEVELOPMENTS
(THROUGH THE EARLY NINETEENTH CENTURY)

Meanwhile, developing along its own way, musical activity in America had produced certain forms that were, in the period after the Civil War, to enter into relationship with institutions of higher education in America and, during the late nineteenth and early twentieth centuries, to become fruitful of educational forms unique in the world today. In this respect, the

[26] Otto Kinkeldey, "American Higher Musical Education Compared with That in Europe," *PMTNA*, Vol. 29 (1935), p. 22.
[27] Earl of Chesterfield, *Letters to His Son*, ed. Charles Strachey (New York: G. P. Putnam's Sons, 1901), pp. 324–325.

situation is not unlike that in the other professions. As in law and medicine, a not too well defined apprenticeship system prevailed during the seventeenth and eighteenth centuries, and various proprietary institutions and examining bodies made sporadic appearances. A few rather colorful individuals in the late eighteenth and early nineteenth centuries projected their own ideal visions into brief existence of amazing brilliance and intensity. This was the heroic period in American education. Partly because of their limited scope and partly because they were rather *ad hoc* forms of musical training, the question of liberal, as distinct from vocational, training seems scarcely to have arisen. There were, of course, professional European musicians on tour, such as Ole Bull, Sontag, and Thalberg, but they were visitors from another planet. Even so important a figure as Lowell Mason "had not the least thought," he said,[28] of making music his profession until well after he was launched on his career.

A fuller account of American developments through the early nineteenth century would have to start with the Puritans' attitude toward psalmsinging. They were distinctly antiprofessional (in the sense of antioperatic), and regarded music more as a manifestation of the Holy Spirit, somewhat as we would regard group prayer: In it, the "whole man" (in his capacity as a Christian) should participate.

Even more intensely oriented toward the "whole man" (as distinct from some special professional skill he might have) was the musical activity among the Moravians in Pennsylvania, particularly at Ephrata. Here a very strong individual leader, Conrad Beissel, was responsible for organizing the life of this celibate religious community down to the last detail of dietary restriction. Though without formal musical training, he harmonized hundreds of hymns and published a system of harmony. Some aspects of the Moravians' activities may now appear eccentric to us, but a connection has been drawn[29] between their publications and the music of the only slightly less freakish late-eighteenth-century Boston composer, William Billings.

In Boston, early in the nineteenth century, the great figure in projecting music into the public schools was Lowell Mason, a superman who could lead four hundred children, in a single group, in a class in note-reading. His Academy of Music, more or less what we would consider today a private music school and pressure group to get music adopted officially in the Boston public schools, was no small operation: Over a thousand students and would-be teachers flocked to it during the year. Mason held ten-day teacher-training meetings, or musical "conventions" as he called them,

[28] Quoted by Frank J. Metcalf, *American Writers and Compilers of Sacred Music* (New York: The Abingdon Press, 1925), p. 212.
[29] Julius Friedrich Sachse, *The Music of the Ephrata Cloister* (Lancaster, Pennsylvania: Printed for the author, 1903), pp. 3, 11.

which by 1850 were attracting as many as fifteen hundred a session. That Lowell Mason could accomplish what he did was due to a number of fortunate coincidences: the times, the need, his personality, the strong assistance that he had from such people as Horace Mann, and his own intuitive grasp of the actual and potential. Within the period from 1827 to 1837, the Boston musical situation was revolutionized, with Mason as the very center-pin of the hub.

The official introduction of music into the public schools there (which was anticipated, paralleled, or followed by introductions all over the country) was a step on the part of musicians to regain some of their lost status: In the curriculum deemed by public authority fundamental for all students, it took its place along with reading, grammar, and arithmetic. Instead of figuring at the upper-division undergraduate level as it had done in the Middle Ages, it now took its place—in a more applied form, of course—at the elementary level, and under civil rather than ecclesiastical auspices.

This particular development is of significance in the fundamental theme of this chapter (the historical background of the relationship between liberal and musical education) for an attempt was made to bring these two branches of education into a harmonious relationship on the elementary level long before it was made on the higher levels. An outstanding figure in American music education for the past few decades, Howard Hanson, stated the point quite forcibly a few years ago when, after discussing "the integration of the arts as a normal part—now necessary part—of life, and therefore of education for living," he said: "It is a pleasure to repeat here what I have said before on numerous occasions, that the public schools have been far more successful in leading the way to such integration than any other branch of the teaching profession."[30] There is a great deal of complaint among college and university teachers that the elementary and high schools are not doing a good enough job; but is it barely possible that they may be doing too good a job, and turning out pupils who will no longer put up with the warmed-over food-for-the-spirit that is sometimes set before them in the college or university?

The academic recognition of music in the elementary schools, achieved in Boston under Lowell Mason's leadership, is significant also because it has certain features that are peculiarly American. *All* pupils must be given a chance to develop their musical potentialities. It is almost as if this were one of the inalienable rights, after life, liberty, and the pursuit of happiness. Music has become as firmly ensconced in the elementary program as it had been in the quadrivium. But this place in the schools is by no means as universal as one might uncritically assume. Instructive in this respect are the reactions of a musicologist and music educator who emigrated from

[30] Howard Hanson, "The Scope of the Music Education Program," *Music Educators Journal,* Vol. 34, No. 6 (1948), p. 8,

Germany to the United States in 1941: Although in general rather critical of the American system of carrying on music education, Manfred Bukofzer thus characterized the American program of public school music: "This phenomenon is unique. Only in this country has the idea of a general musical education been combined with the comprehensive school system of an industrial and democratic society."[31]

Perhaps more immediately significant in our historical account of the developing forms of higher musical education, however, was Mason's idea of the "musical convention." The transformation of the earlier type of singing-school convention into a teachers' institute was something American, somehow different from the English choirs festival or the German *Musikfest*. It was, in a way, a brief music school. After the demise of Mason's Academy of Music, the idea was continued, often expanded to three months in the summer (when it was usually referred to as a "normal institute"), with a staff of five or six, and operating on tuition fees. Eventually some of these institutes became year-round affairs. In some respects, they might be likened to the proprietary medical schools: A distinctly nineteenth-century phenomenon, they especially flourished in the Middle West and South; they were intended to supplement the practical experience of the participants; and they had sprung up in response to a definite need. The interest in music in the mid-nineteenth century was stimulated by a number of developments in addition to the obvious social and economic ones of the Westward expansion: Many excellent musicians from Europe toured America; quite a body of musicians and music-lovers emigrated to America, particularly as a result of the German uprisings of 1848; American manufacturers greatly improved their musical instruments (notably pianos). Music students began to dream of excelling as solo performers. The singing-school, accordingly, became somewhat outmoded as part of its function was taken over by the public school. Private music teaching of the individual student became a much more widespread type of musical activity— though, of course, public school teaching by the special music teacher continued. The normal institute was the main source of teacher training on an organized basis for the mid-nineteenth century.

An interesting account of a week's activities of one of these mid-century music teachers is given by W. S. B. Mathews (1837–1912) in his letter from Aurora, Illinois, to *Dwight's Journal of Music,* which was published in Boston.[32] His week included 28 private lessons (mostly piano),

    [31] Manfred Bukofzer, *The Place of Musicology in American Institutions of Higher Learning* (New York: The Liberal Arts Press, 1957), p. 5. Separate accounts of the educational programs in music being carried out in different countries are contained in UNESCO, *Music in Education* (Suleure, Switzerland: Gassmann S.A., 1955).
    [32] Quoted in Edward Bailey Birge, *History of Public School Music in the United States* (Bryn Mawr, Pennsylvania: Oliver Ditson, 1937), pp. 80–83, from *Dwight's Journal of Music,* Vol. 16 (1859), pp. 309–310.

3 singing classes, 2 public school lessons, 3 choir meetings, and 4 services on Sunday—interspersed with a great deal of traveling by railroad and stagecoach. What is requisite of a music teacher, he writes, is "a good knowledge of music, geniality, good humor, knowledge of human nature and 'soft sawder', and untiring energy." One of Lowell Mason's disciples, Mathews was to become quite influential as an editor and writer toward the end of the nineteenth century. So far as formal training is concerned, he was no doubt typical of the musician of the period: Having studied music privately in his native town of New London, New Hampshire, he came to Boston where he met Mason. He later secured a teaching position at the Wesleyan Female College at Macon, Georgia; and after 1867 he settled in Chicago, where he was active as organist, teacher, choir leader, and writer. He learned, according to Birge in his *History of Public School Music,* by "thinking and working, always busy doing the next thing needed to be done."

As in most other professions, the sheer need for practitioners up through the expansive days of the mid-nineteenth century and the sheer enthusiasm of such men as Billings, Mason, and Mathews caused any serious question about their training to seem superfluous—in fact, a lack of concern over pedigrees and titles was characteristic of the new nation. There is a strange continuity in the idea of what it meant to be a musician in America right on through the Civil War: In Puritan days, if one led the singing, he was supposed to be manifesting the Holy Spirit, not displaying technique; in Revolutionary days, leadership was the result of spirit, nature, actual ability—not of pedigree, tradition, guild, or credentials; right on through the mid-nineteenth century, if one was "good" at leading the group, he led the group. The singing group was the base of activity, and ability, if overtly manifested, was recognized. An exhibitionistic or esoteric type of professionalism, in the sense of solo vocal or instrumental music-making, did not figure prominently in the native musical scene. Family or guild were not important considerations in determining who should be regarded as musicians. This opening up of the profession was also to some extent a phenomenon of nineteenth-century Europe: Whereas Bach, Couperin, Mozart, and others had been outstanding members of families of professional musicians and, from childhood, had received the kind of training best fitted for the professional role they were to play in life, together with an individually adapted introduction to some of the other aspects of life important to them as human beings, Schumann, Wagner, Brahms, and other nineteenth-century musicians entered upon their careers without strongly set predetermining family or professional pattern.[33] The Romantic

[33] Alfred Einstein, *Music in the Romantic Era* (New York: W. W. Norton, 1947), pp. 28–30.

and individualistic tendencies of Europe were simply intensified on American soil.

By the mid-nineteenth century, a truly serious would-be musician would normally complete his studies by going to Europe. Particularly since 1843 when Mendelssohn had become head of the Leipzig conservatory, Germany played an important role in the higher education of American music students. For purposes of contrast between the early nineteenth and mid-nineteenth century, let us consider the way Lowell Mason found his way into music and the way his son William undertook to perfect his musical abilities. In 1849 William went to Leipzig to study, then to Prague, and finally for nearly two years he was with Liszt at Weimar. He played in public at the court of the Grand Duke and in London. Returning to America in 1854, he was active as performer, teacher, and composer in the smaller forms; but particularly he liked to play chamber music with a group of four distinguished string players—music such as that of Schumann and Brahms. Doubtless to him, in his heart of hearts, his father's strictly musical abilities seemed quite provincial.

The Genteel Tradition was quite as much a part of nineteenth-century America as the Jacksonian, and was widespread throughout the country. Posterity has been led to believe that much emanated from the North (and from Boston in particular) that was really arising at the same time in the South and West. The *Boston Musical Gazette,* at about the same date as the announcement of the forthcoming introduction of music into the public schools, printed this revealing little item:

> We are happy to learn that vocal music is successfully taught in the Common Schools of Cincinnati. It is also made a regular branch of study in Cincinnati College, an institution that ranks high in the West. In this we confess they have stolen a march on us. But we would say, "God speed," in so laudable a cause. We only regret that Cambridge has not the honor of first introducing the subject.[34]

Thus, apparently, in 1838 Applied Voice was given credit at Cincinnati College (now the University of Cincinnati).

Early academies and colleges for women did much with music,[35] in close juxtaposition with liberal studies. Among some of these schools there was a feeling that the word "bachelor" in college degrees was inappropriate to their graduates; as Catherine Beecher said in 1835, it caused them "needless ridicule" and "painful notoriety," and would appear as "an attempt to unsex them."[36] As a result, such degrees as Mistress of Polite Literature

[34] *Boston Musical Gazette,* Vol. 1 (1838), p. 117. I am indebted to Arthur Kennedy for calling my attention to this item, which suggests that there was a good deal of music in the schools before Lowell Mason.

[35] A full account is given in Mountney, *op. cit.,* pp. 120–126, 177–186.

[36] Quoted in Thomas Woody, *A History of Women's Education in the United States* (New York: The Science Press, 1929), p. 469.

(M.P.L.), Mistress of Fine Arts (M.F.A.), Sister of Arts (S.A.), and Maid of Arts (M.A.) were awarded. An M.M. degree (Mistress of Music) thus made its appearance. In 1835 the Kentucky Legislature conferred on Van Doren's College for Young Ladies in Lexington the right to award this odd M.M. degree, on an honorary basis.[37]

Considering itself the first authorized degree-granting music school in the United States,[38] Music Vale Seminary for young ladies opened at Salem, Connecticut, in 1835. It taught voice, instruments, harmony, counterpoint, thoroughbass, fugue, etc., and eventually attracted students from all over the country and abroad. Whittlesey, a zealous Methodist (whose death in 1876 the seminary did not survive), conducted the school with a firm hand:

> The young ladies of Music Vale had to rise at five o'clock in the morning and practice from six to seven, and were required to dust their piano prior to commencing practicing. No pupil was allowed to speak during practice time except to her teacher, or to leave the piano, or to play any other composition except that assigned for the practice hour. A student wrote to her Kentucky home: "Strict! You have no idea what *Yankee* strictness means! There is no shirking the rules!"[39]

Not only in special institutions like Music Vale Seminary, however, but also in the more run-of-the-mill women's institutions of the early nineteenth century, music was given a prominent place in the curriculum, as shown by Woody's study of the subjects offered in 162 female seminaries from 1743 to 1871.[40]

ESTABLISHMENT OF CONSERVATORIES AND COLLEGES
(LATE NINETEENTH CENTURY)

Quite naturally, by the middle of the century attempts were made to establish the European conservatory system on American soil. The Peabody Institute in Baltimore, which received its first endowment in 1857,

[37] The Springfield, Massachusetts, *Republican* of March 14, 1835, suggested some further degrees: "M.P.M. (Mistress of Pudding Making), M.D.N. (Mistress of the Darning Needle), M.S.B. (Mistress of the Scrubbing Brush), M.C.S. (Mistress of Common Sense). The Professors should be chosen from farmers' wives and the Laboratory should be a kitchen. Honorary degrees might include H.W. (Happy Wife), H.H. (Happy Husband), and M.W.R.F. (Mother of a Well Regulated Family)." Quoted in Newton Edwards and Herman G. Richey, *The School in the American Social Order* (Boston: Houghton Mifflin Company, 1947), p. 412.

[38] Whether the State Board of Education of Connecticut had the power to authorize academic degrees at this time has been questioned. See Walter Crosby Eells and Harold A. Haswell, *Academic Degrees,* United States Department of Health, Education, and Welfare, Bulletin No. 28 (Washington: Government Printing Office, 1960), p. 177.

[39] Frances Hall Johnson, *Music Vale Seminary, 1835–1876* (Tercentenary Commission of the State of Connecticut Committee on Historical Publications, 1934), p. 13.

[40] Woody, *op. cit.,* pp. 563–564.

has been considered the earliest school of this kind in America.[41]   The groundwork for the Academy of Music of the Peabody Institute was laid much more deliberately than that of Mason's Academy of Music in Boston had been.   While Mason and his associates had shown a fine disregard for money in their enthusiastic efforts but had elicited financial support if and when a real need for it arose, the starting point of the Peabody Institute was a phenomenal grant of money, for which a need was to be created.   In 1857 George Peabody gave over a million dollars for the establishment of an educational institution that would improve "the moral and intellectual culture of the inhabitants of Baltimore," including an Academy of Music "to diffuse and cultivate a taste for this, the most refining of all the arts."[42] It is clear from his letters that the partisanship which was to break out shortly in the Civil War had profoundly shocked him, and in part had prompted him to make this generous (if somewhat unrealistic) move as a hedge against chaos.   The broad social-service and humanitarian aims here are different from the more limited aims of the European conservatory, which was to be imitated in this enterprise during its early years with grim determination.   As events transpired, it was not until after the war (in 1866) that the dedication ceremonies of the Institute were held; at this time the Academy of Music, the spokesman for the Trustees said, "exists yet only in expectancy.   The building necessary to this department is not begun."   The Trustees were quite conscious of the momentous step they were taking:

> Here music has for the *first time* in our country been brought into a system of education, as a coordinate element to hold an equal rank with the other teachings of the University.   We believe, in no other institution of note amongst us has music been assigned a seat in such alliance with philosophy. It is reviving the thought and practice of classic Greece, and carries us back to the Republic of Plato and the Academy of Athens.

Finally a suitable building had been built, a director obtained from Boston, announcements issued, and in the fall of 1868 the Academy opened, with 148 pupils and three professors.   There was no thought here of studies other than purely musical ones: This was a conservatory on the genuine European pattern.   A dozen symphony concerts, for which an orchestra of 41 had been hired, were presented this first year.

Difficulties, however, began to appear as soon as this pioneering conservatory emerged from the realm of idea into that of actuality.   Half of

[41] Kinkeldey, *op. cit.,* p. 26.   Priority, in the sense of the date of the actual opening of the conservatory itself, can be claimed by Oberlin Conservatory which opened its doors in 1865, and the New England Conservatory in 1867, whereas the Peabody did not actually open until 1868.

[42] *The Peabody Institute of the City of Baltimore: The Founder's Letters and the Papers Relating to Its Dedication and Its History* (Baltimore, Maryland: Boyle, 1868), p. 2; *cf.* also pp. 15, 117.

the student body dropped out after the first term, and the attendance at the symphony concerts was poor. Obviously, it was over the heads of the masses in Baltimore. One is reminded of the unexpected results of Thomas Jefferson's attempt, earlier in the century, to transplant the idea of a French university to Virginia. In the annual report for 1870, the director of the Academy of Music, L. H. Southard, seems at a loss to understand the public's response:

> . . . music outside of two or three of the large Atlantic Cities is studied and practiced almost wholly as a domestic pastime and not as an Art.
>
> In music, the most universal art, amateur effort, when confined to the domestic circle, is necessarily crude and unfinished, and as long as it continues unconcentrated and diffuse, must so remain. There will be no well defined standard of taste or of performance, one person's judgment being as authoritative as any other's and no more so—the acquirements and opinions of all being superficial and incomplete.
>
> There is, however, no reason to doubt that in a short time, if the public is properly informed, the Concerts may be made nearly, if not quite, self-sustaining.[43]

But they were not. Next year the chorus dropped from 88 to four members. The symphony concerts, still planned as twelve, closed after the tenth because of insufficient attendance. The director was still puzzled:

> Whatever may have been the cause of this decay of interest on the part of the public, I think it can hardly be attributed to an actual deterioration in the performances of the orchestra, or to a declining taste in the public for classical music. It is to be hoped, therefore, that the causes of this decline are of a temporary nature, which will have lost their influence by another season. [1871, p. 24.]

The director resigned; and a new director, Asgar Hamerick, straight from Europe, proceeded even more firmly to make the Academy of Music what he called "a University for Musical Art, and not a mere school for small girls" [1872, p. 39]. What apparently worried him most was the fact that the wind instruments in the orchestra could not be brought in tune; so the following summer he made a trip back to Europe and bought a new set from Adolph Sax in Paris, and more classical music in Leipzig. In his next annual Director's Report he castigated the laxness of the students. Needless to say, the number of pupils was still declining, but not so drastically. The plans for the symphony concerts were scaled down to a number slightly more realistic—first to five, then to two or three—before they began to come up again.

But there was no relaxation of fundamental idea of direction. In 1874 the name was changed, as Hamerick reported, "from Academy of Music to

---

[43] *The Third Annual Report of the Provost to the Trustees of the Peabody Institute of the City of Baltimore* (Baltimore, Maryland: Boyle, 1870), pp. 49–50. Subsequent quotations are from the various annual reports.

Conservatory of Music—a name which better describes its actual functions" [1874, p. 17]. Hamerick gave lectures on notable European composers: It was more the days of Aristotle than of Plato that had come again. By the 1880's the tension seemed to have lessened, and in 1884 the provost could report of the Conservatory that "through evil report and obloquy it has kept firmly on its way, and the good results are beginning to show themselves on all sides" [1884, p. 20]. As Hamerick, in the 1890's, looked back over his early struggles, they took on a rosy glow: "On my arrival I found matters very satisfactory indeed, the Conservatory had been established on a purely musical basis, everything which did not actually come under this head having been wisely omitted by the trustees" [1893, p. 50].

The diploma given on completion of the courses at the Conservatory was strictly on the basis of musical achievements; but, up to the end of the nineteenth century, only about one was awarded each year, the other hundred or so students not being considered worthy. Toward the end of the century, there was a gradual increase in the student body at Peabody, and by 1914 there were over a thousand enrolled. The director of Peabody Conservatory from 1898 to 1927, Harold Randolph, was much less rigid than his predecessor had been. In commenting on the effects of World War I on music, for example, he urged a less demanding approach to music education:

> . . . are we ready to recognize fully this *universality* of music's appeal, and abandon—or at least considerably modify—our attitude of artistic exclusiveness? No one will pretend for a moment that the world at large is as yet thirsting to hear Bach *Fugues*, Beethoven *Sonatas* and Brahms *Symphonies*, and we know beyond a peradventure that a large portion of it never will, so why not face the fact? At the risk of falling from my proud estate as a "high brow" musician, I am going to say that I think one of the chief shortcomings of our modern methods of musical education arises from a too uncompromising insistence on the "three B's" standard. I hope I need not go through the form of saying that for those of us who have in charge the higher musical education, and especially of such as are making music a life work, the standards could hardly be set too high, but I should like to see a considerable development in our methods of diagnosis whereby we might avoid breaking the spirit of the less gifted by holding them up too rigidly to what for them is an impossible standard. . . . We are making an especial effort at the Peabody Conservatory to solve this problem through application of modern methods of applied psychology and are full of hope as to future results.[44]

Among the courses offered at Peabody some incidentals, such as instruction in language, dramatic expression, and teaching methods, crept in. By the second quarter of the twentieth century, under the influence of the growing importance of music schools in state universities, it had become possible

[44] Harold Randolph, "Co-operation in Music Education," *PMTNA*, Vol. 14 (1920), pp. 15–16.

to take a bachelor's degree by matriculating at Johns Hopkins or Goucher College and taking some courses at the Conservatory. Essentially, however, the Conservatory has remained independent, much as the New England Conservatory is today, or as are some of the great foundations of the early twentieth century like Juilliard and Curtis.

In many ways the experience of Peabody has been like that of other institutions which have attempted to re-create the European conservatory pattern on American soil; ultimately they found it necessary to develop a broader base of operations, and to concern themselves more or less with the masses in some realistic way. Social consciousness was part of George Peabody's original concern (among his other notable benefactions was the endowment of a vast housing project for workers in London, in recognition of which Queen Victoria wanted to give him a baronetcy, but he declined it); the twelve symphony concerts a year were part of the broadly uplifting intention of the foundation. This awareness of the needs of the large, democratic group has, in one way or another, figured as an important element in American institutions of higher education in music, beginning with the conservatories. Frank Damrosch, who in 1905 established one of the notable conservatories, the Institute of Musical Art, and later headed Juilliard School of Music, contrasted the European and the American conservatory thus: "In America the conservatory must aim to make the mass musical, in order to build its pyramid upon a broad foundation, upon which may then be built a structure that may pinnacle in the stars."[45] In summing up the role of the conservatory in America he placed the training of virtuosi and teachers in last place, the education of the masses in first. This trend toward social consciousness in musical training was to be carried on further in the music schools connected with universities, but its presence here in the American version of the conservatory system is noteworthy.

The history of the Peabody Conservatory is an epitome of the problem of the adaptation of the conservatory idea to America. The first too-literal attempt at transplantation resulted in dissatisfaction on the part of both faculty and students. After considerable experience, a modification of the institutional pattern was developed which, actually, perhaps came closer to carrying out the original hopes behind the foundation.

The conservatory in America has had to face a great deal of criticism, particularly from the music educators, because it has adapted itself to its new environment too slowly. Rose Yont, in her valuable early survey of the extent to which music was playing a part in education, could hardly control her indignation at what she found going on in some conservatories:

> A general tendency of purely conservatory training is a drifting away from responsibility, lack of ethical training which is so easily acquired in

[45] Damrosch, *op. cit.,* p. 20.

some scholastic lines, and a narrowing down of the whole viewpoint, as the result of too much specialization along one line, and built upon scant and very often poor school training.

There seems little material in such institutions for instilling lessons in loyalty, altruism, in home life and its responsibilities, or for emphasizing the sanctity and purity of fatherhood and motherhood. The present trend is away from the practical, with an absorption in artistic life which emphasizes the remoteness from real life problems.[46]

The author of this rather sweeping denunciation has started from strong convictions about the moral value of music; one cannot expect her to share Hamerick's satisfaction with an institution "established on a purely musical basis." The only hope for such a monstrosity's moral salvation, according to her, is repentance and turning to "affiliation with some educational institution."[47]

Whether these strictures are still justified or not is beside the point. The conservatory in America has been moving in the direction of a more democratic and socially responsible conception of its role. No doubt some would have had it move faster, but institutions are notoriously slow about changing—particularly when they have behind them a well-established tradition of a few centuries. The director of the Department of Public School Music at the American Conservatory in Chicago assured the Music Supervisors National Conference in 1924 that the Conservatory shared the same aims in music education as the other music schools:

> While the Conservatory gives the major subject the rightful place of greater importance in the "Training of the Supervisor," it also realizes the importance of adequate Academic Training. The Supervisor of Music, if he is to win the respect of his colleagues in the other departments of education, must be more than a musician. The Supervisor must be a teacher of keen insight into human nature; he must have a friendly and sympathetic attitude, not only for his pupils, but also for all other departments of the educational field. With this aim in view, the Conservatory can, must and does stand for a reasonably broad academic training. This problem is being solved by means of cooperation between the Conservatories and the Institutions of higher learning in other fields.[48]

One of the more recent and dramatic moves to revise a conservatory curriculum was that at Juilliard School of Music, carried out by William Schuman shortly after he became president of that institution in 1945, and

[46] Rose Yont, *The Value of Music in Education* (Boston: Richard G. Badger, 1916), p. 267.
[47] More recent, and more temperate, criticisms of the conservatory may be found in John R. Kirk, "Preparation of Music Supervisors," *PMENC*, Vol. 14 (1921), p. 170; Aubrey W. Martin, "The Advantages and Dangers of the Conservatory Feature in Normal Schools," *PMENC*, Vol. 15 (1922), p. 95; and H. D. LeBaron, "The Coordination of Music Studies," *YMENC*, Vol. 28 (1935), p. 392.
[48] O. E. Robinson, "The Training of the Supervisor in the Conservatory," *PMENC*, Vol. 17 (1924), pp. 319–320.

widely influential throughout the country. In place of the department of theory, a department of the Literature and Materials of Music brought the student into direct contact with actual music. Also, the liberal studies were revised, including a program for training teachers. "It should be pointed out," said Schuman,

> that the Juilliard, as a professional music school, does not desire to develop a liberal arts curriculum. The academic division of the School, however, endeavors to offer work commensurate with that of the best liberal arts colleges, the difference being not in the quality of the work but in the scope of the offerings. The courses given at the School in literature, languages, science, social studies (including history and psychology), etc., are designed, then, not only to satisfy the requirements of the University of the State of New York for schools granting degrees, but also to give the young musician an awareness of other areas of learning and some insight into the great issues of the past and present.[49]

In many ways the independent conservatory as an institution has adapted itself to its American environment in response to perfectly real conditions. The Peabody Conservatory, as the first in this field, has perhaps experienced the various stages in this adaptation more intensely than some of the later schools—such as Juilliard, which, of course, could avail itself of the experience of the earlier foundation. From time to time, commentators on the American scene in higher musical education—particularly those whose concepts of education have been long ago established along the lines of the Continental system of strict separation between conservatories and universities—have urged Americans to restore this separation of functions. From the account of the establishment of the purely conservatory type of institution on American soil, however, it is obvious that the proposal thus urged *has* been tried, and that the present situation is the result of a century of very real trial-and-error development.

The early history of another conservatory which can actually claim a slight priority over Peabody in terms of the date on which the doors were opened, the New England Conservatory, deserves to be examined in detail because it is the first example of a music school that in its early years had a connection with a university, Boston University, through which the Bachelor of Music degree was early offered in the United States.[50] Thus, from

---

[49] William Schuman, "On Teaching the Literature and Materials of Music," *MQ*, Vol. 34 (1948), p. 167; *cf. The Juilliard Report on Teaching the Literature and Materials of Music* (New York: W. W. Norton & Co., Inc., 1953).

[50] The attribution of the first Bachelor of Music degree in the United States to Boston University seems no longer tenable (see Mountney, *op. cit.*, pp. 206–212), despite its being widely declared in print (e.g. in Grove's *Dictionary* and in Joseph Nathan Kane's *Famous First Facts* [New York: H. W. Wilson Company, 1950], p. 158). Adrian College, a Methodist institution in Adrian, Michigan, apparently awarded the degree in 1873 (according to the *Report of the Commissioner of Education for the Year 1873* [Washington, D.C.: Government Printing Office, 1874], p. 717), whereas Boston University awarded it first in 1877 (*Boston University Cata-*

considering the independent conservatory, we pass on to considering the university-affiliated college of music. Behind the establishment of this remarkably influential conservatory-college combination stands an unusual individual, Eben Tourjée, a man of the same dynamic promotional ability as Lowell Mason earlier in the century.

Born in Warwick, Rhode Island, in 1834 and obliged to leave school and go to work at eight years of age, Tourjée became interested in music during his early teens through singing in a choir and playing the organ. At seventeen he opened a music store in Fall River, in connection with which he formed several music classes. At twenty-five he became a teacher in the Greenwich, Rhode Island, Seminary, where he had once been a pupil. As eager as Mason had been to show that the supposedly unmusical could be taught music, Tourjée suggested to the trustees that the facilities for doing so be enlarged. "You could as easily make a whistle out of a pig's tail," one of the trustees told him. Tourjée promptly got a pig's tail and from it made a whistle (which later was placed in the New England Conservatory's extensive collection of musical instruments). In connection with the Greenwich Seminary, he founded and secured in 1859 a charter from the state for a Musical Institute, which has been called the "first music school in the true sense"[51] in the country.

The deliberateness of his next step contrasts sharply with the impetuosity of the careers of earlier figures like Mason and Billings. With the aid of a backer, Tourjée went to Europe in 1863 and carefully studied the conservatory system there. Returning, he moved his Musical Institute to Providence and called it a Conservatory of Music. After three years there, he moved it again to Boston and opened it as the New England Conservatory in 1867—an institution which was incorporated by the Massachusetts Legislature as a nonprofit organization in 1870. By that time it had some thousand students in attendance, and could proclaim itself to be "already the largest music school in the world."[52] By 1882 it had a seven-story dormitory housing 550 women, and could claim to have the "largest Conservatory building of the world."[53] Tourjée was a man who "thought big." He had, for instance, much to do with the monster Peace Jubilees held in Boston in 1869 and 1872, at the latter of which he led a chorus of 20,000;

---

logue, 1878, pp. 38–39). What we are more concerned with above, however, is the thinking behind the degree in its early form, rather than the historical fact of the first granting of it.

[51] Arthur L. Manchester, *Music Education in the United States Schools and Departments of Music*, United States Bureau of Education, Bulletin, 1908, No. 4, Whole Number 387 (Washington, D.C., 1908), p. 14. As the first national survey under government auspices, this is an important document.

[52] *New England Conservatory of Music: Boston Music Hall, June, 1869* (Boston: Farrar and Barnard, 1869), p. 4.

[53] *Great Enlargement of the New England Conservatory of Music . . . Calendar, 1882–3*, p. 9.

one of the numbers, played by an orchestra of some 2,000, featured a group of Boston firemen pounding out the rhythm of the "Anvil Chorus" on fifty anvils. The sheer numbers and extent of some of these post-Civil-War operations are hard for us to visualize today.

The New England Conservatory, as set up by Tourjée, was definitely oriented toward Europe:

> . . . the same opportunities for the study of music are demanded as are offered in our seminaries and colleges for the study of literature, or in our professional schools for the study of law, theology, or medicine. Such schools have existed in Europe for centuries. . . . It is the purpose of the Director to place the Conservatory upon as enduring a basis as the great schools of Leipsic, Prague, and Paris. . . . The Course of Instruction is similar to that of the celebrated Conservatories of Germany, France, and Italy.[54]

There is, however, a difference between what the European conservatory meant to Hamerick and what it meant to Tourjée. From the classes he had established in connection with his Fall River music store, Tourjée *knew* that instrumental instruction could be carried on by the group method economically and effectively; what he had seen in the European conservatories was mere confirmation of this inner conviction. When Tourjée said "conservatory," he meant primarily "class instruction." The system in the European conservatory is for a few pupils to come for a lesson at the same time, each being given instruction in turn while the rest sit in the room and observe. It is, of course, a sensible and adaptable system; and Tourjée recognized that it had certain advantages over the prevailing system of purely individual or tutorial instruction.

Tourjée—a person with a very realistic view of things, who had "come up the hard way"—also recognized other aspects of the European conservatory attitude. More than once in his promotional literature he quoted the following words of Mendelssohn:

> An institution such as the Conservatory has this advantage over the private instruction of the individual, that, by the participation of several in the same lessons and the same studies, a true musical feeling is awakened and kept fresh among the pupils: that it promotes industry, and spurs on to emulation; and that it is a preservative against one-sidedness of education and taste,—a tendency against which every artist, even in the student years, should be upon his guard.[55]

Obviously, Tourjée was taking from the European conservatory only certain aspects that made sense to him; he was not undertaking to transplant it intact, as the early directors of the Peabody Conservatory tried to do.

[54] *New England Conservatory of Music* . . . (1869), p. 4.
[55] *Ibid.; cf. Great Enlargement of the New England Conservatory* . . . *Calendar, 1882–3*, p. 11; *New England Conservatory of Music, Franklin Square, Boston, Mass. . . . Calendar, 1890–91* (1890), p. 15.

One of the really brilliant and historically significant things that he did was to enter into a relationship with Boston University which was being organized at about this same time. He served as the dean of its College of Music—the first college of music in a university—and under its auspices the Bachelor of Music degree was awarded. In its inception, the relationship between the New England Conservatory and Boston University parallels that between Tourjée's earlier Musical Institute and the Greenwich Seminary: Here again what he did in mid-career was simply what he had done earlier, but on a larger scale.

To understand how it was that in this country the conservatory idea and the university idea thus made contact—a unique development, unparalleled in Europe—and music again found its way into the university curriculum after having led a peripheral existence, one must understand the way in which an institution like Boston University came into being. It did not start from a college which gradually sent out tentacles into more specialized areas, as the older type of New England institution of higher education had done. Rather, it began as a collection of professional schools, and added a liberal arts college later. As a distinct type of post-Civil-War institution, it merits special attention. First there was a board of trustees, assembled on the basis of a very comprehensive and eclectic plan of what they called "Impartial education," and incorporated in 1869. To these trustees was conveyed, in 1871, the Boston Theological Seminary, a Methodist institution, which became the first unit of the actual university. The following year, two new units were organized, a School of Law and a College of Music—"the first ever established in America, adapted to the needs of graduates of musical conservatories and schools."[56] The implication is that one might graduate from a music school or conservatory, with a diploma, and then go on to the University College of Music for study leading to the Bachelor of Music degree. In 1873, four further units were added to Boston University: a Preparatory Academy at East Greenwich, Rhode Island (an older preparatory school, reopened; perhaps Tourjée had a hand in this, too), a College of Liberal Arts, a School of Oratory, and a School of Medicine (actually, this school was the result of a union between the Massachusetts Homeopathic Medical Society and the New England Female Medical College). Thus the University continued to grow, not only from within in the more traditional way, but also by accretion, from without.

Three leading ideas behind the establishment, all of which have direct bearing on the problem of general and special education, are set forth by

[56] *Boston University Year Book,* ed. by The University Council, Vol. 1 (Boston: H. O. Houghton & Co., 1874), p. 18.

the University Council in the first issue of the *Boston University Year Book* (1874):

> The idea or principle, that a University ought neither to generalize education merely, nor to specialize it merely, but to do both at one and the same time. . . . It should generalize all special training, and specialize to some extent all general. It should do this by carrying the general education of each pupil as high as possible before giving him the special, and by giving the most favored in respect to general education some practical adaptation to serve the world, if only by serving science, literature, and art. [Pp. 21–22.]

The second principle was that comparatively independent professional schools within a university were more effective than one monolithic organization, as is the norm in Continental universities. The third principle was that theoretical and applied study needed to be combined:

> The advocates of the non-professional theory of the University would, as a rule, maintain as wide and deep a gulf as possible between the University and all professional and technical schools. The advocates of the opposing theory would sink and merge the University into one grand polytechnical or pantechnical training establishment. Both classes are equally in error. Each fails to see how vivifying and fruitful are the action and reaction of the two classes of studies and of students upon each other.
>
> A university teaching all branches of human knowledge, but with no reference whatever to their practical applications in the actual world of mankind, is hardly conceivable. Were it conceivable, it certainly would not be desirable. No man has a right to live for self alone, and as little has any class of men, particularly the strong and cultivated. *Non vos vobis* is the language of even a pagan to such.
>
> Nor has there ever existed such an institution. In their most exclusive days, even Oxford and Cambridge were in a sense schools of applied science. They were as studiously adapted to fit men for certain prospective careers in actual life, as is the Law School to fit men for practice at the bar. Still more marked has been the practical character of the historic universities of the continent. Several of them originally grew out of professional schools, and all have ever sought to retain and control the higher professional education of their respective states. In this they have done wisely. Could they have anticipated or accepted the wonderful developments of modern industrial and art education, incorporating them into the life and growth of the University, they would have been still wiser and remained the institutional *Träger* of the intellectual and aesthetic life of their respective nations. [P. 23.]

This forceful statement of faith compels one to honor it by considering it carefully. The pupil "serving science, literature, and art" is here thought of as serving "the world." Obviously, the word "world" is here being used very inclusively, not merely as equivalent to the worldly aspects of existence which, according to the catechism, are wicked. In speaking of "the action and reaction of the two classes of studies and of students upon each other," the Council is admitting the existence of a separation which simply did not exist in the minds of most earlier educators. The Council's statement that "no man has a right to live for himself alone" must, somehow, not be taken as denying the value of contemplation, which Aristotle regarded as the highest (in the sense of the most self-contained) good. After all, for what prospective career in "actual life" did Socrates fit his followers? Certainly not for the career of Sophist as it existed in his day. Or, passing on to the Middle Ages, we must remember that the *collegium* or college was a religious community designed to prepare its members for the service of God in eternity: on earth, this might mean either an active or a contemplative role. These medieval Bachelors of Music were in holy orders, and their "college" was their "religious community." Although many religious communities perform notable works of social service, such as conducting schools, and caring for the sick, these works are incidental—by-products, as it were, of their principal aim. Inevitably, the adaptation of an institutional form that has grown up for the achievement of one purpose to a situation in which the purpose is radically different will have different results. The whole idea of a "college of music" in a university bears the same relationship to the medieval system as an early Italian opera does to a Greek tragedy. Strongly ingrained in the European university and still quite perceptible is a sense of estrangement from the world, of *Weltfremdheit,* which often prevents educated Europeans from accepting uncritically the "wonderful developments of modern industrial and art education" and which would no doubt have made the point of view here expressed by the University Council seem to them quite bourgeois and Methodist.

Within this framework a College of Music, headed by Tourjée (who, incidentally, was also Methodist), was established. The impulse to do so apparently proceeded in the first instance from Tourjée himself, who guaranteed the University that they would lose no money through the operation. Its rationale is thus set forth:

> The necessity of a thorough preparation for the profession of Music is becoming more apparent every year. Such a preparation should embrace not only a comprehensive knowledge of the science of Music, and a good degree of skill as an executant upon some instrument, or as a vocalist, but also a familiarity with two or three of the ancient or modern languages, mathematics, sciences, literature, and the fine arts. The knowledge and general intellectual culture acquired by such a course of study, are needed to give a correct view of the relation of Music to the other arts and sciences. They also enable students to more intelligently interpret and perform the works of the masters, render their services as instructors more valuable, and qualify them to do far more towards elevating the art to its true position in the estimation of the public, than they could otherwise possibly do. Few begin to study for other professions, much less to practice them, until they have acquired such a general preparation as the above course of study

affords; and if important to them, it is not less important for the musical profession. [P. 44.]

It is clear that the Bachelor of Music was here projected as a higher degree than the Bachelor of Arts. Before entering the College of Music, the student would, of course, have studied music either privately or at some conservatory or music school. Then, after three years of study at the College of Music, he might receive the University diploma or, if specially prepared and able, the degree:

> Those who have specially distinguished themselves by their talents and scholarship, will, if graduates of any college of arts, receive the degree of Bachelor of Music. If not graduates of a college of arts, they will be required to pass an examination in English Composition, History, and Literature, a modern language (French, German, or Italian), Latin, or instead of it a second modern language, and Mathematics, before being eligible to the above degree. [P. 46.]

In other words, if the student already had his A.B. before entering the College of Music, he could take his Bachelor of Music degree in three years; if he did not have his A.B., he could show by examination that he had the equivalent of an arts degree. In preparation for those examinations, he would be admitted, without extra charge, to any of the classes in the College of Liberal Arts and the School of Oratory. Of course, one realizes that in actuality there may well have been some leniency in the administration of such requirements; but the idea behind the degree is clear. It is of a piece with the three-year course in theology which led to the Bachelor of Sacred Theology (still, at Boston University, a graduate degree—in the sense that one normally has an A.B. before undertaking it), the three-year course in law which led to the Bachelor of Laws (now practically a graduate degree), and the three-year course in medicine which led to a Bachelor of Medicine or a Bachelor of Surgery degree (now replaced by the M.D.). Under this program Boston University awarded its first Bachelor of Music degree in 1877 to Charles Henry Morse,[57] and continued to grant one every few years —more of the students at the College of Music merely completing their three-year course and receiving the diploma without qualifying for the degree.

There was one slight ambiguity in the status of this original university-affiliated "college of music": Was it to be a "college" or a "school"? In the early years of Boston University, "school" meant "graduate school" and "college" meant something like "liberal-arts college." Thus, from the start,

[57] When Wellesley College opened in 1876, Morse was listed as a nonresident teacher; with his newly acquired B.M. he was responsible for a "Five Years Musical Course" leading to the A.B. there, and in 1880 for a College of Music awarding the B.M. for five years of study; by the end of the century, however, the situation at Wellesley had reverted to the A.B. with concentration in music.

the School of Theology, School of Medicine, School of Law, School of Oratory were consistently named. But the "College of Music," interestingly enough, was the first "college" of the University. It obviously had some features of both a "college" and a "school"; it was as if there were a sign "college" over the front door, and "school" over the back. If the person graduating from it had conceived of it as a college, he could take a diploma; if he had conceived of it as a school, he could take a degree. One may perhaps be inclined to dismiss the difference with a "what's in a name?," but in this instance it points to a fundamental ambiguity of conception which has never been completely resolved to everyone's satisfaction. On the basis of what happened in some of the other professions, one might imagine that the original "college of music" was just a how-to-do-it institution that suddenly began to put on airs by calling itself a college of music. This is not, however, the way it happened. The original "college of music" was a genuinely hybrid conception, with quite a conscious and well-articulated rationale.

The importance of this matter of names arises from the fact that many people think that words such as "conservatory" and "college" and "university" have each one right and true meaning, and that all difficulties can be solved by looking up the word in the dictionary or examining common usage of the particular word and automatically reinstating that as the ideal to be pursued. The whole problem of liberal education for the music student—according to Macdougall, professor at Wellesley during the first quarter of this century—is to be neatly solved by a verbal distinction between the college and the university (the former general, the latter specialized):

> There are many misconceptions both as to scope and manner of musical instruction in the college. The most common one comes about from the lack of the distinction between the college and the university. The university is a school for specialists. Thus Yale University may rightly have a school of music as well as of law, and train professional musicians quite as fittingly as lawyers. The College of Liberal Arts, however, is the school devoted, not to the specialist, but to the man who wishes a broad foundation for culture, a liberal education . . . the college is the place for cultivating the knowledge and the taste of the amateur. The university is the place for making specialists.[58]

This "college of music" of Tourjée's was obviously a daring conception, no doubt as unusual in its day as a "high school of music and art" in New York is in our own.[59]

---

[58] Hamilton C. Macdougall, "The Development of Musical Power in the College Student," *PMTNA*, Vol. 1 (1906), pp. 64–65.

[59] Alexander Richter, "The High School of Music and Art; A Program of Education for the Gifted Child," *PMTNA*, Vol. 33 (1939), pp. 248–255.

The question of whether they were in a "college" or a "school" was clear to the few students who went on to the Bachelor of Music degree; and whatever one wishes to call it, they no doubt did achieve an extensive experience of both the liberal and professional arts. But what of the thousands in the Conservatory, which was the vast reservoir from which the happy few in the college of music emerged? How were they, in their briefer period of attendance, to be preserved against the tendency to one-sidedness, against which Mendelssohn had said the music student should be on his guard? There was great demand for music teachers in the 1880's; and if the student were going to study at the Conservatory for only a year or so— probably working long hours supporting himself (or, more likely, herself) while doing so—he obviously needed something more than mere technical training.

Tourjée's solution to this problem was disarmingly simple: If a few students wanted a class in anything sensible, it would be set up for them. The plan is thus explained in the *Calendar* of 1881–82:

> It is generally conceded that the study of music tends to refine the manners and cultivate the taste. At the same time it is to be regretted that the prevailing impression should be that the concentration of effort necessary to insure the success of students pursuing a musical course precludes all possibility of mental development in other directions. Feeling the necessity of counteracting the evils arising from this erroneous impression, relative to the incompatibility of musical culture and intellectual vigor, the Director of the Conservatory has perfected arrangements which will enable students of the Conservatory to pursue, in connection with their musical course, and without charge, the following studies,—English grammar, rhetoric, literature, reading, spelling, penmanship, arithmetic, algebra, geometry, geography, natural philosophy, geology, botany, physiology, astronomy, history, political economy, mental science, moral philosophy, and Latin—through three years. Classes have just been organized in a number of the above branches, and will be organized in each of the others whenever three or more students shall apply for instruction therein.[60]

Some forty students were enrolled in the three-year College of Music course. It was made adequately clear to them that the fundamental idea of the college was not one of narrow specialization:

> This College is designed for students of the average proficiency of graduates of the best American conservatories. It is the only institution of its grade and kind in America.
>
> The advantages accruing to it from its location in Boston, and from its intimate association with the University, are very great. Few persons devoting themselves to this profession are able to complete a liberal education before beginning their special musical training. Nor, indeed, ought

[60] *Calendar, New England Conservatory of Music and College of Music of Boston University* (Boston: Deland and Harte, 1881), pp. 24–25.

they to do it. The best years for acquiring scholastic culture are also the best years for cultivating the voice, the ear, and the hand. A generous intellectual and aesthetic culture is needed by every professional musician; but it is best acquired, not before or after, but in connection with, his special studies. The lack of opportunities for such acquisition has been the chief defect of some of the most famous music-schools of the world. Had every great national conservatory always presented the collateral advantages for general culture which are here presented, the character of the entire profession would have been favorably affected.[61]

After the mid-80's, however, the tone becomes a little more strident. Merely for *admission* to the first-year class of the College of Music, students who did not already have the A.B. were confronted with this formidable list of requirements (according to the 1886 *Boston University Year Book*):

> If candidates for the degree of Bachelor of Music, and not already possessed of a literary degree, they must also give satisfactory evidence by acceptable certificate, or by examination, that they have been well instructed in (1) English Grammar, Rhetoric, and English Composition; (2) English Literature, and its History; (3) Outlines of Ancient and Modern History, the History of England, and History of the United States; (4) Arithmetic, Algebra to quadratics, and Elementary Geometry; (5) Physics, and three of the following sciences: Geography, Geology, Botany, Human Physiology, Chemistry, and Astronomy; (6) Sight-reading of easy Latin prose; (7) Sight-reading of easy French, German, or Italian prose; (8) Mental Philosophy; and (9) Moral Science. [P. 68.]

And, before actually *taking* the degree, they had "to pass an examination in Logic, and in two of the following works, (1) March's Latin Hymns; (2) Goethe's Faust, Erster Theil; (3) Racine, four plays; (4) Dante's Divina Comedia, one part. . . ." [p. 71]. Certainly this would today be thought excessive—even for a doctoral degree, much less a bachelor's.

The tone of the exhortation to the Conservatory students to broaden their studies also became more insistent:

> *Education is conceded to be the harmonious development of all one's faculties to their highest power, and their application to the noblest uses. It must therefore be symmetrical, for man is a unit, and one part of his nature cannot be developed to the highest point without the cultivation of the other parts.* We may speak of an uncultivated pianist or technician, but to use such a modifying term with the word *musician,* is to associate ideas which are essentially contradictory. *Hundreds of would-be musicians are failing to take the highest positions in our colleges and universities because of their limitations in this respect.* It is our aim to improve this condition of things by affording an opportunity for literary study with specialty work. Accordingly the New England Conservatory of Music has provided, in connection with its regular courses in Music, Art, etc., the following general exercises and facilities which, if appreciated and utilized, will secure

    [61] *Boston University Year Book,* ed. by The University Council, Vol. 10 (Boston: University Offices, 1883), pp. 65–66.

that liberal education which is so imperatively demanded of the representatives of the musical profession today.[62]

No doubt the completely permissive liberal education program had benefited the few students who least needed it, and had left the rest untouched. It is interesting, though, that the reasons for liberal study on the part of the music student are given here as two: the "whole man" idea and teacher training for college and university work. A more definite plan, with diploma-recognition, was accordingly suggested:

> A Course of Reading has been prepared for the students of the Conservatory, under the supervision of Prof. William J. Rolfe, assisted by several leading musicians and literary men, and all students are urged to devote at least *one hour per day* to this essential element in every curriculum of study. It comprehends the careful reading of five volumes per term—three in general literature, and two in some one of the special departments of study, and the completion of the same will be duly credited on diploma. Great care has been taken to select such volumes as will be most likely to interest the students and awaken a desire for further and more exhaustive research. A pamphlet giving details and the list of books, will be sent on receipt of ten cents in stamps. [P. 37.]

By 1890 the New England Conservatory had extended in many directions. In addition to the usual work in music, there was a department of piano and organ tuning, a department of elocution and physical culture, and college of oratory; and there was a department of fine arts. There was also, within its framework, a "School of General Literature and Languages":

> In past years artists as a whole, and musicians in particular, have borne the opprobrium (whether justly or otherwise) of being deficient in general culture, and, so far as this has been true, they have suffered in both reputation and success. It should be remembered, however, that this lack of culture, so far as it may exist today, is largely due to the difficulty—in many cases, we may say, the impossibility—of combining general with professional training. The thorough study of music, for instance, is exacting; and if the student has to seek a separate school, as he is generally compelled to do, for a liberal education, it involves too great a tax upon both his time and purse. To obviate this difficulty, and to afford students the opportunity of obtaining a liberal culture while pursuing their studies in music, elocution, or the fine arts, the above school has been organized. [P. 38.]

Quite an ambitious program was offered by this department of the Conservatory "to meet the wants of the general student, and also to serve as a preparation for the College of Music of Boston University." It included courses in history, English literature, mathematics, natural sciences, lan-

---

[62] *Annual Souvenir of the New England Conservatory of Music . . . 1890 and 1891* (Boston: New England Conservatory Music Store, 1890), p. 34.

guages, and philosophy. In fact, what had come into existence here was a little university in itself.

The Conservatory's program was obviously overextended. Although it had a daily attendance of more than a thousand, it was losing money. Tourjée was quite ill from 1889 on. An unsuccessful attempt was made to secure a subsidy from the state; eventually private contributions and internal reorganization enabled the institution to survive. But at the close of the school year in June 1891 (Tourjée having died earlier in the year), the Boston University College of Music was discontinued and its work transferred to the New England Conservatory.

In announcing the termination of the arrangements between what were henceforth to be two entirely separate institutions, the University Council stated:

> In any case the past is secure, and it will always redound to the honor of the University that in its very infancy it set and maintained a standard of attainment in this department of culture such as no existing American institution had set, and such as no future institution is likely to overpass. So high and strenuous were the requirements of this standard that thus far in the nineteen years of the College's life, notwithstanding it has had in its faculty not a few masters of international fame, but twenty-one students have succeeded in winning the honor of a graduation, and of these but five have succeeded in gaining the Bachelor's degree.[63]

It perhaps seems today slightly odd that an authoritative university body would congratulate itself on the *small* number of students graduated from one of its colleges: Quantity rather than quality is now more commonly a criterion. But like Mason's Academy of Music, Tourjée's conservatory-college combination had burst forth like a meteor and shone for only a decade or so. On American soil a creatively conceived version of the conservatory idea had been planted. Certainly Tourjée was not deaf to the call of a kind of perfectionism that had expressed itself during the early years of the Peabody Conservatory, but he had channeled this desire for perfection into a version of the Bachelor of Music degree and a concept of a university college of music that simply had not existed twenty-five years before. He was intensely aware of the need for liberal education in an institution of higher musical education that might be set up in America, and the span of his concern in this regard ranged from the beginners in the Conservatory to the adepts who emerged from the University as Bachelors of Music. Interestingly enough, his concept of a way in which a university might concern itself with the higher education of musicians has certain terms in common with that which for convenience we might call the "Har-

---

[63] *Boston University Year Book,* ed. by The University Council, Vol. 19 (Boston: University Offices, 1892), p. 80.

vard" attitude on this matter—only Tourjée's attitude was more positive, progressive, and adventurous.

Just to bring to some sort of conclusion the historical account of the two important institutions that have been here touched on—the New England Conservatory and Boston University—we might note that Tourjée's successor, Carl Faelten (a German by birth and early training) had previously taught at the Conservatory in Frankfurt am Main and at Peabody: he tended very strongly to bring the New England Conservatory into line with the best European practice, somewhat as Hamerick had done at Peabody. His successor, the composer George Chadwick, continued to strive toward the independent European conservatory ideal. Writing in 1904, Elson thus characterized the situation:

> Three large conservatories exist at present in America,—those at Boston, Cincinnati, and Chicago. Of the three the New England Conservatory of Boston has a curriculum most nearly approaching that of the great European schools, and this broad course has been largely due to the efforts of Mr. George W. Chadwick, its present director. . . . The curriculum of the conservatory is at present probably the most severe of any musical school in this country.[64]

It is clear that Chadwick's direction was in terms of the genuine European conservatory ideal: he, for instance, told the Music Teachers National Association in 1908:

> The ideal music school in this country cannot arrive until conditions are made favorable for its growth and development. There are signs that these conditions are approaching, and at a rapid rate. An ideal school which is organized and conducted for art's sake alone can never support itself. It needs an expensive equipment. It needs artists and professors whose time and effort command large compensation, it needs permanent support from an enthusiastic art-loving public, and it needs an endowment fund large enough to provide for the entire education and maintenance of highly gifted young people.[65]

This is obviously in a very different spirit from Tourjée, who launched and conducted his amazing enterprise for over a couple of decades solely on pupils' fees, or from Mason, who seems somehow to have elicited financial support as it was needed.

As for the immediate fortunes of the Bachelor of Music degree after Boston University discontinued its College of Music, the New England Conservatory had its own Postgraduate Department, which took over some of the work that had been handled by the College. At the Conservatory during the last decade of the nineteenth century the Bachelor of Music degree led

---

[64] Elson, *op. cit.*, pp. 340–341.
[65] George W. Chadwick, "The Curriculum of a School of Music," *PMTNA*, Vol. 3 (1909), p. 76.

a ghostly existence; if students completed the Conservatory course and passed satisfactorily "examinations in Logic and in two of the following languages, Latin, German, French, or Italian,"[66] they might receive the Bachelor of Music degree from Boston University. Though this reduction of the A.B.-equivalency into an examination in logic and two foreign languages may have been more feasible for the student who might wish to take it, only one did. The New England Conservatory continued to have its own "School of General Literature and Language." A final echo of the earlier grandiose arrangements appears in the 1900 Prospectus of the Conservatory:

> By an arrangement with the Boston University Corporation, opportunity is given to full and regular students in the Post-Graduate Course to pursue the following literary advantages without extra cost, in the Boston University:
>   Languages: French, German, Italian, Spanish, Anglo-Saxon, Latin, and Greek
>   Mathematics and Natural Science: Solid Geometry, Trigonometry, Analytical Geometry, Physics, Chemistry, Biology, etc.
>   History, Literature, and Law: English Literature, Rhetoric, History, Roman Law, Constitution of the United States, Political Economy, etc.
>   Philosophy: Psychology, Logic, and the Theory of Knowledge; Principles of Metaphysics, Theistic and Ethical Philosophy, etc.[67]

In other words, the Boston University catalogue! There is, however, no mention of students taking the Bachelor of Music degree—as a matter of fact, no one had taken it since 1893. While this "list of General Education courses" looks impressive on paper, the practical limitations of time and distance between the two institutions no doubt kept to a minimum the students availing themselves of these opportunities. The New England Conservatory and Boston University had definitely parted after Tourjée's death, and there has existed no organic connection between them within the present century. What general cultural courses the Conservatory has given have been supplied from its own staff or as the result of arrangements somewhat like the one above, but with other institutions in the Greater Boston area. For a while in the early twentieth century, for instance, exchange courses were instituted with Harvard; in 1905, the Harvard student of music theory could take some work at the Conservatory and, vice versa, Conservatory students could take certain courses in English literature, modern languages, physics, and public speaking at Harvard. Again, the physical separation of the two institutions (one in Cambridge, the other in Boston) no doubt meant that very few students made use of these available privileges, though in any metropolitan situation there is always, of course, sporadic exchange of resources among neighboring institutions, usually on an unofficial basis.

---

[66] *The New England Conservatory Calendar, 1893–4*, p. 39.
[67] *Prospectus 1900–1901 The New England Conservatory of Music* (Boston: New England Conservatory of Music, 1900), pp. 49–50.

Meanwhile, during the first quarter of the present century, a Department of Music was organized at the Boston University College of Liberal Arts. Students wishing to take music there might work toward an A.B. with a major in music. In 1928, this department was reorganized as a College of Music, and the Bachelor of Music degree was again granted by Boston University—not, however, quite according to its earlier conception of the degree but more nearly as it had taken shape through the work of the Music Supervisors National Conference and the National Association of Schools of Music in the early 1920's. In the late 1920's, also, both Peabody and the New England Conservatory began granting the Bachelor of Music degree—but this takes us into another era, which will be considered in the next chapter.

Obviously, it would not be feasible at this point to go through the history of other music schools in the country, although each would doubtless yield its particular variation on the professional-liberal theme. Several will be taken up in detail later on in this study, as they are appropriate to particular phases of the investigation. Two which may with some justification claim to be the first conservatories to be opened in the United States, and the initial university-college combination, have been examined from the special point of view of their liberal and professional aspects, particularly as they developed in their earlier years. The account, so far as the present century is concerned, must necessarily focus more and more on the work of associations of schools or the handling of large over-all problems. Just as the account of the eighteenth century had to focus on individuals and the nineteenth on separate schools, the twentieth must focus on aspects involving more than one institution.

Chapter 3

MUSIC CURRICULA TODAY

WHAT IS THE SITUATION TODAY, WITH RESPECT TO THE LIBERAL AND PRO-
fessional component in actual programs of study at institutions of higher
musical learning? The present chapter focuses on the curricula of some two
dozen representative music schools, compares them with the curricula in
the schools of other professions, and tries to concentrate on the twentieth-
century history of the liberal-professional relationship. From time to time,
however, some details of nineteenth-century history may have to be brought
in, for the situation in music, as one of the older of the professional disciplines at the academic board, is not so simple as that of some of the more
recent guests.

Of course the mere analysis of curricula in terms of hour-requirements
for various parts of the students' training gives no final answers to the
questions posed for this investigation. "Liberal education" has been defined
by McGrath for purposes of this study in terms of three functions (somewhat in the mathematical sense of "functions"): breadth of sheer subject-
matter knowledge, intellectual skills, and values, ideals, and attitudes. To
state them more succinctly, we might say: facts, thinking, and character.
An analysis of representative curricula will not show us whether any of
these have actually been achieved, but may be expected to yield data that
bear at least some *negative* relationship to these three functions. *Unless*
something other than harmony or solfège is studied, the student can hardly
be expected to have come into contact with the factual aspects of our Western tradition in any very systematic or intelligible way; he can scarcely be
expected to appreciate, say, the approach of the natural or social scientist
to life by *only* playing his musical instrument; and his intellectual curiosity
is *not* likely to be stimulated by being given an increasingly circumscribed
area in which to manifest itself.

Toward the end of the last chapter the growing importance of associations of music schools in the twentieth century was indicated. Some understanding of how they came into existence and gradually worked out a
relative percentage of professional and liberal studies that they felt desirable

will furnish a necessary background for examination of the actual curricula at some representative music schools.

INFLUENCE OF ASSOCIATIONS

The outstanding development of the present century in higher education in music has been the increasing influence exerted by the national associations. Tourjée was also active in organizing musicians. In 1869, in connection with the Peace Jubilee where he led his monster chorus and orchestra, he was responsible for the first meeting of The National Music Congress —"to arrive at a greater unity of purpose and of method in the musical development of the American people."[1] This organization was primarily effective in developing choral societies and promoting the teaching of music in the public schools, but after a few annual meetings—no doubt having achieved its announced purpose—it passed out of existence.

In 1876 at Delaware, Ohio, however, a national organization that has since been continuously influential and active had its first meeting under Tourjée's presidency, the Music Teachers' National Association. In its inception, this cooperative society of individual musicians, most of them private teachers, had many aspects of a "musical convention"—lectures and discussions as well as concerts. Like the Bachelor of Music degree, it somewhat overshot the mark; as one of its early leaders wrote, in looking back over the early days of the MTNA:

> The main plan was to organize the music profession, or in some way to procure unity of effort along many lines. The scheme was very complete. There was the National Association with its officers and propaganda. Then came the State Associations. . . . All these were to be affiliated and were to cooperate to constitute an organization devoted to the honor, glory and progress of our art. But the plan was too elaborate and did not work. The teachers would not support both the state and the national associations. . . . Moreover, the objects for which all this machinery was created were somewhat obscure.[2]

Eventually, however, it solved its problems of internal organization; and increasingly during the early twentieth century, through the speeches at its annual meetings and through its proceedings (published for many years under the title *Studies in Musical Education, History, and Aesthetics*), it became a factor in the shift of focus in American education from the individual, private teacher, who was often concerned with details of musical

---

[1] Quoted by Edward Bailey Birge, *History of Public School Music in the United States* (Bryn Mawr, Pennsylvania: Oliver Ditson, 1937), p. 231.

[2] Frederick W. Root, "Then and Now—1876–1908," *PMTNA*, Vol. 3 (1909), p. 13.

technique, to the university-sponsored schools of music, which were inevitably more liberal in their orientation.

Reviewing the first five volumes of published papers of the Association, Lutkin, of Northwestern University, pointed out that the majority of the articles had been by men connected with colleges and universities—though there had been no original intention so to limit the Association.[3] At each meeting there had been the address of welcome by the president of the college or university that was host to the national meeting which usually stressed the more liberal aspects of music, and at least one paper by a layman. G. Stanley Hall of Clark University, for example, had quite forthrightly urged the Association to address itself to problems of teacher training;[4] and Nicholas Murray Butler of Columbia, emphasizing the relationship of music to general culture, had said that musicians must

> keep persistently and insistently before the public consciousness the fact that they are dealing with an elementary and fundamental form of human expression which has a splendid history in the progress and development of our modern culture, and that intelligent and well-trained people must know something of its significance, in order not to carry away from their schools and colleges a one-sided, imperfect and thoroughly warped and misleading view of life and the development of the spirit in its manifold forms.[5]

Strongly inspirational, but often quite forcibly to the point of the importance of liberal education to the music student, are many of these addresses before the MTNA. Henry Suzzallo, later President of the University of Washington and of the Carnegie Foundation for the Advancement of Teaching, told the Association in 1908:

> Music in the university should be both liberal and vocational. . . . The average musician is lacking in general culture, too often excused on the basis of artistic temperament, when it is only the bad traditions of his musical training which are to blame. . . . In the first place, students of music should not be inferior in general academic standing to other students. If the entrance-requirements are less for the music student, he will be somewhat less in the social esteem of the college. Music students need to do as well in their general academic studies as their associates.[6]

The address by the President of the Association—always an important feature of each annual meeting—has a constantly recurring theme: as

[3] Peter Christian Lutkin, "Has the Policy Inaugurated in 1906 Been Satisfactory?," *PMTNA*, Vol. 6 (1912), p. 227.

[4] G. Stanley Hall, "The Function of Music in the College Curriculum," *PMTNA*, Vol. 2 (1908), p. 17.

[5] Nicholas Murray Butler, "Address of Welcome," *PMTNA*, Vol. 2 (1908), p. 11.

[6] Henry Suzzallo, "The Place of Music in Higher Education," *PMTNA*, Vol. 3 (1909), pp. 104–106.

John Lawrence Erb of the University of Illinois put it in 1916, the musician needs "to become acquainted with the point of view of the other fellow."[7] In 1940, reviewing the Proceedings published to that time, the editor, Theodore M. Finney, found that the problem of whether music teachers needed degrees—which was basically a question of musical skill vs. liberal training, under various terms—had been a perennial one in the MTNA since its founding.[8] Going back to the initial volume of Proceedings, issued in 1876, Finney found in the preface concern over the narrowness of musicians' training. Returning to the situation in his own day, he quoted a recent statement by the President of the Carnegie Corporation, Frederick P. Keppel, to the effect that only in medicine, law, and the older branches of engineering can the possession of a degree be said necessarily to mean anything.

Because of its original nature as a cooperative association of individual music teachers, however, the MTNA has never really felt it to be within its province to set up an examining body to pass on the actual qualifications of professed teachers or musicians or on the adequacy of curricula at educational institutions. Only with the organization of the National Association of Schools of Music in 1924, avowedly to deal with institutions *as institutions,* has any very effective work been done in establishing standards for curricula—though some very famous institutions (e.g., Harvard, New York University, Princeton, University of Pennsylvania, etc.) do not think of themselves as having undergraduate music schools and consequently are not NASM members. From time to time, the wish has been expressed that some board or examining body would be set up that would exercise authority over the individual musician and the profession as a whole, such as exist in medicine, law, and some branches of engineering; but except in certain limited fields (e.g., the American Guild of Organists) and in some special ways (e.g., the Musicians' Union), attempts in this direction have simply not succeeded.

Within the MTNA, one serious attempt to set up an examining board for all types of musicians, on the model of the London Guild of Organists, was made in the 1880's—the American College of Musicians.[9] Examinations required passing 48 credits in academic subjects, 48 in musical. This "college" would confer degrees of Associate, Fellow, and Master of Mu-

---

[7] John Lawrence Erb, "The Musician and the Community," *PMTNA,* Vol. 11 (1917), p. 17; *cf.* also Waldo Selden Pratt, "Standards in Musical Education," *PMTNA,* Vol. 2 (1908), pp. 63, 65; Rosseter G. Cole, "Musicians and Musicianship," *PMTNA,* Vol. 4 (1910), p. 29.

[8] Theodore M. Finney, "The Problem of Academic Degrees for Teachers of Musical Skills," *PMTNA,* Vol. 34 (1940), pp. 170–174.

[9] Edward M. Bowman, "History of the Organization of the American College of Musicians," *PMTNA,* Vol. 7 (1912), p. 148.

sical Art. An arrangement with the Board of Regents of the State of New York was made, and syllabi were prepared. But, like the early conservatory and the Bachelor of Music degree, it overshot its mark. The examinations were so difficult that few could pass, and the number of applicants had so decreased by 1897 that the project was discontinued.

In 1896 the MTNA, which has carried on most of its work through standing committees, created a Committee on Music in the Colleges and Universities. This has been primarily a fact-finding group and a clearing house for the exchange of ideas. Through questionnaires, for example, it immediately gathered data from 300 institutions: 106 offered opportunities for the study of applied music without credit, 25 had only theory courses, 5 had only applied, and 36 had both. Gradually some picture of the actual situation, in all its variety, began to emerge. The government began to assist in this fact-finding (no doubt at MTNA instigation)[10] during the first quarter of the present century, and foundations like the Carnegie during the second. On the basis of some real information about what was actually taking place in higher musical education, some of the difficulties that these early projects encountered could be anticipated.

The kind of central authority exercised by many institutions and examining bodies in some of the European countries and attempted in the "American College of Musicians" has simply not been possible in the United States. In 1892 a strong effort was made and the National Conservatory in New York City was established with Dvořák as artistic director, but after a few years it was discontinued. Again, in the years immediately after World War I, hopes for a national conservatory revived with the introduction of bills before Congress that might establish a Secretary of Fine Arts in the President's Cabinet. What was envisaged was something that might be to the United States what the Paris Conservatoire is to France. This possibility was discussed pro[11] and con before the MTNA from time to time. Frederick B. Stiven, of the University of Illinois, felt that it would be unnecessary: we already have the state universities. He then proceeded to develop the idea of the school of music being coordinate with the college of liberal arts—a concept quite fundamental to the university-sponsored music school of the day:

> All education can be divided into two branches, vocational and cultural. Music by its very nature belongs to both. The course of study, then, of the ideal School of Music must look constantly at both these goals. There must always be borne in mind the fact that the duty of an academic

[10] A good case in point is the U.S. Bureau of Education survey of 1908, for which Arthur L. Manchester, MTNA President in 1900, was responsible.

[11] John Lawrence Erb, "The Movement for a National Conservatory of Music and for a Secretary of Fine Arts in the President's Cabinet," *PMTNA*, Vol. 16 (1922), p. 31.

institution of music is first of all to provide a foundation of general knowledge, a solid basis, comprehensive in its scope, which will give to its
students a technical and an appreciative understanding of music and its
relationship to the other arts. In addition to this cultural training there
must come some degree of specialization in a particular musical branch—
the vocational aspect of the training offered. Just what the proportion of
these two elements should be is the problem on which leading educators
in music are focusing their attention at the present day.[12]

This "ideal School of Music" is very different from the concept of a
"National conservatory," which might have been an obvious solution to
the problem of standards if it had not been so remote from the actual
thinking of many American educators and musicians of the 1920's. By
this time the intense perfectionism of the late nineteenth century was *passé*.

No simple means—like a central examining board or a national conservatory—would solve the problem of standards for the musical profession
as a whole or change the extreme positions taken by many individual members of the MTNA. Obviously, a *part* of the problem had to be solved, and
the solution—if effective—allowed to influence the surrounding problem
areas. Accordingly, another musical organization, specifically focused from
the start on what is today referred to colloquially as "music ed," and Middle
Western in origin, was founded in 1907: the Music Supervisors National
Conference (later called the Music Educators National Conference, as its
scope widened). This was an outgrowth of the National Education Association, which had been started back in the mid-nineteenth century by that
staunch supporter of Lowell Mason, Horace Mann. The NEA had developed a public school department in 1884; and because the annual meeting of the NEA was often far away, on the East or West coast, a group of
members concerned with public school music decided to meet at Keokuk,
Iowa. The original focus was definitely on the problems of music on the
elementary and secondary school levels, within the public school system.
There has always been a close relationship between the NEA and the
MSNC (or MENC), and a clear awareness of the situation in the Middle
West, with its extensive music programs in the state universities and public
schools. Or, to put it another way, European traditions have seemed
less binding in the MENC than they have in some other groups. One of
the main problems confronting the MSNC in its early days, as recalled by
its first president, Frances Clark, was that music supervisors then were in
an anomalous position—not accepted as "musicians" by professionals, nor
as "educators" by the intellectuals.[13]

[12] Frederic B. Stiven, "The Contribution of a University School of Music to the
State and University," *MQ,* Vol. 9 (1923), p. 399.
[13] Frances Elliott Clark, "Fifty Years of Music Education in America," *Music
Educators Journal,* Vol. 36, No. 4 (April–May 1950), p. 23.

In the early twentieth century, in public school education, there were two antithetical tendencies going on at once: the emphasis on lesson plans, stemming from Herbart, and that on the child as a whole, led by Dewey. Although related and complementary, each of these tendencies had a different focus—one on the teacher, the other on the pupil—and could, on occasion, conflict. In the nineteenth century, education had been simpler —for the teacher. He was primarily showing his pupils how to read, and as the alphabet led to the reading of books, so the scale led to the singing of songs. The music teacher said, "Now follow me right up and down; sound,"[14] and sooner or later—no doubt with a liberal application of "soft sawder"—most did, some one way and some another. But as the new century dawned the teacher had begun to ask himself, "What am I doing, primarily? giving a good lesson? or helping the child unfold?" Although these amount ultimately to the same thing, a cleft between the two had begun to be felt in the minds of many. By the scale method, prodigious feats of sight reading had been achieved among groups of children before the nineteenth century had come to an end; the only trouble was that the children thus taught to read music did not seem to care for it much. "We might say," observed Birge, president of the MSNC in 1910, "that the children possessed the music, but that the music did not possess the children."[15] During the early part of the twentieth century, the MSNC stressed the idea that the "whole child" was necessarily involved in the process of learning music, and that the child rather than the subject was the paramount concern of music educators and, consequently, of the educators in university-sponsored music schools who were confronted with the task of preparing students to take their place as teachers in the public schools.

The influence of the "whole child" approach has penetrated all aspects of education in music, higher as well as lower. Waldo Selden Pratt, at one time professor at the Hartford Theological Seminary and president of the MTNA, wrote:

> When we talk of "musical education" we tacitly admit that education in music is not all of education. We all know this to be true. The process of bringing to light whatever is best in personality and fitting it for usefulness in actual life—which is the essence of education—may be operated along several different tracks, only one of which is that of musical culture. Yet there are hosts of music teachers who practically never instigate pupils to study anything but music. And so there are hosts of music-pupils growing up with no strong and sound mental discipline except in music. Every such teacher and pupil is more or less a foe to the best interests of musical art

[14] *American History and Encyclopedia of Music, History of American Music— Music in America*, quoted by Birge, *op. cit.*, p. 13.
[15] Clark, *op. cit.*, p. 24.

and liable to become a menace to society. Mentally he is one-sided and defective. He is apt to have some of the unlovely attributes of the bigot or fanatic, and his influence is likely to prejudice the non-musical against music and to mislead the musical into being proud of an intellectual isolation of which they ought to be ashamed.[16]

Many developments of the early twentieth century combined to make the music teacher's role much more varied than it had been before. The development of the phonograph made it possible for each child to discover music for himself, yet at the same time to enter into a nonparticipating relationship with the music—a relationship which, in comparison with that to music in the singing school, was most ambiguous. There was consequently development of "music appreciation"—too little for some commentators on the scene, too much for others.[17] Music no longer meant singing church hymns and related forms; it had begun to mean many different things, but, especially, instrumental music. In high school there was class teaching of, first, the violin, then the piano, and later the orchestral instruments. High school bands and orchestras had made sporadic appearances, particularly in the Middle West, in the late nineteenth century. World War I gave a great impetus to them: During the war there were high school ROTC units for marching music, and after the war many returning bandmasters became instrumental teachers in the schools. The town band, which had played regularly during the summer in the square or public park, was replaced by the school band, which played at the football games. The promoting, organizing, and maintaining of a complex enterprise like this involved a great variety of managerial skills that had not usually been considered a concern of the music teacher back in the nineteenth century. Public school music teaching became something infinitely more complex, in certain ways, than it had been—something much more institutionalized. This was not, of course, peculiar to music: Every profession at the turn of the century shared somewhat in this sudden increase in the number and types of different things that its members were expected to do. Public school music was a particularly active area in these changes, and the MSNC a focal point within it, growing as if by chain reaction: Its membership was some 150 in 1910, 1,500 in 1920, 4,000 in 1930, and is about 25,000 today.

The ideology which this movement represented, however, was very

[16] Waldo Selden Pratt, "The Ensemble Idea in Music-Education," *PMTNA,* Vol. 14 (1920), p. 28.

[17] Contrast, for example, Roy Dickinson Welch, *The Study of Music in the American College* (Northampton, Massachusetts: Smith College, 1925) and Carl Engel, "Views and Reviews," *MQ,* Vol. 11 (1925), pp. 617–629. They are, of course, talking about music in colleges and universities; but the same considerations apply, the changes that had taken place in the lower levels of education having now begun to make their presence felt throughout the whole educational structure.

different from that which had appeared in the nineteenth-century attempts on the part of conservatories and universities in America to deal with music, and even different from Mason's idea of morally reforming America by teaching all school children sight singing. In 1915, at the request of the MSNC, Karl Gehrkens of Oberlin formulated this statement of purpose: "The ultimate aim of music teaching in the public schools is to cause children to know, to love, and to appreciate music in as many forms as possible, and thus to bring added joy into their lives and added culture and refinement into their natures."[18] Smooth as this statement is, one must recognize that it does not have quite the same intensity of wind-pressure (to use a metaphor from organ-building) as Mason's advocacy of the teaching of music as "a sure means of improving the affections, and of ennobling, purifying, and elevating the whole man."[19] Viewing this matter of fundamental aims and intentions from the vantage point of the mid-twentieth century, moreover, the veteran music educator, Will Earhart, has pointed out some shortcomings of "enjoyment" as a criterion:

> . . . to *feel* that music is good is not enough. One who has only that basis is likely to succumb to the scientific outlook (which is applicable to technical and vocational efficiencies only) or to be seized by the fear that the feelings of others are just as authoritative as his. Then the many whispering voices of those others—and they are the voices of adults, not children —begin to sound in his ears. Music is an "escape" (and, curiously, an escape *from* what to what does not appear to be defined); or it is an entertainment; or it must be "functional"; or the real music for Americans, because expressive of the "American spirit," is the twitching, hiccoughing, syncopated energy of jazz, or the cacophonies, the wild, aimless improvisations, the ugly noises of mistreated woodwinds, muted trumpets, and sliding trombones that mark the neural sprees indulged in by our "dance bands." We have all seen instances—although, thank goodness, rarely—where such voices have insidiously influenced the educational music program; and such instances grow more and more rare. But we still see large and gorgeously caparisoned bands led by prancing drum majorettes and outfitted at a cost of thousands of dollars, when at a fraction of that cost—indeed, at no cost except for printed music, and that the bands, too, must have—those youths might be in a chorus singing the music of Palestrina, Bach, or Brahms.[20]

In 1915, however, the "party line" of the music educators, as expressed through Gehrkens's statement of purpose, was not particularly moralistic, and it was very simple and clear: Pupils should enjoy music.

In 1919 Gehrkens was appointed to head a committee of the MSNC on

[18] Birge, *op. cit.*, p. 249.
[19] Lowell Mason, *Manual of the Boston Academy of Music* (Boston: Carter, Hendee & Co., 1834), p. 35.
[20] Will Earhart, "A Philosophic Basis for Aesthetic Values in Education," *Music Educators Journal*, Vol. 37, No. 2 (November–December 1950), p. 17.

the Training of Supervisors of Music. By questionnaires, he determined that about a hundred schools in the country were offering such training courses; about half of them were two-year, 20 were three-year, and 25 were four-year. Most of the four-year courses led to a bachelor's degree (12 B.S., 5 B.M.). As for entrance requirements, 89 required four years of high school, with most requiring some preliminary musical training. As for academic work during the music supervisors' course, 71 required some sort of nonmusic work, usually English.

Obviously, the situation which the MSNC committee faced was a rather formless one. A great deal of discussion—some of it also a little formless —took place before it became clear what should be done. Heacox, of Oberlin, for example, wished to canvass the then leading supervisors of music to see how *they* had been prepared for their work, and to build a curriculum on this information:

> As of old, there are giants in these days. If we want to know how to develop the ideal supervisor, why not tabulate the recipes which have produced the giants who now lead in their profession, those who have had the enterprise to organize and foster the growth of the MSNC, the vision and diplomacy to work wonders with school boards, the musicianship to prepare books of beautiful music such as former generations never knew, and the zeal to study pedagogical questions and courageously discard useless and outworn methods? Or, to be even more specific, why not have the Danns and Dykemas, Birges, Baldwins and Beatties, Millers and McConathys, Giddingses, Gartlans and Gehrkenses, Fullertons and Farnsworths, the Woods, and many others I should like to take the time to name, write for us brief autobiographies, *including their confessions,* and let us tabulate the evidence and accept the composite thus obtained as our ideal supervisor?[21]

It is hard to know whether he was perfectly serious about this (after all, these people named would have been present there before him, no doubt pleased to hear their names read off as if they were already semi-legendary figures in some great epic roll of heroes): Discounting the possibility of there being some "soft sawder" here, one can imagine that Gehrkens's committee, had it made such a canvass, would have been still further confused by the variety in existing patterns of training the supervisor.

There is a strange similarity between the recommendation that was made by Gehrkens's committee (and that subsequently became the basis for curricular recommendations of the associations) and the pattern of higher education in music that had long before been developed at Oberlin. For that reason, some understanding of the background of the

[21] Arthur E. Heacox, "In the Curriculum for Supervisors, How Can We Maintain a Proper Balance between Subjects of Purely Musical Nature and Those of General Value?," *PMENC,* Vol. 14 (1921), p. 161.

Oberlin Conservatory is here appropriate. Its beginnings go back to 1834, when the legislature incorporated the "Oberlin Collegiate Institute." The catalogue of 1835 lists a "professor of sacred music," and in 1838 George N. Allen—probably a pupil of Mason's—held that post until well on into the Civil War. It is said that he was riding the stagecoach through northern Ohio, stopped in Oberlin to pass the Sunday, and when his musical talents were recognized was asked to remain—first as student, then as teacher, and from 1841 on as professor.[22]

After Allen retired in 1864, the "Oberlin Conservatory of Music" was started, for the modest purpose—according to its first catalogue—"of advancing Music, by furnishing systematic and thorough instruction at low rates, and encouraging the investigation and prosecution of Music both as a science and an art. . . . Persons desiring to study Music in connection with studies in the College can choose such branches of study as they wish to pursue."[23]

During its first decade or so, however, the authorities were more concerned with making sure that the student was well rounded *within* music —being not merely a pianist, for instance, or merely a singer. For the diploma awarded by Oberlin College he had to complete—according to the 1883 catalogue—four branches (in the sense of piano, organ, voice, theory, etc.) and to show "satisfactory evidence of proficiency in the fundamental branches of an English education"[24]—by which is meant, no doubt, the ability to speak and write acceptably. Students of the Conservatory could take a course in the College at half-fee, and were urged to do so for the sake of symmetrical self-development, social acceptability, and diversion —the latter of these contrasting with Tourjée's more ambitious suggestion of preparation for teaching on the college level.

By 1896, a slightly more pressing plea for attention to liberal study was made:

> Years ago a smattering of harmony and, perhaps, a side-long glance at counterpoint were considered quite enough for the average student. Very few went so far as to investigate the intricacies of fugue or pure part-writing. As to academical or collegiate education, its lack among musicians was the fashion to such a degree as to bring the stigma of narrowness upon the entire profession. But the student of to-day, looking out upon greatly changed conditions, finds that his natural gifts, however great, are not sufficient in themselves, or even with moderate training, to enable him to cope successfully with the great problems of musical classicism and roman-

[22] Rose Yont, *The Value of Music in Education* (Boston: Richard G. Badger, 1916), p. 136.

[23] *Catalogue of the Conservatory of Music, Oberlin College, 1869–70* (Cleveland, Ohio: Fairbanks, Benedict & Co., 1869), pp. xi, xix.

[24] *Ibid., 1883,* p. 17.

ticism. They must be subjected to a thorough technical and aesthetical training and be supplemented by a liberal education.[25]

Just what academic subjects a Conservatory student could or should take at the College, however, were not prescribed, but were to be arrived at by individual conference:

> Conservatory students are recommended, as far as practicable, to avail themselves of this privilege, that they may secure symmetry and breadth of culture, as well as the ability to use their musical powers to better advantage.
>
> College students also will find facilities unusually good for carrying on their work in music at the same time with their literary studies. The work in harmony, and, for advanced students, vocal and instrumental study, is permitted to count in the college course.[26]

An important aspect of the Oberlin situation was this easy reciprocal relationship between Conservatory and College.

It was not until 1905, however, that Oberlin announced that it would award the Bachelor of Music degree. Instead of presupposing an A.B. or its equivalent, however, it simply required that "Before entering upon the senior year, students must have completed a course of literary work equivalent to that of the College entrance requirement as defined in the Oberlin College Catalogues."[27] In other words, this Bachelor of Music degree was the counterpart, for music students, of the Bachelor of Arts for regular College students.

The developing rapprochement between Conservatory and College which can be observed at Oberlin was rather typical of many institutions in the Middle West. In 1912 the Director of the Conservatory of Music at Wooster, Ohio, commented before the MTNA on this phenomenon:

> Except in the East, especially New England and the Northern Middle States, nearly every college and a goodly proportion of the universities possess a Music Department, organized more or less along conservatory lines and often bearing the name "Conservatory." This is overwhelmingly true of the coeducational schools and those for women only—in fact, so much so, that it might almost be laid down as a universal fact that only colleges for men rarely possess a conservatory. But colleges for men alone exist almost entirely in the East, so the college conservatory is well nigh universal except in New England and the North Atlantic seaboard. To illustrate with the state of Ohio, with which I am best acquainted statis-

---

[25] *Ibid., 1896*, pp. 5–6.
[26] *Ibid.*, p. 29.
[27] *Oberlin Conservatory of Music, 1905* (Cleveland, Ohio: F. W. Roberts Co., 1905), p. 15. Some of the Bachelor of Music degrees awarded in 1905 were retroactive, three of them to members of the class of 1873. They were for applied music, and represented a five-year program. See Virginia Ruth Mountney, "The History of the Bachelor's Degree in the Field of Music in the United States" (unpublished D.M.A. dissertation, Boston University, 1961), p. 205.

tically, out of more than sixty institutions of collegiate rank, fifty-four or fifty-five possess conservatories, and of the five or six that do not have them, four are in large cities and the fifth is a men's school.[28]

In examining the development of Oberlin Conservatory, accordingly, we are concerned with a rather distinctively American, and Middle-Western, institution—quite different from the independent conservatory like Peabody and the New England Conservatory.

By the 1920's, the requirements for admission to Oberlin Conservatory had been brought even more into line with those for admission to the Oberlin College of Arts and Sciences on the apparent assumption that the status of the two degrees should be still further equalized. It was this background of experience and intention that guided Gehrkens and his committee, charged with proposing a workable curriculum for training the music supervisor. If they had been guided solely by their surveys, made and suggested, they might have come up with something that resembled a Gothic cathedral. Instead, they projected a plan of the utmost simplicity. What they were doing was projecting on to the national situation a version of the curriculum that had been developed at Oberlin.

They recommended a four-year minimum professional course, with a four-year high school prerequisite, including two grades of piano as set up by the MTNA, sight singing, dictation, and the like. This four-year supervisors' training course should qualify the student for the Bachelor of Music degree and should consist of approximately three-fourths professional and one-fourth academic or cultural courses. On a 120-hour basis, this would mean 90 hours of professional work (including 60 hours of music and 30 of pedagogy) and 30 hours of academic work which would include "such subjects as English, History, Dramatic Expression (Speech), Modern Language, and Science."[29] Unanimously accepted by the MSNC, a description of the recommended course was printed and distributed the same year, and, since then, only minor changes have been made.

Considering the complications involved in state teaching-certificate requirements, the development of advanced degrees in music with their requirements, multiple-subject teaching, and the improved musical training on the high school level, this is a remarkable tribute to the work done by the original committee. The basic idea of one-half music, one-fourth education, and one-fourth general culture, within a four-year pattern, preceded by four years of high school (including Grade 2 Piano) has a mathematical harmony to it that would, perhaps, have delighted the medieval Bachelor of Music who was preparing to lecture at Oxford on Boethius—though he

[28] John Lawrence Erb, "The College Conservatory of Music," *PMTNA*, Vol. 7 (1913), p. 60.

[29] Karl Wilson Gehrkens, "Report of the Committee on Training Courses for Supervisors," *PMENC*, Vol. 14 (1921), pp. 216–231.

would, of course, have been puzzled by some of the other aspects of the degree. At all events, this curriculum has been a strong factor in making definite the twentieth-century conception of the bachelor's degree in music.

As published in 1951, the MENC-approved "Course in Music Education Leading to the Bachelor's Degree" is as follows:

```
General Cultural (Academic)  .  .  .  .  .  .  .  .  .    30 hours
     English (including Speech)  .  .  .  .  .  .  . 12
     Social Studies (History, U.S. Government, Sociology,
         etc.)  .  .  .  .  .  .  .  .  .  .  .  .  6
     General Psychology  .  .  .  .  .  .  .  .  .  3
     Electives (completion of a minimum of 15 hours in
         either English or Social Studies is recommended) . 9
Education  .  .  .  .  .  .  .  .  .  .  .  .  .  .  .    21
Theory of Music and Other Technical Courses .  .  .  .  .   30
Applied Music  .  .  .  .  .  .  .  .  .  .  .  .  .     30
Free Electives  .  .  .  .  .  .  .  .  .  .  .  .  .     9
                                                       ───
                                                       120
```

It will be noted that generous provision has been made for electives, 9 semester hours of which are free and thus applicable to any of the subject groupings. Such flexibility is necessary in view of certification requirements in certain states. Where no certification problem exists, the student may apply electives in such a manner as will contribute most to his needs and interests. . . . These suggestions represent an attempt to meet the necessities of certification through the use of free electives while still adhering to the principle that a collegiate course for the training of teachers of music must place chief emphasis on music.[30]

Changes have been made from time to time. In 1953 the joint approval of the MENC, NASM, MTNA, and AACTE (American Association of Colleges of Teacher Education) was secured for the following music education curriculum:

I. GENERAL CULTURE
   Minimum requirement suggested: 33% of the total (120 semester hours) required for an undergraduate degree. . . .
   A. Non-music subjects, to include a non-music minor if required.
   B. Any psychology course other than Educational Psychology.
   C. Music literature, history, and/or appreciation.
   D. The basic survey type of course, where required: 1. Humanities; 2. Social Sciences; 3. Natural Sciences. (In some cases subjects listed under A, B, and C above are, or may be, included in certain surveys.)

II. BASIC MUSIC
   Minimum requirement suggested: 14% of the total (120 semester hours) required for an undergraduate degree

[30] Hazel Nohavec Morgan, ed., *Music Education Source Book* (Chicago: Music Educators National Conference, 1951), p. 43.

III. MUSICAL PERFORMANCE
      Minimum requirement suggested: 33% of the total (120 semester
      hours) required for an undergraduate degree
IV.   PROFESSIONAL EDUCATION
      Minimum requirement suggested: 20% of the total (120 semester
      hours) required for an undergraduate degree.[31]

It will be recognized, however, that this is a variation on the theme originally adopted in 1921.

Noting particularly the General Culture or Academic portion, however,
one observes an odd change that has occurred between 1951 and 1953:
In the 1951 schedule there was an item "Electives," recommended as being
interpreted as English or Social Studies—quite understandable as belonging
under this general heading—but in the 1953 schedule there has appeared an
item "Music literature, history, and/or appreciation," which would more
logically, on the face of it, seem to belong under Basic Music. This anomaly
was an outcome of a meeting of representatives of the NASM, MENC,
AACTE, and MTNA at Chicago in 1952, which will be considered again
in Chapter 5; no doubt a factor in producing it was the complexity of state
teacher certification. Here we can only observe the clearly intended and
stated fact, that four courses are to be allowed to count as *either* General
Culture *or* Basic Music, depending on the pleasure, convenience, or need
of the one figuring up the components of any particular music education
curriculum: music literature, music history, music appreciation, and history
and appreciation of music. One observes also the disappearance of the
"Free Electives" item—a move rather characteristic of the mid-century.
There has been an increased allotment of time to "ed courses." Thus the
professional component of the curriculum has been expanded; the nonprofessional, contracted or denatured. The interlarding of the General
Culture area with music courses was an anomaly destined to spread, as we
shall see, and by 1962 to appear in other Bachelor of Music curricular which
had not the possible excuse of being under pressure from state certification
requirements.

The steady work of the MENC in its special field of music education
has had a certain effect on the MTNA, which in 1948 set up a committee
under the chairmanship of E. W. Doty of Texas to study the question of the
possible certification of the private music teacher. The committee gathered
information; but encountering so many problems peculiar to individual states,
they reported that the MTNA should simply encourage states wishing to
set up plans and should act as a clearing house for information. Then, in
1953, the MTNA reactivated this committee under the chairmanship of
Hyman Krongard of New York City. The cooperation of the NASM was

---

[31] "Evaluating the Music Education Curriculum," *Music Educators Journal,* Vol.
39, No. 5 (April–May 1953), p. 34.

secured, and a panel discussion on the problem was held at the annual meeting. Eventually, at the 1955 MTNA convention, a recommended curriculum for the private studio teacher was passed. It was outlined as a four-year program leading to the Bachelor of Music degree with a major (applied music) in pedagogy, as follows:

A. Performance . . . . 40 sem. cr.
B. Theory, History, and Literature 32
C. Professional Education 6
D. Pedagogy 10–12
E. General Culture 30–32
 Social Sciences, Humanities, Arts and Literature,
 Sciences, Foreign Language
      Minimum total . . . 120[32]

Behind this schedule, however, one again recognizes the outlines of the 1921 MSNC curriculum for music supervisors, and behind that the concept of a B.M. developed at Oberlin.

Perhaps more important than the mere setting up of a neat schedule of credit hours is the kind of person who is envisioned as being produced by the operations of such a set of courses. Gehrkens thus described the ideal music supervisor:

> . . . the supervisor of music . . . more and more in the future is to become the leader of and authority in all musical education in the community; . . . not only able to organize and supervise work in music in the grades with its emphasis upon appreciation rather than upon mere performance, . . . able to direct with authority a fine high school chorus, singing standard choral works; . . . conducting an orchestra of 25, 40, 60, or 80 pieces . . . knows music theory well enough to teach a class in harmony, counterpoint, or composition, or to combine all three in the same course . . . teach a class in what is commonly called musical appreciation; . . . *ex officio* assume the leadership of the various phases of community music and . . . take charge of community singing with all of its possibilities in the direction of inspiration, socialization, and Americanization; and . . . has taste, discrimination, and valor in the selection of music, and . . . because he knows the classics and at the same time knows people, will sometimes not begin his musical instruction with a thing which is so far beyond the comprehension of his pupils that they would probably at once become discouraged and give the whole thing up as hopeless. This involves fair ability in playing the piano . . .: all of these things of course imply a musician of broad scholarship, of wide experience, and of real discernment.[33]

Especially striking here is the consciousness of the relationship between school music and the community. This represents a great change from the

[32] John Crowder, "Presentation and Comments on the Curriculum for Training Private Music Teachers," *NASM Bulletin,* No. 41 (January 1956), p. 12.
[33] Karl W. Gehrkens, "The Music Supervisor of the Future," *PMTNA,* Vol. 14 (1921), pp. 39–40.

"art-for-art's-sake" point of view of the old-line private studio teacher, the extreme professionalism of the conservatory, and the extreme intellectualism of the nineteenth-century Bachelor of Music. Music is thought of here as primarily a contributing factor to life in a democracy.

Viewed less sympathetically, however, it perhaps has the shortcoming of not really expecting the music supervisor to be able to *do* anything, in his own right—except to achieve fair ability at the piano. He is definitely more a supervisor than a musician. And as the pattern becomes further extended to other B.M. curricula, its essentially administrative character shows up perhaps even more prominently.

In a somewhat more realistic vein, Gehrkens formulated his conception of the need for liberal or general education on the part of the music supervisor in a music education textbook written in 1929:

> The musician is often accused of being one-sided and narrow in his interest, . . . for this art of ours is so fascinating, so completely satisfying, that it seems unnecessary for the musician to go outside of it for further types of satisfaction. But . . . this narrowness is today wholly inexcusable, and in a member of the public school system . . . almost criminal, for the very foundation upon which our public schools are built is breadth of preparation, universality of interest, and cooperation of members. . . .
>
> One difficulty here is, of course, the fact that the technical side of music study takes so much time that general culture is apt to be entirely crowded out. The fact that so many high schools are now offering credit for music should help at this point, however, for in this way the prospective musician is enabled to remain in school instead of dropping out in order to study music as he used to do. While studying music he is thus enabled also to come into touch with literature, history, science, government, etc., and may thus establish certain tastes which in later years will be developed through general reading and may thus eventually become the basis of a broad and comprehensive culture.[34]

The same consciousness of the claims of society on the individual appears in the explanation by the NASM of the presence of the General Culture requirements as one-third of the course:

> This area of preparation should assist the individual (prospective teacher) to take his place in a democratic society and a world order; to gain a cognizance of the scientific contributions to mankind; to recognize and accept the responsibility of living in a social relationship; and to evaluate the cultural heritage. He should be able to use, adequately, the English language and should acquire the ability to recognize and solve problems independently.[35]

[34] Karl Wilson Gehrkens, *An Introduction to School Music Teaching* (Boston: C. C. Birchard & Company, 1929), pp. 93–94.

[35] *NASM By-laws and Regulations, 1949*, p. 20, quoted in "Evaluating the Music Education Curriculum," *Music Educators Journal*, Vol. 39, No. 5 (April–May 1953), p. 34.

Needless to say, this official statement of aims for the General Culture portion of the curriculum was formulated long before such an item as "Music literature, history, and/or appreciation" was inserted under it, as if—by some obscure reasoning—it might be thought of as an example; for if one may count all nonperformance music courses as General Culture *ad lib.,* one can wipe out that whole nonprofessional sector of the curriculum.

The concept or ideal behind the General Culture requirement as originally projected showed a high degree of social consciousness. Other conceptions of why some form of general education was important for musicians have been urged. Frank Damrosch, for example, who spoke from a more independent-conservatory and individual point of view, thought that a knowledge of mythology would be more important to the music super-visor:

> In addition to the usual academic and pedagogic training, I feel that he needs a special training in those subjects which are the sources from which poets, painters, sculptors and musicians, have drawn their chief inspiration, namely mythology, folk-lore and romance.
>
> These were evolved in the human mind when the world was young and they still carry their message to the young world: the child, the youth and to all whose heart has been kept young by love of beauty, goodness and truth. They contain all the wisdom of the ages and the beauty of the human soul seeking the light. Also, they give expression to every emotion of which the soul is capable.
>
> Equipped with such knowledge, the Supervisor could accomplish wonderful things in stimulating the child's imagination, broadening his vision, awakening him to a realization of a world beyond the narrow confines of his home. Much good and beautiful music has been written on the inspiration of such themes and it is desirable that our children be brought under its influence.[36]

This is obviously a different, more romantic and individualistic, less groupy idea of what a music supervisor should be, couched in a set of terms that seem to be in a different language from that in which the other MSNC deliberations—some of them rather metallic-sounding—were being conducted.

Clear and reasonable as the MSNC pattern for raising the standards of the curriculum for their particular conception of the ideal music supervisor is, the approved curriculum was simply recommended and could in no sense be enforced. The non-"music ed" Bachelor of Music degree, moreover, was completely out of the MSNC's jurisdiction, as also some borderline applications of the degree (like that for the private studio teacher) were felt by some to be. The MTNA, consisting only of individuals *as musicians,* was also reluctant to exert any pressure on institutions, although

[36] Frank Damrosch, "The Mental and Musical Equipment of the School Music Supervisor," *PMENC,* Vol. 13 (1920), p. 42. He is here rather consciously answering Gehrkens's blueprint for a Supervisor of Music as presented in *An Introduction to School Music Teaching.*

through its meetings and reports of its committees the fact was amply clear that the Bachelor of Music degree was beginning to mean all things to all men. As recalled by Hanson,

> To understand those days, which can only be described as pioneering, it is necessary to remember that conditions in professional music education on the eve of its induction into the academic service were more than mildly chaotic. The basic professional degree, the Bachelor of Music, taken over originally from English practice, had almost lost any academic significance. In certain institutions the degree represented five, or even six, years of professional study beyond high school graduation. In other schools it might be granted without even the mildest academic pre-requisite of high school graduation, or might be granted while the student was still in high school.[37]

The chaotic state of the B.M. degree is what one would expect: Left at the end of the nineteenth century in impractical form, it had been quietly adopted here and there as a school-music supervisors' degree, and suddenly it was given a quasi-official status and definite rationale—in the latter role —by the MSNC. At the MTNA meeting of 1923, for example, Fredrik Holmberg, Dean of the School of Fine Arts at the University of Oklahoma and Chairman of the State Music Examination Committee, observed:

> a Bachelor of Music degree may mean anything from two years of high school plus the ability to play . . . or to sing . . . up to a general and musical education that compares fairly well with the requirements for a Ph.D. As it is now, unless a person is intimately acquainted with the details of the work at each institution granting music degrees, it is practically impossible to judge what a student must know before he is granted a degree by any particular school.[38]

Holmberg proceeded to urge the MTNA to set up a recommended Bachelor of Music curriculum, and to work to get the Education Department in each state not to recognize a substandard music degree. He explained that his school was considering abolition of the Bachelor of Music degree and substitution of a Bachelor of Fine Arts degree in Piano, in Voice, in Violin, in Painting, or whatever the major might be, much as at the College of Liberal Arts there was a Bachelor of Arts in Geology, in English, in Modern Languages, etc. Quite apart from the question of what letters were to be used for the degree,[39] several things appear clearly from Holmberg's remarks: that the old Bachelor of Music degree, as such, had gone in all different directions; that there was need for some clear counterpart of the

---

[37] Howard Hanson, "Professional Music Education in the United States," *Musical Courier*, Vol. 151, No. 3 (February 1, 1955), p. 63.

[38] Fredrik Holmberg, "Standardizing Music Degrees," *PMTNA*, Vol. 18 (1924), p. 141.

[39] Actually, over half a dozen institutions do grant a B.F.A. with music major. *See* "List and Classification of Institutional Members of the NASM," *NASM Bulletin*, No. 21 (April 1945), pp. 10–24.

A.B., only for the undergraduate professional school; and that the ghost of the late-nineteenth-century Bachelor of Music degree could not be laid merely by the MSNC's passing a recommended curriculum.

The MTNA felt that its proper role was not to act as an institutional pressure group. The threatened flight from the Bachelor of Music degree to new and even as yet unheard of degrees by individual institutions would only have complicated the situation still further, and would have caused the loss of much that had been gained by the MSNC since the opening of the 1920's.

Accordingly, from a conference of the directors of some of the leading institutions of higher education in music the National Association of Schools of Music was formed. It is an organization which has become the principal accrediting agency for music schools. The initial assumption was that an institution which could develop and maintain a proper curriculum was worthy of membership in the Association, and currently over two hundred schools are members. Working relationships with the MTNA, MENC, AACTE, and other groups have considerably extended its influence. A significant development in the field of accreditation occurred in 1949 with the formation of the National Commission on Accrediting, which for the music part of its jurisdiction relies heavily on the NASM; accordingly, the President of the NASM could report in 1960:

> Instead of being responsible only for the welfare of our 250 member institutions we now have upon our conscience the standards of the music content courses in the music education program of hundreds of additional institutions preparing music teachers and the total responsibility, too, for accrediting the degree programs in applied music, theory, composition, music history and literature, musicology, music therapy, church music, and the A.B. programs in music, in every institution of higher learning in the United States.[40]

Membership in the NASM itself is now based on a number of criteria —equipment, faculty, organization, student body, and actual teaching results, as well as simply curriculum. Regular review and visitation of member schools are maintained. Minimum curricula for undergraduate and graduate degrees have been set up, the Bachelor of Music degree being defined somewhat along the same lines as the MSNC concept of it. The greater part of the student's program, of course, is specified as being devoted to his professional studies; but "a minimum of eighteen and a maximum of thirty semester hours in subjects of a general cultural value shall be required." As this is in terms of a 120-hour total, the upper limit of this range is still the same as that of the old ½–¼–¼ formula. Two questions, however, might well here be raised: In the absence of the one-fourth education component, should the general cultural component really be so low?

[40] "President's Report," *NASM Bulletin*, No. 48 (February 1960), p. 14.

Is the possibility of its being still further reduced almost to one-seventh of the total, desirable? From coordinate status, the liberal arts aspects of the degree have undergone something of a *diminuendo,* from Tourjée through Gehrkens to the present.

What kind of Bachelor of Music is envisaged is thus formulated by the original chairman of the Commission on Curricula of the NASM, Howard Hanson:

> What should we expect of the professional music student upon graduation? I should answer, first, that he be able to play his instrument or sing in an acceptable fashion for the specific work that he intends to do; second, that regardless of his "major" instrument he should have a sufficient grasp of the piano so as not to be handicapped in the pursuit of his theoretical subjects; third, that he should have a thoroughgoing and reliable ability in the fields of sight-singing and ear-training; fourth, that he should have a working knowledge of the basic subjects of harmony, including keyboard harmony, counterpoint, form, music history, and, if possible, orchestration or instrumentation; fifth, that he had sufficient training in subjects outside of the immediate field of music to give him at least an introduction to literature and the arts allied to music, the beginning of at least one foreign language, and the ability to properly speak and write his own language. This, in a very general way, might be considered a primer of curricular requirements.[41]

This description, with its coordinate emphasis on technique, musicianship, sight singing and ear training, harmony, and semi-professional or supporting studies (i.e., the humanities), is more professionally and individually— less socially—oriented than Gehrkens's description of the ideal school music supervisor.

The relegation of a possible fourth of the program to subjects of a nonmusical nature was obviously a matter of acute concern, as Hanson continues:

> The day of the musician who knew nothing but his instrument is past, to be followed by an era of broader development of the individual. This is entirely laudable. I should add, however, a warning to those universities and colleges that insist that their music students study so many other subjects that it becomes impossible for the music department to function adequately. In these cases the student becomes involved in a mad marathon from class room to class room. This is allowing the pendulum to swing rather too far in the opposite direction.[42]

Judging from some of the discussions at the time, one concludes that this was the most daring part of the NASM's standard curriculum—the inclusion of as much as a fourth for nonmusical studies. Another member of this same Commission and later its chairman, Earl V. Moore, Director

[41] Howard Hanson, "A Discussion of the Curricula of Schools of Music," *PMTNA,* Vol. 22 (1928), p. 59.

[42] *Ibid.,* p. 62.

of the University of Michigan School of Music at the time and former president of the NASM and MTNA, stated:

> The requirement of a definite proportion of study in fields other than music —literature, science, languages, etc.—is in line with current tendencies in other professional fields. The musician, performer or teacher, is preparing to take his place in a social organization, in which more and more of general culture is necessary. Approximately one-fourth of the student's program may be elected in these cognate fields of human activity. The practical result of the adoption of this provision was the closer affiliation between the professional schools offering no "cultural" courses, and the academic institutions in which little or no music was available. The purpose of the introduction of these "cultural courses" into the music curriculum was to bring the music student into close contact with scholarship in other fields under the most advantageous conditions. Regardless of the intensity of professional training, the candidate is deemed to be preparing for life, and for its manifold interrelationships.[43]

That this "general cultural" provision has been no mere gesture is shown by the report of an NASM examiner, Harold L. Butler, Dean of the School of Fine Arts, University of Kansas, and former president of the NASM, on the basis of his visits to music schools in 1930:

> Naturally, all colleges and university schools of music are strong in academic subjects, and such teaching is the principal job of colleges and universities. All varieties of academic teaching are found in the independent schools. . . . The independent schools were urged to have all academic work done in academic institutions wherever possible. In case this was not practicable, the schools were urged to employ adequate and experienced teachers and to offer an academic course, which gave three hours credit, one hour each day, three days in the week.[44]

Obviously, this type of concern over the nonmusical component of the music student's curriculum is necessary to keep it from becoming a mere legalistic paper-requirement; and no doubt much careful and conscientious work has been done by individual examiners under the aegis of the NASM.

Special curricula for various kinds of music training have been worked out and published; but the basic idea of 18 to 30 hours in nonmusical courses prevails. Its significance has been pointed out by Earl V. Moore, thus: ". . . in the B.A. or B.S. degrees, music has relatively the same status as a subject of general culture as have the arts and sciences in the B.M. degree. The definition of music as cultural or professional credit depends on the perspective from which the courses are viewed."[45] In other words, there is the same sort of adjustment between the aims of the liberal arts college

---

[43] Earl V. Moore, "The Standardization of the Bachelor of Music Degree in the United States," *PMTNA,* Vol. 25 (1931), p. 32.

[44] Harold L. Butler, "Observations on the Examination of the Schools in the National Association of Schools of Music," *PMTNA,* Vol. 26 (1932), pp. 62–63.

[45] Moore, *op. cit.,* p. 32.

and the music schools as we observed first taking shape in the interrelation-ship between the Conservatory and the College at Oberlin; and by way, first of the MSNC, and then the NASM, it has become a vital part of the higher education in music in this country. Considering the great diversity of such institutions, one must marvel at the speed with which some order appeared within the chaos that prevailed on the subject of the music degree earlier in the century. Where the medical and legal professions took almost forty years to straighten out their curricula, the results of the NASM were quickly apparent. With funds provided by the Carnegie Foundation, a survey was made of the results of the NASM's first four years of activity, and it was found that by 1928 almost fifty of the leading schools of music from coast to coast had agreed on the minimum requirements for the Bachelor of Music degree. The NASM accordingly issued a booklet de-scribing the minimum requirements for the B.M. and M.M., with particular adaptations of the basic idea of the program to students majoring in piano, in voice, in organ, in orchestral instruments, and in composition. Basic requirements were also set up in the fields of theory, history, and ensemble. Specimen examinations in harmony, counterpoint, analysis, and ear training were made available. From time to time, further curricula have been added, and other problems have been dealt with, much as one would expect the responsible central agency of a profession to do.

Partly as a result of the efforts of the associations, the independent conservatory has moved closer to the university school of music and the college music department—a fact recognized by the director of the Chicago Musical College, Rudolph Ganz, in an address to the MTNA at their 1940 meeting:

> Some years ago a dear friend of mine, colleague in "education through music" . . . said to me, "May be that—in future times—the professional conservatories will give B.M.'s and M.M.'s, while the Music Departments will be satisfied with offering B.A. and M.A. degrees." On the other hand, another equally prominent colleague had stated, some eleven years ago, that "there would be no professional schools of music existing by 1940." Both of these assertions were well meant but did not materialize. The picture of the entire situation has changed. While the professional schools extended their curricula by including a greater number of academic courses in their collegiate departments, the music departments are giving greater attention to so-called applied music. . . .
>
> The N.A.S.M. has done remarkable work in establishing certain stand-ards of instruction and requirements, with the result that there has been greater confidence among the student body.[46]

The NASM has been an effective focal point for the work of all the associations devoted to special areas of music study. The three large, in-

[46] Rudolph Ganz, "The Professional School and Its Function," *PMTNA*, Vol. 35 (1941), pp. 256–257.

clusive organizations—MTNA, MENC, and NASM—have worked closely together, their officers meeting jointly each year at the NASM convention. The AAUW, the College Band Directors National Association, the College Music Association, the Society for Music in Liberal Arts Colleges, the American Musicological Society, the National Association of Teachers of Singing, the American Guild of Organists, the American String Teachers— to mention only a few—have worked together with the NASM, and its influence has constantly increased since its founding in the 1920's.

In view of the cardinal importance today of the NASM schedules for curricula, they deserve careful scrutiny. As given in the *NASM By-laws and Regulations* for 1959, they are set up in eight forms, of which the first six lead to the Bachelor of Music degree, the seventh to the Bachelor of Music Education degree, and the eighth to the Bachelor of Arts degree with Music Major. Thus there are three patterns of relationship between liberal and professional components of the curriculum: the B.M., the B.M.E., and the A.B.

In the Bachelor of Music pattern, the requirements are classified as (1) Applied Music, (2) Music History and Theory, and (3) Academic Courses. The underlying idea is clear enough: "Applied" means actual instrumental or vocal work; "Music History and Theory" means solfège, harmony, and music literature; "Academic Courses" means "subjects of general cultural value"—the primary concern of this monograph. These "Academic Courses" are assigned from 18 to 36 semester hours in, for example, the B.M. with Instrumental Major. This is, of course, not very high: 18 to 36 hours normally constitute about 15 to 30 per cent of the total program (or, as the total number of hours in a B.M. program approaches 148—as sometimes happens—18 hours could be as low as 12 per cent). Contrast, for example, the 50 per cent endorsed by the National League of Nursing in 1950 or the 75 per cent by the American Council on Education for Journalism in 1953.

The Bachelor of Music Education degree is set up a little differently: General Culture, 33 per cent; Basic Music, 14 per cent; Musical Performance, 33 per cent; and Professional Education, 20 per cent. The first category, "General Culture," is still characterized thus:

> This area of preparation should assist the individual (prospective teacher) to take his place in a democratic society and a world order; to gain a cognizance of the scientific contributions to mankind; to recognize and accept the responsibility of living in a social relationship; and to evaluate the cultural heritage. He should be able to use, adequately, the English language and should acquire the ability to recognize and solve problems independently. (*NASM By-laws and Regulations,* 1959, p. 25.)

In terms of this statement of aims, "General Culture" should mean liberal or general education. "Basic Music" means ear training, harmony, composition—Theory in the previous schedules. "Musical Performance" means Applied. "Professional Education" means "ed courses." The idea of the distinction among these four categories is logical and consistent within itself.

Under the heading of "General Culture," however, some specific examples are given which—we have seen—crept in shortly after the mid-century and which are liberal or general education in rather another sense of the term than the one used in this monograph:

> The courses in this area include the following, some of which may be specific institutional or state requirements:
> *a.* Non-music subjects, to include non-music minor if required.
> *b.* Any psychology course other than Educational Psychology.
> *c.* Music Literature, appreciation and/or history.
> *d.* The basic survey type of course, where required: (1) Humanities, (2) Social Sciences, (3) Natural Sciences. (In some cases subjects listed under *a, b,* and *c* above, are included in certain surveys.) (*NASM By-laws and Regulations,* 1959, p. 25.)

Quite apart from the question of the number of hours allotted to General Culture and the possible discrepancy between the idea and the examples of it, are there not here two different principles of dividing up the curriculum—as between the B.M. and the B.M.E. schedules? To rephrase them, in the B.M. we have (1) Applied, (2) Music History and Theory, and (3) Academic Courses; in the B.M.E., (1) General Culture, (2) Theory, (3) Applied, and (4) "ed courses." Like the classical concerto, the B.M. has three movements; like the classical symphony, the B.M.E., four. The B.M. schedule moves from the more practical to the more theoretical; the B.M.E., vice versa. History and Theory of Music are lumped together in the B.M. schedule; in the B.M.E., they are separated, the History of Music figuring in the General Culture component.

Thus, for the B.M.E., "music literature, appreciation and/or history" can come in under "General Culture." It will, of course, be recognized that if a music student takes a course in "music literature, appreciation and/or history" it is not exactly liberal or general education as outlined by McGrath in Chapter 1 of the present study. But no doubt there are practical reasons—particularly in view of the very complicated requirements for state certification of music teachers—for considering these music courses as part of the student's general cultural background. The B.M.E. schedule doubtless has a rationale of its own, and historical and actual reasons for being as it is. Its "General Culture," however, does not mean quite the same thing as "Academic Courses" in the B.M. schedule.

In the abstract, this point may seem picayune. But, to be concrete, in 1960 the NASM approved a revision of the *By-laws* which somewhat fuses (or confuses) these two types of schedule by transferring an item bodily from the one into the other. The nonprofessional component of three of the B.M. schedules was raised from an 18-hour minimum to a "suggested requirement" of "approximately 40 semester hours of academic and cultural courses, including courses in music literature, music appreciation and/or history."

The intention behind this move is reasonably clear. The 1959 Annual Meeting had been concerned with the problem of liberal or general studies in music schools; the NASM had realized that here it was in a vulnerable position. The President of the Association, E. William Doty, opened by stating that the minimum requirements in liberal education in the music curricula no doubt should be raised "since a recent survey indicates that this will work no hardship for a majority of our membership." The principal addresses at this meeting, by Earl J. McGrath and Howard Hanson, had focused on problems of General Education and Music. McGrath, in the course of his review and appraisal of the situation, had said: "Depending upon the particular organization of courses in a given institution, these general education requirements would probably require 40 of the 120 or more hours usually required for the Bachelor's degree."[47] In the light of the discussion at this annual meeting, the subsequent annual meeting approved a change in the *By-laws* according to which the B.M.E. "General Culture" component of 33 per cent or 40 hours should be applied to three of the B.M. schedules. This revision was voted to go into effect in 1962.

One certainly cannot accuse the NASM of unawareness of the situation or unwillingness to try to do something about it. The result, however, presents an anomaly, emerging from the historical sequence of events by which these schedules have been thus revised. Consider again the resulting B.M. schedules, which might be summarized thus:

1. Applied Music—during each year
2. Music History and Theory Courses—28 to 32 semester hours, including sight singing, harmony, survey of music literature and history (as given in the Lower Division), literature of the major instrument, etc.
3. General Culture—40 semester hours, now *including music literature, music appreciation and/or history*.

The number of total hours for General Culture has been raised and the name changed from Academic Courses to General Culture, but the categories have been confused. Do not "music literature, music appreciation and/or history" belong in Category 2 rather than 3? Do "literature of the major instrument" and "music literature in general" logically belong in different subdivisions of the curriculum? What can music appreciation legitimately be but music history and theory, in a somewhat popular or nontechnical vein? Why should a B.M. student be taking a music appreciation course anyway? If he does not appreciate music, how did he get in

[47] Earl J. McGrath, "General Education in Music: A Review and an Appraisal," *NASM Bulletin,* No. 47 (February 1959), p. 5.

the music school? What the "and/or history" means is not crystal clear: Does it mean history in the sense of European History from 1792 to 1914? Surely not. But if it means *music* history (as it *must* mean), why does the phrase not read "music literature, appreciation, and/or history"? And— more important—if it means music history, it is a duplication of an item in Category 2. Doubtless some esoteric distinction is conveyed by the connective "and/or" which is felt necessary by some music educators who have wrestled with the intricacies of state certification, but the force of that "and/or" hardly comes through clearly. It was clearer back in 1953. Apparently what has happened is the transference of an element from one context, where it makes sense, to another where—on the face of it—it does not. This is the sort of thing that often happens when curriculum revision is undertaken in terms of details rather than of the whole.

One of the recommendations that will be made at the end of this monograph is that the NASM reconsider these schedules in terms of ends rather than of means, and that there be an over-all unification of them. Why some of the schedules should be expressed in hours, some in percentages; why some should be arranged from the specific to the general and others vice versa; whether words are really used consistently and clearly throughout the various schedules (coming, as they do, from various sources and having been formulated at different times, and often revised and amended)—this sort of genuine stylistic overhauling needs to be undertaken. As these schedules stand, they are an accumulation rather than a clear-cut set of expressions of idea. There will, of course, soon be an up-to-date reprinting: The use of the 1959 *By-laws and Regulations* with an inserted sheet of *Revisions* and with necessary reference to other issues of the *By-laws* is obviously only a temporary expedient. It reminds one a little of the situation encountered in the regulations for state certification (which will be considered in the next section of this study), except that when one consults those various state regulations one finds the situation *really* confusing. Before the NASM issues its *By-laws* in a revised form, a searching and thoroughgoing revision should take place, both in terms of ideas and in terms of style.

The NASM in the 1960's—thanks to the backing of the National Council of Accreditation—finds itself in a position where it can be of influence as never before. But if that influence is based on a position of increasing ambiguity, it can be quite dangerous. In terms of the *By-laws* revisions that go into effect in 1962, it would be possible for a school to claim that it had sanction for going as far as it wished in wiping out the nonmusic part of the B.M. curriculum, allowing a student to sign up for music literature, music appreciation and/or history (whatever that means) in all the hours when he was not occupied with applied or music history and theory courses. Perhaps it is unfair to suggest that any institution in the NASM would want to do this, or that the NASM officials would countenance it for a moment if they heard about it. But the clear-cut, objective backing for measures to be taken if and when such a thing might happen has disappeared from the *By-laws*. Viewed merely as a requirement, the former provision that a minimum of 18 hours in academic courses "is required" had a definiteness that has been lost in the new "suggested requirement" of 40 hours "to include . . . music literature, music appreciation and/or history." What has occurred here in the liberal component of the music school curriculum is not so much increase as inflation.

Before the *By-laws* are reissued in this decade, there should be a clearer idea of what "General Culture" within the B.M. curriculum means. Does it *really* mean what the revisions that go into effect in 1962 say it means: for music students, courses in (among other matters) "music literature, music appreciation and/or history"? Back in 1925 Carl Engel had some rather cutting remarks about music appreciation as a music school or university study:

> Imagine a university devising courses in law for non-practicing, nonprofessional students of law! or holding a clinic for non-practicing, non-professional physicians!! You can not blame college presidents for losing patience with their musical faculties, or for looking upon them with an air of slight disdain, if "Musical appreciation" is to be the sum and substance of the proposed academic training in music. . . .
>
> There is a place for the teacher of musical appreciation, and a wide place. The schools must have a share in it, wisely apportioned. That the American universities should foster that brand of popular instruction is to be questioned.[48]

Although a case could be made for the inclusion of music appreciation in the "music ed" curriculum (perhaps some course dealing with the possibilities, problems, and various ways of teaching music appreciation), it is difficult to see how a plain, old music-appreciation course can be justified in the B.M. program at all, and particularly in the part of that program which was originally intended to be devoted to the liberal or general—that is, nonprofessional—sector of the student's education.

The last of the eight schedules is that for the A.B. with Music Major. It is set up in terms of General Academic Requirements (Natural Science, Social Sciences, Humanities), 65 to 78 hours, and Music Requirements (concentration in History and Literature, in Theory, or in Applied), 40 to 42 hours. This schedule is followed by a quotation from the A.B. Committee report, concluding:

> Within the usual 120–130 semester hours the prospective teacher can go a long way toward satisfying his special institutional and state require-

[48] Carl Engel, "Views and Reviews," *MQ*, Vol. 11 (1925), pp. 620, 629.

ments. Of course, the completion of such work will require either a heavier than average load during his four years, one or two summer sessions of additional work, or a fifth year.

But the combination of a broad general education and an adequate professional training in any field requires more than a minimum amount of undergraduate work, and the short and long range values of this program justify our highest recommendation.[49]

Many aspects of this schedule for the A.B. with Music Major (which has been worked out within the past five years) strike one as being more clear-cut and well-thought-out in terms of ends as well as means than the corresponding features of the somewhat older B.M. and B.M.E. schedules. One knows what is meant, what is intended in it. Could not the schedules for the B.M. and B.M.E. emulate it—not so much in the quantity of hours allotted for various subjects, but in the sheer stylistic quality of inner logic and consistency?

What these rather well-worn B.M. and B.M.E. curricula need is quite thorough overhauling, not just a little tinkering here and there. This suggestion is made in full cognizance of the delicacy of some of the adjustments and calculated ambiguities that have been arrived at over the years. The time has come for a genuine rebuilding from the ground up, in terms of what is actually envisaged—what is really wanted as the intended result— and how the parts fit together to form the whole. This is the sort of thoroughgoing change that can proceed only from within the ranks of the musicians themselves. It cannot be forced from the outside, or imposed from any higher academic authority. It really can scarcely be outlined or suggested by the outsider. For such a change to have real coherence and relevance, it must come from within. It may even require the leadership of some individual or individuals of the dynamic qualities of a Mason or a Tourjée. Back in the 1920's Gehrkens provided another example of the right man at the right time who was able to project a coherent image of a plan, which can still be seen glimmering through the music curricula today, after almost half a century of storm and stress. This is not to imply that there is no leadership today. But some kind of really imaginative personal vision of what the curricula in music schools can be, and why in the 1960's they should be that way, will no doubt have to be brought to bear on the problem.

INFLUENCE OF STATE CERTIFICATION

In addition to the influence of the MSNC and NASM in standardizing the curriculum and assuring in it a place for nonmusical pursuits, there is a source of influence that has operated more in the direction of varying

[49] *NASM By-laws and Regulations, 1959,* p. 30.

the situation, injecting sometimes more liberal courses, sometimes more professional education courses. This is the arrangement by which practically all the states set up their own requirements for teaching certificates, usually quite different in each state. The associations have acted more as clearing houses for information and as agencies where an attempt is made to reconcile the varying demands. In many individual instances, complete reconciliation of these demands is scarcely feasible within a four-year framework —even of the specifically school music teacher's degree of B.M.E.—and the result has been the unofficial lengthening of the course of study by a summer term or an additional year, where the student has wished to qualify for a particular state certificate that makes unusual demands.

The course of development in this respect is reflected in reports made before the various associations. At the 1923 MTNA convention, Birge reported for the Committee on Public School Music that five states had no special music certificate requirements, leaving the decision about the fitness of the special music teacher up to the local school board, and that the rest required college work as follows: 2, one year; 18, two years; 3, three years; and 3, four years.[50]

The requirements had, however, increased by the 1929 meeting of the MSNC, at which Dykema reported that only 3 states now required one year or less, and that 10 now required four years. So far as liberal arts subjects were concerned, several states required more than the 30 hours suggested in the 1921 MSNC recommendations: Wisconsin specified 30 to 50; Michigan, 34; New York, 36; Ohio, 36; Maryland, 42; and West Virginia, 60— or one-half of the entire four-year program. Dykema's committee felt that the 30-hour provision represented the most practical course that could be set up for a "well balanced education" though "the necessity for education which provides a general background of knowledge needs no argument."[51] The only recommendation of the committee was that the General Cultural component be described as 10 hours of English Composition, Literature, and Speech, and 20 hours of "Electives chosen from various fields in accordance with interests of students; languages, social science, pure science, mathematics, art, psychology, philosophy and so on."

At the 1930 MTNA meeting Hanson pointed out the widely varying requirements of General Academic subjects specified by 12 states. The highest state requirement in this respect, however, was not nearly so high as it had been a decade before: The top requirement was now 34 hours,

[50] Edward B. Birge, chrm., "Report of the Committee on Public School Music upon State Requirements in the United States. . . . A Survey," *PMTNA,* Vol. 18 (1924), pp. 167–177.

[51] Peter W. Dykema, "Report of the National Council of Music Education," *PMENC,* Vol. 22 (1929), p. 26.

specified as English, Language, Social Science, Biology, Physical Science, or Mathematics.[52] Instead of the original MSNC recommendation of 30 hours of General Academic subjects and no Electives, the NASM recommendation was now 18 hours of General Academic subjects and 10 hours of Electives. This decline in the total was reluctantly suggested, but was thought to represent a more realistic approach to handling the quite various state certification requirements.

Continuing the re-examination of the general outlines of the B.S.M. degree in a report before the 1931 MTNA meeting, Boyd pointed out that the original MSNC schedule specified 60 hours of Education and Academic Subjects, but the current NASM schedule specified only 44 hours (12 hours General Education [i.e., pedagogy], 14 hours Music Education, 18 hours General Academic Subjects); however, the 10 hours of Electives made that total potentially 54 hours—still a little short of the original 60, the 6 hours having gone to Music Theory.

The whole problem of state certification of music teachers is quite complex. A study of the situation was undertaken in a Master's thesis at Eastman in 1945: By that time all states except Massachusetts had state-wide certification (and Connecticut seems to have been slightly hazy on the subject). Some states had two or three different types of initial certificates for teachers of high school music; in all, there were some 82 possible initial certificates. The years of college required were as follows: 5 required five years; 57 required four years; and the remainder, fewer years. The comment of the author of the thesis points to a real problem for the curriculum planners of the undergraduate professional music degree:

> Certification, it seems, does not assume a particularly high degree of importance in a number of states. This point is shown partly by the fact that in some states certificate regulations in existence at the present time are ten to twenty years old. The bulletins, pamphlets, mimeographed sheets, etc., on which certification regulations are set forth in many states are so incomplete and the material presented so vague and confusing that comprehension of their actual regulations (if they have a "set" of regulations) would be a task for a genius. Either the laws which govern certification should come under observation and, if necessary, be revised, or a "shake-up" in some state departments of education is essential! Certainly certification of teachers is not so unimportant that regulations need not be presented in a logical and orderly manner.[53]

Woodbury's conclusion is that greater uniformity and simplicity are sorely needed: Perhaps only one certificate per state for teachers of high school music would be enough. "The music teacher's background in general

---

[52] Howard Hanson, "A Training Course for School Music Supervisors," *PMTNA,* Vol. 25 (1931), pp. 87–96.

[53] Ward Woodbury, "State Certification of Music Teachers," *Music Educators Journal,* Vol. 32, No. 2 (November–December 1945), p. 20.

education," he adds, meaning by this phrase the music teacher's liberal studies,

> should not be disregarded in requirements for certification. In a report of the state committee on teacher education and certification of the Louisiana State Department of Education, a required minimum of 50 semester hours in general education is given. . . . That it would be desirable for a teacher of music to have 50 semester hours of general education background is undeniable. However, the musical preparation of the teacher of music demands so much time that in four years of college work a prospective music teacher cannot spend 50 semester hours in general education courses. . . . Of the states which require general education in the certification of teachers, the median and mode in number of hours come at 30 semester hours. . . . The author suggests that 10 semester hours should be required in each of at least three of the following general areas: social sciences; language arts; science and mathematics; psychology, philosophy, and ethics; and practical arts.[54]

Here again, as when Gehrkens faced the chaotic situation in the Bachelor of Music curriculum a quarter of a century before, the only feasible procedure seems to be to project some simple pattern and wait for some order to appear if the pattern is found helpful. In this instance, the 30-semester-hour pattern was still the same one projected in the early 1920's.

In 1956 a report to the NASM by Hodgson of the University of Texas pointed out that state legislatures still were unexpectedly injecting liberal studies into musical curricula—little items like Texas history, etc.—with resulting problems for the balancing of the curricular budget:

> These requirements are frequently in such fields as American government and history. Colleges under the jurisdiction of private boards and church schools have had parallel demands. The fear and hysteria responsible for this suddenly required cramming in American history may well be at the point of receding. The fact is that I see little reason to believe that there will be any lessening of these requirements in the foreseeable future. (In my own special institution, two years ago three hours of Texas and National government were required of all students. At the present time, six hours of government is required and six hours of American history is required for every student graduating from a state institution.)[55]

The general education movement, which came into full sway at the mid-century, also resulted in music students' taking more academic work—in this particular instance, at the University of Texas, some 6 to 9 hours. Also, there have been further demands by some state educational agencies to increase the course requirements in professional education. The extent of these three sources of pressure (state legislature, general education, and professional education agencies) varies in different states and situations,

[54] *Ibid.*, p. 65.
[55] W. H. Hodgson, "Report of Teachers College Committee," *NASM Bulletin,* No. 41 (January 1956), p. 35.

but, wrote Hodgson, "I find, as I talk with various deans, a number of very resourceful and imaginative contrivances which have been developed to cushion the shock."

In commenting on these external pressures that exert themselves on the music school, Doty of the University of Texas has made some very incisive observations:

> The purpose of these well intentioned efforts was to make sure that the graduates of state supported education knew our national traditions and how our government operates so they could be useful, effective citizens. It is useless to deny that these developments plus the tremendous growth in the sciences and social sciences have posed some real problems for our professional curricula in music.[56]

The pressures, he points out, are of the same order as have always existed under patronage—and music is here being supported by the civil authority.

> In the judgment of many it is only enlightened self interest that our aims and objectives should be conceived in some relationship to our whole educational institution. We are fortunate that in our contemporary society there are so many schools serving different and useful functions. Nearly everyone will agree that these many schools exist to teach something. In higher education there is practically complete agreement on the fact that that something is the power to think. Up to this point we can agree with our academic colleagues. We part company with them when they assert that a given package, such as that represented by the Harvard Report, or the forty-eight hour rule, or a requirement that all freshman and sophomore courses must be taken only from the liberal arts core, that any *one* of these formulas is the *only* way a man can acquire the power to think and to continue to grow as an intelligent citizen.

The demands of governing and academic bodies, according to Doty, have their justification; so far as possible, however, they are better kept in terms of ends rather than means:

> On their part, our colleagues in the liberal arts should, and for the most part do, recognize that the liberal arts include the fine arts both as intellectual and emotional disciplines. Furthermore, the professional schools are forced to demonstrate, and the liberal arts people are compelled to admit, that many of the professional courses can and are being taught as courses which train the mind to think clearly, independently, and creatively, and that they do so as efficiently as the courses in the forty-five to sixty hour package. It should also be noted on a logical basis alone, and every true scholar has to recognize the force of logic, that if there are so many "*only*" proposals, doubt is thereby cast on any *one* procedure as *the* means of guaranteeing the educated man.

[56] E. William Doty, "A Pattern for Producing an Educated Man," *NASM Bulletin*, No. 41 (January 1956), p. 18. [Extracts quoted on the pages following are from this same article.]

Some canny suggestions about strategy on the part of the professional school in dealing with outside pressures are given:

> Discussions about the amount of course work to be taken in social science, science, communications, and the humanities outside of music, are better avoided unless your strategy is to involve the several parties in disputes among themselves. It would seem more convincing, however, to compare the freshman music or fine arts students in two ways: first, in contrast to all entering freshman students; and second, comparatively with all students who have completed the four year, 120 hour program when they too are at the point of graduation. These scores to be valid should of course be in terms of nationally recognized tests and preferably those which are designed to test the power to think.
>
> Compared with other entering college students it is significant that freshman majors in the fine arts score above the average entering college student. In addition, the tests of graduating seniors in all subjects demonstrate that while music majors take by far the smallest number of hours in general education they rank above the average in general education attainment in national test scores. (Florida State University Studies.)

Doty attributes the high scores of professional music majors on general education achievement tests to the stimulus of music itself and to the fact that only superior students are able to carry on school work plus private music lessons during their precollege years. He concludes:

> It is indeed a pleasure to report that the outcome of discussion between these points of view can be a recognition that a University is such because it offers *both* professional and liberal education; and that music, with the other arts, continues to take its proper place as an indispensable part of the training of the liberally educated man, as well as to serve the society which supports us all by training professionals in the arts who alone can preserve, create, and recreate the art of music in our time for that society.

To trace in detail the effect of state certification requirements and other pressures from governmental and academic bodies on the curriculum of undergraduate students of music is obviously beyond the scope of this study. But they are unquestionably factors to be reckoned with; and they constitute a force, by and large, more in the direction of liberalizing than of professionalizing the study of music—if one understands by "professionalism" the emphasis on sheer performance skill. If, moreover, one understands by "professionalism" the emphasis on pedagogy instead of performance, the influence of these bodies in the past few decades seems to have been more in the direction of stressing academic subjects and liberal values as these are understood in the present investigation.

The very diversity of these state requirements for certification to teach has placed on schools of music an almost unsolvable problem so far as balancing the professional and nonprofessional aspects of the training are concerned, and yet enabling the graduate to apply for regular certificates in a satisfactory number of states. The granting of "emergency certificates" by state agencies only makes the normal situation one of increasing "emergency." A complicated institutional structure has grown up around some of the states' requirements, as one or another state higher educational institution may have adapted itself to a particular set of state requirements like a glove to the hand; as a general thing, however, the graduating student wants to be able to teach in more than one state—to go where the opportunities are best. In the resulting tension, the liberal component of the student's education often receives the full impact of the pressure, despite the fact that music educators usually are, personally, more acutely aware of the values of some nontechnical education for their students than are the teachers of performance skills.

To anticipate a recommendation that will be made at the end of this monograph, the situation presented by state certification needs to be more directly worked on by the MENC. All means of active propaganda and persuasion should be brought to bear on the states to make their requirements more sensible and even, in some instances, more intelligible. In comparison with the only slightly tangled NASM *By-laws* the state certification requirements are a howling jungle, and it is the duty of the MENC— and of any other bodies that are so minded—to begin to chop a path through it. So far, the associations have performed valuable service in reporting on the situation. But actual manipulation of it should be undertaken; otherwise the liberal education of music students will continue to suffer, despite pious wishes to the contrary by all concerned. Most of the associations have been too much preoccupied of late with problems of accreditation and have neglected the really crying problem of certification. In full awareness of the difficulties involved, the recommendation will be made at the end of this study that state certification be actively worked on by any of the music agencies that will dare to depart from the former, rather passive, merely reportorial role that has been traditional and that has permitted the situation to deteriorate. A first step would be the revitalizing of existing committees that nominally are devoted to this matter. No doubt support would have to be sought from foundations. The situation would have to be presented in as clear-cut and complete a way as possible, for at present a music educator who wants to find out *exactly* what is required must write to all the states individually and assemble this extremely miscellaneous body of data; and keeping it up to date and interpreting it—not to mention translating it into terms of the curricula—are most difficult. There are inadequacies in the purely informative role the associations have so far undertaken. Exactly what steps could be taken to simplify things here and there can scarcely be suggested by an outsider, but unquestionably there *must* be *some* simple and logical changes that would be immediately recognized by state certification agencies, particularly when their practices were brought into juxtaposition with those of other states and some obviously feasible suggestions were made. As an ultimate step, there would perhaps have to be recourse to lobbying and other forms of political pressure. The matter is so crucial that it simply cannot be allowed to continue in the aimless way it has in the past.

<h2 style="text-align:center">ANALYSIS OF REPRESENTATIVE CURRICULA</h2>

Recognizing fully the many pressures that operate to make actual curricula at music schools quite different, we might yet expect to hear faintly through them some echo of the simple one-half music, one-quarter education, and one-quarter general culture "music ed" curriculum devised back in the early 1920's by the MSNC, or the one-third musical performance, one-third basic music and professional education, and one-third general culture arrived at by the combined associations at mid-century. So far as associations are concerned, the principal influence today is the NASM, which up to 1962 has recommended that at least 15 to 25 per cent of the B.M. curriculum be in subjects "of a general cultural value."

The phrase "of a general cultural value" and the rather wide range within the recommended percentages obviously leave considerable latitude —for very good reason, as we have seen. For our present purposes, a more specific way of characterizing the nonmusic courses is desirable. McGrath has suggested in Chapter 1 that courses be considered on the basis of their relative function in the curriculum: their contribution to breadth of knowledge, degree of intellectual stimulation, and assistance in the formation of values. Although *any* course may be taught liberally or illiberally, there is a presupposition—other things being equal—that harmony or applied music will, for a music student, be more directly professional than a course in chemistry or political economy. Some courses occupy a middle position and might be characterized as semi-professional or supporting courses: For a music student, the whole humanistic area might be so considered, since music is usually classed with the humanities, which have in common a somewhat similar framework of historical knowledge, way of thinking, and set of values (as contrasted with the sciences). The presence of electives in a curriculum is, for our purposes, an x-quantity: Unless restrictions are placed on their use, they may be an encouragement to greater professionalization or greater liberalization of the program, depending on the student. Only in terms of general attitudes and individual transcripts of grades (which will be considered later) can the significance of electives be assessed. The heading "Other" in the ensuing table means any courses

TABLE 1. Per Cent of Total Curriculum Devoted to Various
Classes of Subjects in Selected Schools of Music

Program for Bachelor of Music (Applied)

Music Schools	Sciences	Social Sciences	Humanities	Professional	Electives	Other	Total Semester Hours
1.	4	13	20	59		3	138
2.	6	5	15	61	9	4	131
3.	6	8	11	63	6	6	131
4.	6	2	16	52	19	5	134
5.	2	6	16	74		3	136
6.	3	10	9	65	10	3	124
7.		5	16	74	3	2	132
8			20	66	9	5	130
9.	2		18	56	21	3	126
10.			20	80			128
11.		5	13	66	17		132
12.			16	68	16		124
13.	4	4	8	82	1	1	134
14.		5	10	67	12	6	128
15.			15	56	27	2	124
16.		2	10	71	13	2	126
17.	4		9	68	16	3	136
18.		5	8	74	13		128
19.			9	66	20	4	127
20.		4	4	62	24	6	139
21.			8	78	12	2	124
22.		2	5	62	22	8	135
23.	2		5	80	10	3	132
24.			6	63	27	3	126
25.			5	75	18	2	120
26.			5	73	19	3	127
Mean	1.5	2.88	11.4	67.85	13.34	3.03	129.63
Range	0–6	0–13	4–20	52–82	0–27	0–8	120–139

such as physical education and ROTC which do not fall into the usual categories of natural sciences, social sciences, humanities, or professional subjects.

In Table 1 the programs of 26 schools of music in the United States have been analyzed. They do not, of course, constitute a statistically representative sample of all the schools of music in the country; but they do represent a number of different types of programs at schools selected from among the members of the NASM in terms of such things as variety of geographical location, affiliation (or lack of it) with public or private institutions, secular or religious ties. Three of the curricula offered by these

TABLE 1, *Continued*

PROGRAM FOR BACHELOR OF MUSIC (COMPOSITION)

Music Schools	Sciences	Social Sciences	Humanities	Professional	Electives	Other	Total Semester Hours
1.	4	13	20	59		3	138
2.	6	5	16	63	6	4	128
3.	6	6	11	68	2	6	128
4.	6	2	16	52	19	5	136
5.	2	4	23	70		2	138
6.	3	10	9	60	15	3	124
7.		5	14	74	6	2	125
8.			20	66	9	5	130
9.	2		25	56	15	3	126
10.			18	82			130
11.		7	11	74	8		132
12.			16	69	15		124
13.	4	5	8	78	5	2	133
14.		5	10	60	20	6	133
15.			15	56	27	2	124
16.	2	2	8	69	17	2	127
17.	4	4	11	62	16	3	136
18.		5	8	83	5		128
19.			9	66	20	4	127
20.							
21.			8	72	19	2	123
22.		3	5	58	26	8	131
23.	2		4	84	7	3	138
24.			6	70	21	3	125
25.			5	75	18	2	120
26.			5	74	18	3	130
Mean	1.66	2.98	12.02	67.97	12.53	2.84	129.25
Range	0–6	0–13	4–25	52–84	0–27	0–8	120–138

various music schools were selected as representative: piano or applied music as representing the instrumental or vocal majors, composition as representing those more oriented toward theory, and music education. Not all institutions offered all three types of program, but they did all offer a Bachelor of Music (Applied); accordingly, this program was taken as a basis for organizing the three charts. The schools are listed in order of decreasing percentage in the B.M. (Applied) curriculum allotted to the liberal or general education area (sciences, social sciences, and humanities). In the middle six columns of each chart the figures are percentages of the total program rather than number of credits (since the various programs range from a total of 120 to a total of 155 semester hours, as indicated in

TABLE 1, *Continued*

PROGRAM FOR BACHELOR OF MUSIC EDUCATION

Music Schools	Sciences	Social Sciences	Humanities	Professional	Electives	Other	Total Semester Hours
1.							
2.	6	7	16	60	7	4	127
3.	6	11	4	66	8	6	141
4.	6	5	17	63	4	5	127
5.	8	10	12	66		5	139
6.	7	11	10	68	1	3	139
7.	6	10	7	69	7	2	128
8.			15	71	9	5	132
9.	5	5	19	60	9	3	132
10.	4	8	14	73			142
11.		9	11	73	7		132
12.		6	12	73			122
13.		6	7	81	1	1	138
14.	12	12	8	62		6	155
15.	5	7	12	74		2	129
16.		9	10	75	4	2	126
17.	4	4	11	76	2	3	136
18.	5	5	8	75	8		133
19.		5	9	73	9	4	127
20.		9	4	67	14	6	140
21.			8	82	8	2	122
22.		3	5	64	20	8	131
23.	2	2	4	77	12	3	145
24.	2	5	8	71	11	3	131
25.		3	5	80	11	2	120
26.		2	5	79	11	3	132
Mean	3.61	6.0	9.63	71.2	6.51	3.05	133.07
Range	0–12	0–12	4–19	60–82	0–20	0–8	120–155

the last column, and the actual number of credit hours at the various institutions would therefore not be strictly comparable). There are also apparent anomalies resulting from the fact that some schools operate in terms of quarters rather than semesters, and that percentages have here been rounded off to the nearest whole number. The purpose of the table is more one of comparison: It is intended to give relative rather than absolute information.

In Table 1, the most important portion for the present investigation is the "general" area, representing the work in the sciences, social sciences, and humanities. Here the combined mean requirements on all these curricula stand between 15 and 20 per cent, or barely above the NASM recommendation (in force at the time this survey was prepared) of a 15 to 25 per cent minimum in subjects "of a general cultural value." Of course, the letter of this provision may be covered within the framework of the electives and "other" courses; but whether it actually is so covered depends on the spirit in which they are utilized. Though the ghost of the original idea that a third or a fourth of the Bachelor of Music curriculum should be devoted to general studies hovers over these curricula, various pressures have obviously acted to keep it from manifesting itself too palpably.

Within this 15 to 20 per cent general component, the ratio between sciences, social sciences, and humanities courses is roughly 2:4:11—that is, almost three-fourths of the general courses are in the supporting or semiprofessional area of the humanities, and barely over one-fourth are in the sciences or social sciences, which, for music students, might be considered truly nonprofessional. Perhaps the principal exception would be acoustics, which traditionally has formed a part of the curriculum of music students, and which has definite professional implications; normally, it introduces the music student to a quite different body of knowledge, way of thinking, and set of values from the ones that underlie the bulk of his work, and consequently is assigned here to the area of the sciences. English Composition is normally a prominent course in the humanities area and, particularly if taught by graduate students in English, can easily turn into a course where the emphasis is on how, or how not, to "do it"; however, as a subject, it obviously belongs in the semiprofessional or supporting area.

Of course, the fact that the studies in Table 1 are expressed in percentages prevents one from telling at a glance how much credit or how many courses are required in the general area. But, roughly, four or five percentage points indicate a requirement of one or two courses. A 15 to 20 per cent component of a four-year course would represent only a little over one semester out of the eight.

Viewed in the abstract, and quite apart from the actualities of pressures operating upon the music school from all sides, the requirement in the general category seems relatively small. A constant source of controversy between music faculties and university curriculum-planning bodies is the question of how music history is to be counted: Is the subject in the music school curriculum usually labeled History of Music to be thought of as professional or nonprofessional, as music or as history? Whereas no one would wish to be put in the totally untenable position that it *cannot* be taught liberally, and whereas it is closely related in subject matter to the liberal study of history per se, and whereas the advent of musicology on the American scene (which will be considered later) has brought it much greater academic respectability as a course—and other whereases—there are considerations on the other side of the ledger that would justify its being classed as a part of the professional (or, certainly, semiprofessional) component of the music curriculum.

Music differs from some of the other arts and sciences in that the actual realization in sound of the historical heritage of scores is the main concern of most musicians. The painter or the physicist, on the other hand, is concerned with the past only as a point of reference or comparison. To a dentist the past is only a matter of historical curiosity. But to a musician it is the very stuff of what he is doing most of the time, as a professional man. The question of whether a course is professional or nonprofessional ultimately depends on what student is being considered: To a law student, a course in music history as taught in the music school would, obviously, be nonprofessional as would be a course in the history of law to a music student. In Table 1, the history of music has been considered a professional course inasmuch as the facts, way of thinking, and values which the music student is likely to gain from it are centered within his professional area. The human values that are *other than* those of music are not only central to building the broad frame of reference that ought to distinguish the professional person who has a liberal education; they also have great significance in music because this field is so directly concerned with human beings in an inner and personal way. Would not schools of music do well, therefore, to increase requirements in the general area to at least the equivalent of a full year—i.e., to something nearer the one-fourth (or even one-third) of the curriculum that has been arrived at on various occasions in the music associations as a desirable proportion of liberal studies in the music program?

The proportion of liberal studies in the curricula of other professional schools is, on the whole, much greater than that in music schools. Of course some of the professional schools, like those in law and medicine, are virtually graduate schools; others, like business, education, and public relations, are so verbalistically oriented as to find no difficulty in working great quantities of general studies into their programs. For purposes of comparison, however, three quite nonverbalistic professional disciplines might be considered: engineering, nursing, and pharmacy. An analysis of the curricula in 30 accredited schools of engineering, selected on a basis somewhat comparable with that used for Table 1 above, showed that the mean per cent of the curriculum devoted to liberal and semiprofessional courses was 45.5, that to professional courses was 44, and the rest was elective and miscellaneous.[57] Similarly, in nursing, an analysis of 31 curricula showed for general and supporting courses 40.6 per cent as the mean, for

[57] This survey, made by Herbert Miller in 1958, is reported in Edwin J. Holstein and Earl J. McGrath, *Liberal Education and Engineering* (New York: Bureau of Publications, Teachers College, Columbia University, 1960), pp. 74–75.

professional courses 51.7 per cent, and the rest elective and other courses.[58] In pharmacy, an analysis of 22 curricula showed for general and supporting courses 48.6 per cent, for professional courses 46.6 per cent, and the rest elective and other.[59] Approximate equality between professional and non- or semiprofessional study is apparently not unattainable in the curricula of these highly technical fields.

One other aspect of Table 1 should be noted: the range of difference within each column, and within the first three columns of percentages combined. A relatively narrow range in the difference between the lowest percentage in an area and the highest indicates a tendency among music schools to agree on the importance of that area. Vice versa, a greater range of difference indicates less agreement that the particular area is important. Thus, in the B.M. (Applied) curriculum, the range of difference on the professional courses is 30, that on the general 32; in the Bachelor of Music Education curriculum, the range of difference on the professional courses is 22, that on the general 25. Apparently there is less agreement among these schools about the importance of general studies than about the importance of professional ones.

Within the general studies area, moreover, the range of difference is greater for the work in the sciences and social sciences than it is for the supporting or semiprofessional work in the humanities. In the Bachelor of Music Education program, for instance, the range of difference in the area which for the music student is most clearly nonprofessional, the sciences and social sciences, is 0–24, while that in the supporting area of the humanities is 4–19, or a difference of 15. The fact that nine schools call for no work in the sciences and social sciences on their B.M. (Applied and Composition) curricula is not without its significance: Whereas the "music ed" curriculum is subjected to all sorts of pressures from without and within, the straight applied and composition curricula should have more leeway to take the forms that the music school faculty members really think desirable for an educated member of the profession. The absence, there, of provision for liberal training in the curriculum confirms the generalization made earlier, that the effect of the various external pressures on the "music ed" curriculum has been to liberalize it, and suggests the generalization (which will emerge from the viewpoints of faculty, deans, and students to be considered in the next chapter) that there is less agreement in music schools about the importance of liberal education for their students than there is about the importance of professional training.

Before proceeding to deal further with the attitudes of music school

[58] Charles H. Russell, *Liberal Education and Nursing* (New York: Bureau of Publications, Teachers College, Columbia University, 1959), p. 47.

[59] James Newcomer, Kevin P. Bunnell, and Earl J. McGrath, *Liberal Education and Pharmacy* (New York: Bureau of Publications, Teachers College, Columbia University, 1960), p. 39.

TABLE 2. TOTAL CURRICULUM DEVOTED TO LIBERAL ARTS CONTENT, ACCORDING TO NASM SURVEY (1960)

	DEGREE			
	B.M.	A.B.	B.M.E.	B.S.
Total response	107	83	62	21
General culture requirement:				
Nonmusic	31.8	54.6	33.5	38.4
Music	6.6	5.9	5.3	4.5
Total	38.4	60.5	38.8	42.9

NONMUSIC CONTENT IN MUSIC CURRICULA

	DEGREE				
	B.M.	A.B.	B.M.E.	B.S.	B.F.A.
Total cases	97	88	64	22	7
Below 25 hours (below c. 20%):					
Cases	20	3	4	2	0
Average	15%	13%	16%		
25–30 hours (c. 20–23%):					
Cases	14	0	3	0	1
31–35 hours (c. 24–27%):					
Cases	24	1	8	2	1
36–40 hours (c. 28–31%):					
Cases	27	2	13	4	1
Above 40 hours (above c. 31%):					
Cases	63	82	36	14	4
Average	39%	57%	41%	46%	54%
Median	36%	58%	39%	47%	57%

faculties toward liberal studies, the results of another recent survey of the relationship between professional and nonprofessional study in member institutions of the NASM should be brought into the discussion, by way of comparison with the foregoing table. This NASM survey, results of which were published in the 1960 *Bulletin,* was conducted by means of questionnaires returned by 144 institutions. It thus has a much wider coverage than that of the previous survey, which was based on analysis of only 26 representative institutions.

The results of the two surveys are close enough to indicate that they are dealing with the same situation. For example, the number of semester hours in the various music programs showed a wide range on this NASM survey, as they had done on the earlier survey undertaken for this study ("music ed" curricula ranging from a total of 120 to 150 semester hours), and the mean was within one point of that given for the "music ed" curriculum in the previous survey.

To facilitate comparison, the figures on the NASM survey are here translated into percentages of the total program rather than presented in semester hours as they are in the 1960 *Bulletin* report. The first section of Table 2, thus translated, gives the portion of the curriculum reported by the member schools as general or liberal. That is, these figures show how the schools make up their requirements under the "General Culture" category—what part of this nonprofessional portion of the music curriculum actually consists of music. "Since some of the music courses are quite commonly considered as having *general education* properties," writes the chairman of the Research Committee in his remarks prefatory to the tables, "an attempt was made to secure information on the extent to which member schools were able to include such courses toward general education *requirements*." Hence, there is this separate listing of nonmusic and music courses that are counted as fulfilling the General Culture requirement.

Although—as one would expect—there are differences between this 1960 survey and the one previously presented, the results are at many points quite close. On the B.M. curriculum, for instance, the total of non-music courses was found on the survey presented in Table 1 to be slightly over 32 per cent, whereas here it is reported as 31.8 per cent. What this *c.* 32 per cent may mean is to be gathered from Table 1.

As pointed out in the discussion of Table 1, the Humanities are, for a musician, a semiprofessional or supporting area; Electives are an x-quantity (unless restrictions are placed on them and then, to that extent, they are no longer really electives); and, so far as "Other" courses are concerned (e.g., physical education and ROTC), about all one can say is that they are just nonmusic. The NASM Committee on Research pointed out in connection with the Report that

> A number of directors responding took pains to point out that the totals did not include required credit in physical education. There seems to be no fool-proof conclusion possible that all of the figures do not include this subject, however. Whereas physical education may have been included in the totals for graduation, credits in physical education are less likely to be considered as "liberal arts" or "general culture" in the columns specifically so labeled.[60]

Perhaps the omission of physical education credit from the totals of some of the programs may explain why the figures for the nonmusic component

[60] "Report of Committee on Research," *NASM Bulletin,* No. 48 (February 1960), p. 69.

of the curriculum are even a little lower on the NASM survey than on the survey made for this study.

Whether, for music students, music courses *should* legitimately be counted in the General Culture requirements on the basis of the claim that they have *general education* properties is a question that needs very serious consideration by the music teachers and schools themselves—and no doubt the way in which the point is phrased by the Research Committee indicates that this question is already the subject of soul-searching on the part of many music educators. Of course, practically all music courses *do* have *"general education* properties"—but for whom? Unquestionably, many music teachers feel that these courses *have* to be so counted, to "get everything in" or to meet some odd state certification requirements, or to "make the totals come out right"—but whether they *should* be so counted is the question. The NASM survey shows that they *are*.

In the second section of Table 2 (also from the NASM survey), 20 curricula for the B.M. are six-sevenths music, 14 are four-fifths music, 24 are three-fourths music, 27 are over two-thirds music. In other words, the majority of the B.M. curricula reported have less than one-third of the work nonmusic, and the distribution of this majority is fairly equal along the line between one-sixth and one-third.

The situation indicated for the B.M.E. is that of a higher nonmusic content, of course, but four cases are reported with nonmusic content of only about one-sixth of the curriculum. Think, for a moment, of what this means. In four schools only about 21 semester hours of "General Cultural" courses are required—perhaps only three real full-year courses, of which English Composition would be one. On the basis of a couple of courses the individual prospective teacher is to be assisted in "taking his place in a democratic society and a world order . . . gain a cognizance of the scientific contributions to mankind . . . recognize and accept the responsibility of living in a social relationship . . . evaluate the cultural heritage . . . and . . . recognize and solve problems independently." How has the NASM allowed such manifest discrepancy between intention and achievement to come into existence? Two extenuating considerations may be urged: This information comes from the *Bulletin* of the Association itself, where it is no doubt intended as a step in the correction of such situations; and the stated requirements are not crystal clear. No doubt what is observed here is a result of this ambiguity. Also, it may be urged that the situation in the B.M.E. curriculum as a whole is better than that reported for the curriculum in these four member schools. The majority of the institutions reported that more than one-third of their curriculum was devoted to nonmusic content, as recommended by the NASM. In the light of this 1960 NASM survey, however, it is hoped that exception will not be taken to the recommendation at the end of this monograph that the NASM require accredited institutions at least to meet their minimum standards. This may seem a rather sharp rebuke to an association which has obviously been trying to do the right thing in this respect. But the ambiguity of including under "General Culture"—clearly defined as the liberal or non-professional part of the curriculum—courses in "music literature, appreciation and/or history" has created an area of meaninglessness in the standards which, according to the *Revision* of 1962, is on the point of spreading.

Referring again to the 1960 NASM survey, we find in the latter part of Table 2 that two member schools reported that the B.S. was granted for work in music that had practically no liberal or general content. The Committee on Research thus reported:

> There is a significant preponderance of conservatories among the relatively few schools reporting degree patterns requiring fewer than 25 semester hours of liberal arts content. One institution indicated a range of 9–24 hours of non-music for the B.S. degree "depending on choice of second high school teaching subject, which might be in this area."[61]

Obviously, here the nonmusic portion of the curriculum was frankly being used for professional rather than liberal or general aims.

Perhaps a summary of the line of reasoning taken in the last chapter and in this will be helpful toward placing in its historical perspective the recommendation that music schools liberalize their curricula. The original idea behind the university college of music seems to have been equality of music and nonmusic (or professional and liberal) studies. In the 1920's

TABLE 3. MEAN PERCENTAGES OF NONMUSIC COURSES FOR THE B.M.
(FROM TABLE 1)

	DEGREE	
	B.M. *(Applied)*	B.M. *(Composition)*
Sciences	1.5	1.66
Social Sciences	2.88	2.98
Humanities	11.4	12.02
Electives	13.34	12.53
Others	3.03	2.84
Total	32.15	32.03

the MSNC set up a "music ed" curriculum that was half music and half nonmusic, the latter being conceived of as pedagogical and general courses. Thus, quite understandably for "music ed," the liberal component became a fourth instead of a half. But then the "music ed" curriculum began to influence the applied curricula and there, too, the liberal portion became

[61] *Ibid.,* p. 69.

only a fourth of the whole. Whether, in all instances, this was an entirely well-considered move, or whether it was just a matter of general drift toward conformity and administrative neatness would be impossible to determine; at any rate, it happened. Then various pressures began to operate on the "music ed" curriculum—notably the somewhat antiquated system by which each state sets up different certification requirements. Soon—reluctantly—the music educators were allowing more and more latitude in the liberal education part of the degree requirements. Consequently, the general area in the program has been creeping, *de facto,* in the direction of one-eighth. In counterpoint, this is what is known as diminution.

A certain curricular inflation has not helped the situation: The associations still talk in terms of a 120-hour degree, but of the 26 curricula analyzed, only one had a 120-hour total. In itself, this is not too important; but it suggests, symbolically, that the present situation is not perceived with perfect accuracy by those charged with responsibility for it. What is really much more important is that the clear, incisive, intense attitudes of such men as Mason, Hamerick, Tourjée, and Gehrkens—odd as some of their ideas may seem to us today—no longer figure prominently in the world of the music schools, and the response of students is often lacking in strong conviction.

Chapter 4

ATTITUDES IN MUSIC SCHOOLS

TWO BODIES OF DATA ILLUMINATE THE MUSIC SCHOOL FACULTIES' ATTI-
tude toward liberal studies in the curriculum: one, a questionnaire survey
conducted by a consultant to the Institute of Higher Education, Paul L.
Dressel, to determine the points of view of staff members in several different professions; the other, a series of visits to half a dozen music schools
throughout the country. For the first body of data, 182 colleges partici-
pated in the Dressel survey, with over three thousand faculty members returning the completed inventories, among which were 351 from individuals
in 26 schools of music. The results of this survey, published in 1959,[1]
enable us to examine the attitudes of a few hundred music school faculty
members objectively and to compare them with those of faculty members
in other professions. As for the second body of data, personal visits to six
music schools, made at about the same time as the Dressel survey and involving at each school some thirty interviews, each about an hour in length
(ten with administrators, ten with faculty members, ten with students)
and, of course, some on-the-spot investigation and observation, helped to
clarify the thought and feeling behind the responses given in the survey
and the attitude manifested in the then existing situation among these music
schools.[2] Both bodies of data were made possible only by a very generous
cooperative effort on the part of a great number of institutions and individuals, indicating in itself a lively desire to clarify this aspect of the professional school students' training.

MUSIC IN THE DRESSEL SURVEY

In general, the Dressel survey reveals that technical and professional
faculties are interested in and favorable toward the liberal arts: 97.4 per
cent agreed that all students should be required to take liberal arts courses,

[1] Paul L. Dressel, Lewis B. Mayhew, and Earl J. McGrath, *The Liberal Arts as
Viewed by Faculty Members in Professional Schools* (New York: Bureau of Publications, Teachers College, Columbia University, 1959).
[2] Two of these visits were made by Arthur W. Kennedy, of Boston University,
one by Charles H. Russell, then of the Institute of Higher Education staff, and three
by the author of this monograph.

90.4 per cent rejected the idea that liberal training should be postponed for adult education, and 85.5 per cent felt that those with both liberal and specialized training were better off vocationally. The divergences among teachers in the different professions, however, was marked when it came to questions of how much and what kind of liberal arts were to be required. Of the nine professions investigated, music stood at the bottom of the list, tied with engineering for last place in the "index of favorable attitudes toward the liberal arts"—that is, the music school and engineering school faculties were less favorable toward the liberal arts than such faculties as those in schools of agriculture, home economics, and pharmacy. Nursing and journalism headed the list.

The dim view of liberal arts taken by the musicians may seem at first a bit odd, for music—traditionally one of the liberal arts—was conceived of by many of the great nineteenth-century composers such as Liszt and Wagner as deserving a position at the very center of all the arts and sciences, as the leader in cultural progress. By no means does it have so high a sheer technical content as, say, nursing, which headed the list of the nine professions in order of warmth of endorsement of liberal arts courses and their values. The consequences of a wrong note are not quite as serious as those of a wrongly administered set of directions a nurse may be given, and the intensity of the desire to establish professional standards is perhaps greater in nursing, in its close relationship with the medical faculty and the hospital world—certainly one could not impute to the nursing faculty any lack of occasion for stressing the sheerest professionalism in their curriculum, if they had been so minded.

The difference between the nursing and the music faculties' attitudes, however, is consonant with the terms in which their professional associations formulate the desirable proportion between the liberal and professional components of the curriculum. The National League of Nursing Education in 1950 established a 50–50 division between professional and "general collegiate" studies.[3] In the Dressel report, moreover, journalism stands second to nursing; and it is interesting that the accrediting agency in journalism, the American Council on Education for Journalism, endorses a ratio of 25 per cent professional courses and 75 per cent liberal arts.[4] The music accrediting agency, the National Association of Schools of Music, however, operates on a proportion more the opposite of this; and, as we have seen in the preceding chapter, there is a tendency in actual practice for music schools to scale the nonprofessional part of the program down to the minimum. While this tendency to fall a little short of the ratios

[3] Charles H. Russell, *Liberal Education and Nursing* (New York: Bureau of Publications, Teachers College, Columbia University, 1959), p. 42.
[4] Paul L. Dressel, *Liberal Education and Journalism* (New York: Bureau of Publications, Teachers College, Columbia University, 1960), p. 35.

promulgated by the accrediting agency is not peculiar to any one profession, the Dressel survey shows that a considerable number of the music school faculty members think they would be happier if there were still less liberal arts work in their curriculum than there is.

The respondents to the Dressel survey were asked whether they agreed or disagreed with this statement: "Students majoring in your specialty are now commonly required to take an excessive amount of liberal arts work at the expense of needed specialized courses." Of music faculty members, 17.4 per cent said "yes," in contrast to 8.3 per cent of pharmacy, 7.7 per cent of engineering, 7.4 per cent of agriculture, 7 per cent of education, 4 per cent of business and journalism, and 1.9 per cent of nursing faculty members. To the statements "Liberal arts courses to be taken by professional or technical students should be specifically adapted to the needs of such students, such as English for Engineers, or Economics for Business Administration students" and "In adjusting the balance between liberal and professional requirements, the number of liberal arts courses rather than the number of specialized courses should be reduced," a greater percentage of music school teachers said "yes" than did the teachers in any other professional school. In other words, the excuse sometimes heard, "We couldn't permit more nonprofessional work or we would lose our accreditation with the NASM," only dodges the issue: The NASM reflects what the music schools want, and the music schools reflect what their faculties think they want or feel they have to put up with. If anything, when the matter is brought down to the individual level, an even more forthright attitude is usually encountered than at the level of the association or institution—and it is this attitude which the latter part of this chapter, based on personal interviews, undertakes to explore.

The response to one of the questions is very interesting in the light of the frequently heard remark that the music school curriculum should be extended to five years in order to get everything in that seems desirable. The following statement was given on the Dressel form: "More liberal arts courses should be introduced into most technical and professional curricula even if this would somewhat lengthen the time required to earn a degree." The majority of the home economics, engineering, agriculture, and music replies were "no," while the majority of the business, nursing, pharmacy, and journalism replies were "yes." This negative answer on the part of the majority of the music school faculty is very interesting because the music school curriculum has *de facto* become a somewhat lengthened program, involving in many instances four years and a summer at least; in some curricula, particularly in some state-supported institutions, it has officially become a five-year affair; and some of the requirements have been shifted from the bachelor's to the master's and doctor's degrees, with a phenomenal growth in the number of people taking these latter degrees. All these developments have, whether one realizes it or not, considerably lengthened the time required for acceptable professional training.

This extension of the curriculum no doubt will continue, either overtly or insidiously; and it will create tensions, whether understood by the people involved or not. One student interviewed at a Middle-Western music school said that her mother had been there twenty years before as a student, and had had a major and two minors, whereas now you scarcely could get in a major and one minor; the girl herself had the impression that the school was really more specialized and professionalized now, that the courses were more specific. This impression of hers no doubt resembles that of most people as they think back in their own experience to the academically *laissez-faire* days after World War I: The curriculum, somehow, did not seem to have quite the tension to it that there is now and that will no doubt continue for some time to come. Fork-of-the-road situations will occur in which decisions will have to be made to let something expand and to crowd something else out. So far as the personal wishes of the music school faculty are concerned, they would jettison liberal arts courses if anything has to go (keeping, no doubt—as Polyphemus promised Odysseus he would do—Freshman English to the last). As individuals, music school faculty members do not appear, according to the Dressel survey, as enthusiastic about liberal arts courses as are members of most other professional school faculties.

The majority of music school faculty members, like that of faculty members in other professional schools, favored spreading the liberal arts courses over the four years in a limited core of required courses. In general, the pattern of the first two years devoted to nonprofessional study—the junior college or general college idea—did not find much favor among professional school faculties. A concentration of nonprofessional work at any one point in the four years is, of course, particularly hard to adapt to the needs of the music school, where it is widely felt that the student requires a continuing experience of practice and performance. More than in any other professional school faculty, however, a considerable minority of the professors in the schools of music would just as soon allow the students to take the nonprofessional courses at their convenience: 15.7 per cent so indicated, as compared with 12.6 per cent in agriculture, 11.1 per cent in engineering and home economics, and under 10 per cent in the rest of the professions.

As to the courses preferred by the music faculty for their students, English composition stands in a virtually unchallenged position. The majority in the music school would also include history, literature, and foreign languages. To Dressel, it has seemed that these are closely related to the professional area; and certainly, in the abstract, it would seem that for music students they would come under the general category of supporting or semiprofessional studies (as would the rest of the humanities), much as for nursing students some of the work in the sciences (chemistry, biology, psychology, nutrition) would be classifiable as belonging to their supporting or semiprofessional area. Even within the humanities, some subjects seemed to those filling out the questionnaires of doubtful value for the music student: The queen of the sciences, philosophy, would be required by only a fourth of the musicians, whereas a third of the nurses and journalists, and three-fifths of the business people would like to see it required of their students.

Of course, as one ventures into the natural and social sciences, one is (in the eyes of the music faculty) descending into the lower circles of Inferno: biology, for instance, 8 per cent of the musicians would require but 15.7 per cent would discourage or prohibit (75.5 per cent would consider it optional); physics, 7.1 per cent would require but 11.9 per cent discourage or prohibit (despite the obvious subject-matter relationship between music and acoustics, long recognized as highly important for musicians); chemistry, 2.3 per cent would require but 23.4 per cent would discourage or prohibit. Is not this chemistry a case in point?

Certainly the experience of taking a course in chemistry would be *other than* the experience of taking more music courses. But whether it would be for that reason harmful or meaningless to a music student is a discussable subject. It is just possible that a student, becoming aware of the amazing recurrences in the table of chemical elements, would suddenly achieve a genuinely personal sense of what rhythm and periodicity mean, not merely in music but in the whole of reality, and would then realize that music is a symbol-system for formulating that reality just as much as mathematics or chemistry is. It is just possible that the full, first-hand impact of the great shift in human thinking that took place in the light of the chemical experiments of Lavoisier (from the older phlogiston idea, a subtractive process, to oxidation, an additive process) would illuminate in a flash for a music student, as for any thinking human being, the difference between the music of Bach and of Beethoven. That a student will achieve any revealing insights from a course in chemistry, however, is by no means certain: some remember only that bad smells were generated. But there is the same possibility of meaninglessness in any *ostensibly professional* course. Many music students carry away from harmony and counterpoint courses only a confused idea that these were "much ado about nothing"; and the most generally criticized courses in the interviews with students were the education courses, which usually represent vocationalism with a vengeance.

Many reactions of the music school faculty, as recorded in the Dressel survey, would have puzzled Bach or Beethoven. Should mathematics be a required study? Next to English composition, mathematics would be re-

quired by the largest proportion of the faculty in professional schools generally. Dressel feels that this is a supporting course in many professions.
Historically, it is no less so in music, as music was for many centuries
studied as a branch of mathematics—much as, in the nineteenth century,
sciences were often listed in the curriculum as "natural philosophy." From
the days of Pythagoras and Plato, mathematics has played a basic role in
all branches of learning: supposedly, a statement about the necessity for
studying mathematics before entering was inscribed over the entranceway
to Plato's Academy—not for professional purposes but for purposes of
understanding Socratic philosophy. One has only to glance at such a book
as Fux's *Gradus,* the textbook used by Bach and Haydn with their pupils,
to realize how fundamental mathematics still was in the Classical period,
or at Schönberg's *Harmonielehre* or Hindemith's *Unterweisung in Tonsatz,*
to realize how basic it still is to an understanding of music, particularly on
the professional level. But in evaluating mathematics as a possible study
for the music student, only 13.7 per cent of the music faculty would require
it, and 9.7 per cent would discourage or prohibit it. In evaluating religion
as a course for the music student, 10.3 per cent of the music faculty would
require it, 6.5 per cent would discourage or prohibit it. Bach studied theological tracts. What can the *St. Matthew Passion* mean to a student for
whom the events and ideas around which it revolves are as remote and
vague as some episode from the *Mahabharata?*

One subject that came up for evaluation by the music faculty was music
itself. This created a unique situation in the Dressel survey, in that no other
professional school faculty had occasion to rate as a subject what they taught.
Agriculture, for example, is a school and not a liberal arts course. Music,
however, is both. As pointed out at the beginning of Chapter 2, music is
alone in this respect among the professions included in this project by the
Institute of Higher Education. When the members of the music school
faculty were requested, with respect to music itself, to "Indicate your judgment concerning the desirability of *some* work . . . for *students in your
own specialty,"* 64.4 per cent would require it of all, and .6 per cent would
discourage or prohibit it. Exactly what that three-fifths of one per cent
thought it was voting against is not too clear, nor is the thinking behind the
64.4 per cent who would require it of all, in contrast to the 97.9 per cent
who would require English composition of all. No doubt the request was
variously understood by various people filling out the form—particularly
as *"in your own specialty"* might be taken by a music teacher to mean violin if he were a violinist, piano if he were a pianist. But Bach would have
laughed.

Regardless of the implication of various details in the evaluation of
music by the music faculty, however, there is one sobering aspect to the
percentages resulting from this item in the survey: 64.4 per cent of the

music faculty would require it, whereas among the professional schools as a whole only 13 per cent would require it and 6.4 per cent would discourage or prohibit it. The disinterest which the music people feel for some of the disciplines other than their own is returned in kind; and, as repeatedly came up in interviews with music school faculty members, "We're as much to blame as they are; we haven't, somehow, got through to *them* any more than they have to us." Some of the recent discussions in the professional music magazines, incidentally, stress exactly this same point: the need of the music faculty's "getting through" to those people around a university who are involved in the other professions.[5] A simple way to do this would be for the musician to interest himself in what they are doing— it is no more mysterious than that.

With respect to this same problem of isolation, art encounters somewhat the same response as music, but a little more so: only 12.1 per cent of the faculty in the professional schools as a whole, and 29.1 per cent of the music school teachers, would require art.

The social sciences fare not much better at the hands of the music faculty than the natural sciences did: 14.2 per cent would require and 6.5 per cent would discourage or prohibit sociology, 4.8 per cent would require and 14.5 per cent would discourage or prohibit economics, 7.4 per cent would require and 13.7 per cent would discourage or prohibit political science.

Dressel's interpretation of these figures stresses the obvious fact that professional groups favor subject matter that reinforces or is related to their own professional activities. Musicians, for example, largely ignore the sciences and mathematics, as agriculture, engineering, "and, in fact, all the other professional fields completely disregard music."[6] Among all the subjects considered, the three rated lowest by the combined professional faculties are music, art, and religion. It will be readily recognized that in any survey of this type words may be taken in different senses by different people and when the results of their reactions are tabulated, a misunderstanding or deviation in one direction will be offset by a misunderstanding or deviation in an opposite direction, and useful generalizations may be derived. What we have here is more a pastel than a bas-relief, more a halftone than a dry point.

Whether religion is the least professionally related of the subjects listed and English composition the most, or whether the relationship is the exact opposite, is perhaps a debatable question. One wonders whether the music faculty members have really debated some of these matters in their own minds. Consider this bit of the data accumulated: Of all the faculty in

[5] For example, Earl V. Moore, "Music in Higher Education," *Music Educators Journal,* Vol. 47, No. 5 (April–May 1961), pp. 54–60.
[6] Dressel, Mayhew, and McGrath, *op. cit.,* p. 32.

professional schools, 7.7 per cent would require religion and 8.7 per cent would discourage or prohibit it—thus religion is even more shunned than art and music. This odd fact may be interpreted in a number of ways. Is religion, like Christ, here being rejected? Is it, perhaps, the *most* professionally related, but the professional school faculty members feel that precisely because there is so much dynamite in it and because there is opportunity to deal with it seriously through other channels within the community, it is something that should not be carried on in the classroom (with textbooks, syllabi, lectures, recitations, quizzes, papers, grades, attendance records)? The fact that religion stands lowest in the list might be interpreted as indicating either a very reverent or a very irreverent attitude. Yet the result is that more professional school faculty members would like to see their students *not* take a course in religion than would want them to do so.

English composition, on the other hand, is more harmless as a subject. The student sometimes writes a great many themes on personal experiences and on his reading. Perhaps he reads a few novels that were considered shocking back in the 1930's or whenever the person who has made up the course was in college. No doubt the student reads some essays, usually of about the caliber one encounters in the *Atlantic Monthly;* perhaps he writes a comparison or contrast between two such essays that happen to be related in subject matter. Most important, he has an opportunity to hold forth—in class discussion and in writing—on some fields of knowledge about which he knows little in any formal or organized way. This is important because he is usually allowed to do this in freshman English with a freedom that is not often permitted in courses formally labeled Economics, or Logic, or Political Economy, particularly if they are conducted mainly through large lecture groups. Although any generalization about the way freshman English, as distinct from other liberal arts courses, is handled is likely to oversimplify the situation, we may assume a few things: the classes are likely to be small, the students full of a great variety of thoughts and feelings, and the inner pressures to let off steam quite high. Of course, there are many exceptional courses in other liberal arts fields but, as a general rule, the student is not given quite the same freedom to formulate and express himself in all the chaos of his aboriginal ego. When—in, say, a history or geology or psychology course—he ventures to express himself, he usually does so only after careful preliminary channeling of his impulse to self-expression—only after he has been given some glimpse of the overwhelming bibliography of the subject and the bullet-proof set of terms and concepts in which respectable work within that field operates. When he has finally come to formulate a few ideas which he thinks are his own, he is usually made painfully aware of the fact that his teacher has already spent years in a field that he himself has been studying only a few weeks or months; and unless he has skin like elephant hide he usually keeps a respectful silence, especially if he is in a group of a few hundred and is hearing the exposition of the material through a public address system. The English instructor, on the other hand, may be a young graduate student, quite close to the freshman's own level. The author of the present monograph, who began his college teaching a quarter of a century ago as a freshman English instructor and who has been in touch with the developments in that course ever since, finds the characterization of freshman English implied by Dressel and the respondents to his survey rather embarrassing. "English comp" is a course without a definite content; how then can it be related or not related to some other body of subject matter? In terms of McGrath's definition of liberal education, freshman English is more likely than not to be a liberal course. It would, however, fall more into the category of the humanities, of which music is one. Dressel is correct in suggesting that the high estimate placed on the desirability of including freshman English in the music school curriculum represents a tendency by musicians to favor semiprofessional or supporting courses. But why should fewer of the music school faculty favor requiring the music student to study music itself? Certainly there seem to have been some differences of intention and some sheer inertia about these evaluations of various liberal arts courses. Some features of the responses are explicable, perhaps, only on historical grounds.

An understanding of how the human body operates, for example, is not irrelevant to the things a music student ought to learn. Until he has become aware of his hands, his major muscles, his lungs, his lips, his eyes, his ears, he has scarcely got beyond the amateur stage. As a dilettante, making music only for his own and his friends' amusement, he may well dispense with any concern about what his body is doing when it makes these interesting sounds. But there usually comes a time in his development when he grows aware of these matters; and, particularly if he is going on to become a teacher and have assigned to him the responsibility for starting off countless young people in a way that is either helpful or harmful, he ought to know a great deal about the inner structure of the human body. Yet, as a subject for music students, physiology would be required by 5.4 per cent of the music faculty and discouraged or prohibited by 17.4 per cent. Such a relationship of percentages makes sense perhaps only on the basis of sheer custom: It has not been usual to formalize such instruction into a course, but rather to leave it to the various music teachers to introduce if and as they perceive the need for it—just as foreign language diction is often inculcated by the private voice teacher on the basis of the song being studied. A *course* in physiology is not usually available, convenient, or customary.

In their responses, sometimes the members of the music school faculty are merely giving in detail what is the usual thing for music students to take, and are letting their reactions color this; at other times they are no doubt indicating what they would like to see in existence. Dressel tried to separate these two types of response by giving separate sections of the questionnaire to items about what was desirable and what was actually the present state of things, but this subtlety did not yield significant results, other than suggesting that many members of professional school faculties were vague on what was currently required of their own students. Detailed consideration by Dressel of five institutions, for example, did not yield evidences of a high degree of enthusiasm for liberal arts at one institution and not at another: The faculties of engineering, agriculture, and music—at whatever institution considered—tended to "include significant numbers of persons whose attitude toward the liberal arts is negative or at best neutral," regardless of whether or not the particular institution may have a program of broad general education courses. Where such programs exist, there seems to be a slightly larger percentage favoring them; but it is a matter of only a few points. By and large, the faculty members in the professional schools seem to feel that the liberal arts faculty is doing its best: "They have their problems and we have ours," seems to be the implication of the preponderance of the replies, "and however they want to do it is all right with us so long as there is still room enough for us to breathe."

Who, in the university hierarchy, is thought to be most eager for more liberal arts work for professional students? In the eyes of the faculty of the professional schools, according to the answers on the survey, the order seems to be: liberal arts faculty, president, dean of the professional school, student personnel worker, department head in the professional school, and faculty member in the professional school. Two principles seem to be implied: self-interest and rank. The deans of the professional schools normally have practised and taught in their profession, but as deans they apparently become more eager for their students to do more liberal arts work. Similarly, only to a lesser degree, ordinary faculty members undergo this change when they become department heads, according to the picture of the state of things that exists within the minds of those in the professional schools. Advancing age and the acquisition of higher and higher degrees seem also to predispose professional school faculty members to the liberal arts. Although some features of these generalizations may seem truisms, there is a slightly disturbing aspect to all of them: The interest in the liberal education of the student seems, on the face of it, to be not so much a grassroots matter as something that is (or is thought by the faculty member to be) imposed from above.

In the old days—we like to think—as one got older and higher up in the academic hierarchy one got narrower and more set in his ways; progress, or at least change, was supposed to ascend from below, like moisture coming up through the roots. The results of this survey seem to point to a reversed relationship. Curriculum reform becomes a more fascinating activity for the administration than it is for the faculty, who reluctantly go through the motions of sitting on committees, but really are more and more concerned about the fact that they observe their students' education suffering in the process. The course requirements change so often that the teacher no longer knows what his student is supposed to have studied. At more than one institution students were interviewed who were "still taking courses under the old plan"—that is, at any one moment there is likely to be a heterogeneous group of curricular requirements actually in operation. One would think that extensive curricular changes would be made only after a particular plan had been allowed to operate through at least the time-span of a few four-year college classes, and after the results of the operation of one plan (in the form of scores on recognized tests, etc.) had been compared with the operations of another plan or so, perhaps tried out in a limited way on some pilot or control groups. But such procedure is rare today. Think, for a moment, of the deliberateness with which Peabody and New England Conservatories were launched. Nowadays curricula are instigated rather quickly, and they give the impression—at least within the minds of the professional school faculties as reflected in the Dressel survey—of coming "from the top down." True or not, this image invites the appearance of many features of an authoritarian system: With a faculty that is unsure, under shifting leadership, suspicions arise, and the most innocent and well-intentioned moves are then misinterpreted.

Judging from the Dressel survey, one might say that, for some reason, the individual younger faculty member in the professional school seems to have misinterpreted the concern over the liberal or general education of the professional school student—a concern that has been constant ever since Tourjée fantastically insisted that a Bachelor of Music be able to read *Faust* or four of Racine's plays or one whole *cantica* of the *Divine Comedy* in the original, a concern that was unquestionably very real when Morley took his degree (one has only to glance at his *Plain and Easy Introduction* to realize that he was a man of real wit and learning)—as merely a move on the part of his hard-working liberal arts fellow faculty members to get more students. Instead of regarding the university as a place directed to the best interests of the student, it begins to be thought of as a racecourse where different faculties jockey for the inside position. Of course it is possible that one may be misinterpreting the data from the survey. Only through actual interviews can one hope to find out what the faculty members of the professional schools have in mind.

To conclude the review of Dressel's survey in terms of its music school aspects, one might note a passage in which he speculates on why the musicians may not have been able to "get through" to the rest of the teachers in the professional schools:

> . . . mathematics, English composition, and speech were seen as desirable requirements by substantial majorities of all professional faculty members, regardless of their specialties. This was in contrast to the relatively small number of people who would see art, music, philosophy, and religion as desirable requirements for students in technical and professional fields. Here again it should be noted that first courses in mathematics, English composition, and speech have reasonably clear connotations in terms of content and procedure, and they represent attempts to cultivate basic skills of communication long deemed desirable for the educated person. In contrast, the nature and significance of a first course in art, music, philosophy, or religion is relatively obscure.[7]

The implied suggestion is that if music teachers would get together and agree on an approach to music there might be a chance of its figuring in the nonprofessional training of students generally (as it unquestionably should, for music has more relevance to the life of people today than does the material usually read in freshman English).

This may or may not be a practical suggestion. The connotations of first courses in mathematics, English composition, and speech no doubt seem clearer to some people than to others. One music student interviewed said that she had taken a course in general mathematics, designed in all good faith for nonmathematics majors. It was supposed to convey the thinking involved in mathematics, the essence of the subject; numbers were not used, but only dots, circles, squares, and plus and minus signs; nobody could understand it, she said, and at the end of the year she expected to flunk but almost fainted when she got an A. She said that music had been brought in a time or so, when the instructor superimposed two sine curves or alluded to the principle of the octave. But, she added, "you can't retain something if you don't have a purpose or reason for retaining it."

First courses in English and speech can be entirely different within the same department and under the same instructor—more so than almost any other courses in the curriculum—for they are really courses with a content usually defined in terms more of manner than of matter. "Clear, correct, effective expression" or some such formula, usually used in explaining the aims of a first-year English course, is a matter of *how,* rather than of *what.* Even when a formula like "a review of fundamentals" is included in the prospectus of the course, this very seldom means a straight confrontation of English grammar as a body of subject matter in itself, such as, say, a mathematics course that deals with a certain segment of the mathematics field. Normally, freshman English has very little subject-matter content, in the sense of covering definite areas in grammar, rhetoric, or any other

[7] *Ibid.,* pp. 58–59.

aspects of the English language or literature as an organized body of knowledge. Rather, its subject-matter aspects are more likely to lie in other fields, such as philosophy, politics, psychology, and just generally unclassified areas of the student's own personal thought and experience.

English and speech are the media through which practically all courses are conducted in American universities. They are means rather than ends. It is interesting that in European universities (as in American universities before the last century) a course in writing in the vernacular is practically unknown. When the present writer was an exchange student in Germany, he found some little difficulty in explaining to his fellow students that there was actually in America a university course in writing English; the idea of such a course, when fully explained to them, seemed as odd as a course in breathing or the digestion of food. To isolate writing and speaking from what it is you are writing or speaking about is to follow the model provided by the cat in *Alice in Wonderland* when it gradually disappeared but left only its grin leering between the trees.

This is not to disparage English and speech as courses; obviously they have proved their worth and are highly regarded, and at their best they represent liberal or general education in its quintessential form. They are the latter-day descendants of two members of the medieval trivium, *Grammatica* and *Rhetorica, Logica* having been unseated during the period of the Enlightenment and having retreated for security to the upper divisional area of the curriculum. Like music, freshman English and speech are the scions of a noble line, so far as their liberal arts ancestry is concerned; and, rightly taught, they can be truly liberal. But in their original form of *Grammatica* and *Rhetorica,* they were Latin, not vernacular, grammar and rhetoric. And while a show is still made of investing these courses with grammatical and rhetorical content, it is often just a matter of window dressing. The freshman English course as it is actually given at American universities has many aspects that are peculiarly American. Under proper instruction, English composition and speech deal quite forthrightly with matters of fact, thinking, and character—the components of liberal or general education. But why English and speech seem so simple and utilitarian while an education methods course often strikes the would-be teacher as the very opposite is something of a mystery.

No doubt the history of academic curricula has something to do with all this. Mathematics was a requirement when Plato set up his Academy. Freshman composition is Latin composition in slightly altered guise: The very word "composition" suggests a "putting-together" of Latin words and phrases. Speech was there when the curriculum started. The suggestion that musicians might do well to create a general impression that there is one clear, simple, definite, usable approach to their area—as the mathematicians and composers and speakers of English apparently have done—

is here passed on to those members of the music faculty who have expressed in interviews their concern that their offerings are not more widely accepted by other members of the institutions which they serve. For some reason, music seems to many to be relatively obscure of access.

VISITS TO MUSIC SCHOOLS

A report on the extensive interviews at six schools of music throughout the country is perhaps best approached within the framework of the Dressel survey. The purpose of this report is not to expose individuals or schools as such, or to denigrate one or another of the institutions in the eyes of the public. Rather, it is to articulate points of view encountered and to draw relationships that might not at first be apparent to those who are preoccupied with the day-to-day situation in their own institutions. Thus in the presentation of these viewpoints there will be a certain degree of anonymity that may at first seem a little irritating. The decision to adopt this style, however, was a policy decision made by the Institute of Higher Education rather early in its plans for this study.

Also it must be recognized that since these visits in 1959 changes have occurred at these institutions; two have been extensively reorganized, and no doubt at all these schools changes of detail have occurred, are occurring, or will occur even as these lines are being read. The direction and intention of these changes, however, are mostly in the line of tendencies observed at the time of the visits; and by a long enough view of the past the general nature of future developments may be surmised. Whether individual bits of these many changes are good or bad is not for the present writer to say, especially in an account that is intended to be basically reportorial. Fundamentally, the ensuing reports are in terms of the situation as encountered on the visits, as it is anticipated that these will be read more in terms of the light they may cast on the underlying liberal-professional problem and not as merely factual accounts of the practices and procedures at these institutions at the present moment. To keep up with the latter this monograph would have to be revised at a breath-taking rate. The question that the writer would like to raise is whether there is not perhaps too much *change* in the situation—just "change" in the abstract—for the students' own good. To anticipate one of the recommendations that he will make in the final chapter, he would suggest that in this matter of curricular change there be a slight *ritardando*.

The six institutions—all members of the NASM—are widely separated geographically: one on the West coast, one in the Southwest, and the rest rather in the Central and North Central areas. Relationship to college or university differs considerably, from a very close tie-in with the college, through status as part of a school of fine and applied arts, on through autonomy as a separate school of the university, to loose affiliation between conservatory and university. With regard to the favorableness of the professional faculty toward the liberal arts, the "index," as Dressel terms it, seems to be highest in the first of these relationships. The greater the degree of segregation of the music faculty from the rest of its related institution, the greater the coolness between them.

There are, of course, difficulties of sheer space in trying to reproduce the essence of these extensive interviews, and necessarily a great deal of repetition in attitudes encountered at various places. On the other hand, without some fullness—some attempt to recreate the personal aspects of emphasis in each conversation and the details of the situation at each place —much of the real point of this discussion of attitudes is lost, and we might as well rely on the objective data that have been presented so far in this chapter. Rather than trying to reproduce all the interview data, the writer has thought it more useful to concentrate on the extremes and to leave it to the reader's personal experience and imagination to supply the obviously intervening shades. An institution visited where the attitude of favorableness to liberal arts was indicated by the Dressel survey as very high, and one visited at which it was indicated as low, will be dealt with in some detail—more as examples of extremes than as individual institutions being examined merely out of curiosity.

At the institution shown on the Dressel survey as having quite a high "index of favorable attitude toward the liberal arts" for all the professional faculties, the attitude of the music faculty toward the liberal arts was found to be favorable among the theory, composition, and musicology people (of whom the last named seemed rather to be in control). On the other hand, some of the performance faculty seemed to be opposed to liberal studies and some of the students, particularly the older ones, were bitter about the work they were taking. The interviews suggested that there is quite a difference between a genuinely liberal element in the curriculum and merely a certain academic dimension to it.

The very extensive state-wide higher educational system of which this institution is a part was founded in 1868. Today, in this particular state, when the "state university" is mentioned, the term covers the whole group of seven campuses, with all their ramifications of academic and professional schools and colleges, divisions, departments, museums, libraries, institutes, bureaus, and foundations. On the campus to which this visit was made, a state normal school had been established by the legislature in 1881, and by 1919 it had become a branch of the "university" in this particular part of the state. In 1937 a resolution was passed that a professional or vocational college be added to the state system. As this particular state normal school had become first a teachers' college and then a school of education, with emphasis more on the upper level and graduate divisions, some of the courses that had developed within its framework were left stranded; and these departments—art, home economics, mechanic arts, music, and physical education—were grouped together to make up a new college with "curricula of a professional or vocational character," which was opened in 1939 as a College of Applied Arts. The direction of change is significant: The year after the visit was made this college was reorganized as a College of Fine Arts; by 1962 the B.S. curricula in business education will be discontinued, by 1964 the B.S. curricula in apparel design and apparel merchandising will be discontinued, leaving only an A.B. program with majors in various branches of art, music, and theater. This particular "state university" is an educational operation of considerable magnitude: At present there are some fifty thousand students, and by 1970 there will presumably be over a hundred thousand.

Many features of the situation here are quite different from, for example, Boston University of a century before with its pride in having graduated only five B.M.'s in nineteen years. One factor contributing to the high "index" on the Dressel survey is the newness of the situation. At the time, the College of Applied Arts was just emerging. Another factor is doubtless the administrative structure, for this is a department, functioning within a collegiate structure, rather than a separate school. The department is here the constant element, the college the variable one: The music department existed before the College of Applied Arts came into existence, and continued after it had been transformed into a College of Fine Arts. At the time of the visit, practically all the music students were enrolled through the College of Applied Arts, though a few were enrolled through the College of Letters and Science. In view of the institutional structure, the high "index of favorable attitude toward the liberal arts" on the Dressel survey is rather what one would expect as there is not much occasion for the development of a sense of otherness between, say, the music teachers and the English teachers, any more than there might be between the chemistry and the philosophy teachers. It is a little like the 64.4 per cent of the music faculty who feel that music should be required of all music students.

So far as the music department here was concerned, both local and world-wide events in the 1940's were guiding the development of the faculty in a direction that was more academic than perhaps had been envisaged in the original resolution to establish a college with "curricula of a professional or vocational character." Two musicologists were added to the staff and became increasingly involved in giving direction to the department's development, and the activities of Hitler in Central Europe gave a powerful impetus to musicology in America. Thus, within a decade, the department had quite changed its inner character.

No doubt alarmed by the tendencies of the higher educational institutions of the state to go out in all directions at once, the state Regents in 1948 were responsible for a report which established a division of labor among the junior colleges, state colleges, and the university. Roughly, the junior colleges were to offer technical and vocational work, the state colleges were to train teachers, and the university was to concentrate on the professions and graduate study. The particular institution here under consideration thus had high encouragement to re-examine the nature of its offerings in career areas and eliminate what might be considered vocational-type courses. Apparently courses oriented toward research passed muster, but those oriented toward "doing" were eliminated: the University Course Committee, for example, rejected 25 courses from the department of physical education, but was inclined to leave the music department's courses alone. The setting off of the music, art, and theater departments into a separate college, away from the business education, home economics, and physical education departments, is a further step in the same direction —away from vocationalism. Shortly before the visit, the report of 1948 had been reaffirmed by a re-study, so that the ideological framework within which the viewpoints were expressed in the interviews had been made quite explicit.

Although this institution had undertaken no notable general education program, the president had had considerable experience with general education, having set up outstanding programs at two universities which he previously had headed. No doubt he was in some way behind the pressure for more liberal arts work; certainly he was not against it. Thus is borne out a general principle suggested by McGrath at one of the planning sessions on the present project—that academic leadership is important, that there is often striking similarity between the attitude of the dean, the faculty, and the students, and that students even parrot the dean's words.

At the institution discussed here, the individual most immediately responsible for the leadership of the music faculty is the chairman of the department. At the time of the visit, the person in that position had been on the staff of the institution for some twenty years and, while inclined to disparage the importance of his role as being mere "impresario" work of arranging schedules, no doubt exerted a good deal of influence. A musicologist, he is personally favorable toward liberal arts, believing that they give the student perspective and enable him to see his specialty against the total background of human society. Although sheer performance skill frequently develops in a vacuum, he said, research, teaching, and composition tend less to do so; composers are often more liberally educated than performers: Witness the notable American composers who have graduated from Harvard where the Department of Music places heavy emphasis on general liberal arts education. Having a Master's degree from Harvard, he approved of the situation there. With the assistance of some of the other musicologists on the staff, he was leading the current revision of the music program in the direction of increasing the amount of general liberal arts work, and of reorganizing the program so that the students might take related humanities subjects such as art history or the history of the theater as part of the music major. It will be recognized that this is a trend in the same direction as that which had brought the institution, in a couple of decades, from the mere remnants of a teachers college to an academically very impressive branch of the university.

Perhaps the major educational issue before the music faculty and the institution as a whole, according to the then head of the music department, was that of finding means to ensure that students used their electives to take liberal arts courses rather than merely more courses in their professional field. He felt that specific liberal arts courses that the student might take in order to meet university requirements should be named. In the major itself there were only eight credits in specifically named courses; the intention was to double this aspect of the requirements, so that what had been taken for some sixteen credits would be specified—perhaps in history and musicology.

There was also a move to limit the amount of credit for performance work. During the time the interviews were taking place, a committee of the school passed a resolution to limit the amount of performance work in any major to sixteen credits. The rationale behind this move was that each credit of work should require from three to four hours outside of class in preparation. For their performance organizations students are not required to do outside preparation. This reduction of credit hours would create more space on the program for academic-type courses. Certain specific theory courses, in place of so much performance, were mentioned.

In the light of this move to pack tighter the music student's program, it should be mentioned that the music major is already large. It consists of twenty-four credits to be done in the freshman year, and thirty-six credits in the junior and senior years. Majors in other departments of the college run twenty-four to twenty-six credits rather than thirty-six.

As then being revised, and as it has subsequently developed, the music program would emphasize more exclusively one major, the Bachelor of Arts in Music. In addition the student might take work in education to qualify for a general credential for teaching; this work was being put into a fifth year, to be taken at the School of Education. This would eliminate a so-called special credential for teaching in secondary education, which had formerly been fitted ostensibly into the regular four-year program (though, as pointed out by one of the music education professors, in actuality students were generally taking four and a half to five years to finish the old program). This overt move to a five-year program is often envied by teachers in the music schools of privately endowed institutions as a solution to the problems of "fitting everything in"—a solution more feasible for a state-supported school, particularly in a carefully planned state-wide system. The pattern for the five years that seemed to be evolving here was that the basic work in music and the other liberal arts should be completed in the first four years, and the education work in the fifth year, thus extruding the education matrix from which the school arose.

Although there is a rationale behind this four-year undergraduate music and fifth-year education program, is there not some danger in allowing the student to go along for four years without really raising the question of what he is going to "do" with all this training in music, and then in the fifth year bringing him suddenly face to face with the actualities of the situation? This is the reverse of the situation in general education, where the majority of the professional school faculties do not like the idea of the student doing all his liberal arts work in the first two years and then suddenly plunging into professional study. Though there are advantages in this plan for the terminal student, the disadvantages outweigh them; and, according to the Dressel survey, the professional school faculties strongly favor that the liberal studies be spread over the four years. Vice versa, is there not greater advantage in spreading the education work (for "music ed" students, a truly professional study) over the whole program?

At the time of the visit, there were supposedly two other areas of music offered for the degree—one in performance and the other in opera—but few students were taking these programs. As a result there was a desire on the part of some to raise the entrance requirements in performance skill and to give so-called master classes in the school, thus reducing the total length of these programs from five to four years and giving these students substantially the same program as the others except that they would be in classes that required a more advanced level of performance.

Before proceeding to consider the attitudes toward liberal arts encountered in interviews with faculty and students, one might perhaps wish to have some idea of what the professional and liberal components of the curriculum were at the time of the interviews. There was a comparatively large provision for liberal studies, as music curricula go. This was in part inevitable when the music faculty was a department under collegiate jurisdiction and subject to the same requirements as the rest of the college or university. Thus, whether one were taking home economics, music, or whatever it might be, he had to comply with certain requirements which had been set by the Academic Senate for all campuses of the university throughout the state. While the faculty was represented in the formulation of these requirements, the representation was channeled through a long series of steps: the individual teacher could propose a change to the chairman or the curriculum committee of his department, which in turn might decide to convey it to the committee of the college, which in turn might pass it on to the course committee of the Academic Senate, where it might be brought before the Educational Policies Committee and the Budget Committee, etc., and eventually there would come some final action—as one would expect, quite deliberate and well considered. As established for all branches of the university throughout the state, every student on entering had to show certain proficiencies in English and mathematics, or else had to make up his deficiencies without credit. There were, of course, ROTC and physical education requirements. There was a general curricular requirement in foreign language and/or science which might be fulfilled in any one of three ways: 16 units of one foreign language, 12 units of science, or 16 units of two foreign languages and 9 of science. Every student, moreover, had to take three full-year courses in three of the following seven fields: English and speech, foreign language, mathematics, social science, psychology, philosophy, and music or art. The new set of requirements promulgated since the visit is even more sharply defined: Instead of three alternative ways of adjusting the relative claims of foreign language and/or science on the student's time, the new list has only two possibilities: 12 units in one foreign language or 16 in two, and 9 units of natural science. Instead of a choice of three courses among seven areas, the new list calls simply for 9 units of natural science, 9 units of social science, and 9 units of humanities. Curricular change, however, is always bound to create problems in the programs of individual students who may have started under one plan and find it suddenly shifted. The new catalogue states: "As changes in major requirements occur, students are expected to satisfy the new requirements insofar as possible. Hardship cases should be discussed with the departmental adviser, and adjustments approved by petition when necessary."

As will be observed, there is a comparatively high liberal arts requirement in the curriculum of this music department. At the time of the visit, the way the electives were managed and the inclusion or omission of education courses made a difference in the totals. If no education courses were taken, 50 per cent of the work was professional, 25 to 36 per cent liberal, and the rest elective; if education courses were taken, 65 per cent was professional, 25 per cent liberal, and the rest elective. The extrusion of the education work into the fifth year, of course, has strengthened the former pattern. The apparent intention was that the musical and nonmusical components of the curriculum should form more or less of an equilibrium, so far as the allotment of hours is concerned. In its local context, this idea of a 50–50 ratio between music and nonmusic courses seemed something of a compromise, as another branch of the state university had a 70 per cent liberal arts and a 30 per cent music relationship, and still another branch reversed this ratio, with 30 per cent liberal arts and 70 per cent music. From both sides, as one might expect, there was criticism of the

50–50 arrangement: In the eyes of some musicians it was too liberal, of some liberals, too musical. It seems, however, a sensible enough proportion, and is by no means out of line with the thinking in some other professions.

Two of the members of the faculty interviewed—both musicologists— suggested that the performance people were less interested in the liberal arts than were the musicology and theory people. This was also the interviewer's impression.

One faculty member, trained at a conservatory as a pianist, had then decided to become a composer and, to get a liberal arts education, had taken his Bachelor's and Master's degrees at Harvard. He considered the liberal arts indispensable to composition; in the creative arts, he said, one cannot grow unless one grows in personality, and in order to grow in personality one needs to study something outside music. The performer, he thought, does not need liberal arts education. Primarily the teacher and the composer do because they need to be able to draw on other fields in order to do their own particular work. The liberal arts work at present taken by the professional students was sufficient, but for the teaching and composition students should be increased—rather in the humanities area. The sciences, he continued, were not especially important for people in music, and he would not recommend them to students in the school—an attitude which he believed the faculty shared (this was confirmed in at least two of the interviews with students who said the faculty tended to steer them away from science). He thought that the students do not get a liberal arts education because they are too closely restricted by the present program, in which there is too much emphasis on quantitative requirements and too little on its qualitative aspects.

This belief that the requirements a student must meet are too cut and dried was shared by another, somewhat older member—who, ironically enough, was currently chairman of the curriculum committee—although he thought that the 50–50 proportion of music and nonmusic credit was all right. This feeling that the requirements might be too rigid ran counter to the tendency already noted at this institution to specify many requirements that previously had been unspecified.

Rather more outspokenly enthusiastic about the liberal arts was another, somewhat younger faculty member, who said that the nonmusic fields are especially important for a musician, who deals in a nonverbal form of expression and needs to translate his thoughts into words rather than simply into music. For instance, in rehearsal or in teaching or as a critic, the musician needs verbal skills and familiarity with ideas outside of music. The musician needs awareness of values in philosophical, aesthetic, and historical context, and in science as well—particularly scientific method and the nature of scientific truth. This faculty member thought it was necessary for students to understand how values are established in these fields, and their various methods of development. He also thought that students should be acquainted with great works of art. Particularly he stressed the need for languages because of the semantics training they provide, and because the study of a foreign language would give awareness of another culture. Lacking such an opportunity the student is doomed to being provincial. This faculty member believed that courses dealing with the cultural history of other societies were more important to these students than, for instance, courses dealing with international politics. He also believed that in any course there is a core of things which are in essence liberal arts and that the focus should fall on these matters—on the essentials rather than on particulars.

An exceptional member of the staff who was interviewed is a famous young composer, who felt that liberal arts are extremely important. He said that he himself had had practically none in formal education, having been a product of the European system. A person who wants to be more than a tootler of a horn all his life, he asserted, must have liberal arts interests. Obviously, this particular young composer and conductor is one of the poetic types of person who somehow gets a liberal education without having to go through the formal steps that provide it. He said that he was at present teaching only four hours a week and had very little to do with the total curriculum. Thrilling as contact with him unquestionably is for a few advanced composition students, or the members of an orchestra he might have occasion to lead, he really plays more the role of composer-in-residence. The present writer is convinced that the department would benefit if it gave more importance to the somewhat individual and unorthodox approach to liberal training that a person of this type could provide.

Another member of the faculty interviewed, a music educator, was slightly more cautious in endorsing the liberal arts program: Teachers should be interested in the world and be able to relate music to the society in which they live. But the sciences, languages, history, and other branches of the humanities require too much of the student in the light of his heavy commitments elsewhere; perhaps he should be allowed to continue with Spanish if he likes—a view in opposition to the current move to require all music students to take the more academically sanctioned languages of French, German, or Italian. Also, particularly for "music ed" students, there is special merit in the social sciences, such as anthropology and psychology, since social studies might be a good second subject for a music teacher to have. This particular faculty member believed that the performance end was sometimes slighted here, and that some students actually lost skill; in general, the music program seemed rather academic.

Still another faculty member felt that the performing student should have more than half his program in music, but needed to have the outside liberal arts in case he could not obtain employment in performance. When asked what liberal arts courses the student should take, he said he had never given it much thought—none especially. Composers and musicologists should have languages. If a student intended to be a composer he advised him to take more composition; if a musicologist, more history; if an educator, more education.

Quite different was the attitude of another faculty member, who said that liberal arts are especially important to the composer who needs as broad an education as possible. It is not only technique in composition that counts, but what one is saying—and what one is saying grows out of what one is. What he had in mind was more the general education type of course, such as Contemporary Civilization and Humanities A at Columbia (where he had taken his A.B.). He would favor four years of liberal arts with a music major and then further work outside on one's own. He did not feel that the performer needed a substantially different program—only supplementary work on the outside.

Another faculty member favored liberal arts work because, he said, one cannot have a true profession which is isolated from the community. One cannot interpret music to society as a performer if there is no contact with society itself. As a composer one must understand the society for which one is writing. As a teacher one must understand the society in which one is teaching. As a musicologist one must be able to place music in the context of its time. He believed languages to be crucial, but also favored history, science, philosophy, literature, and so on. He felt that there could be a certain amount of reduction—perhaps four or eight points —in the professional instruction to make room for more liberal arts.

Finally, another faculty member—a musicologist (Columbia University A.B., and very much in favor of the general education program there) —was all for stiffening the liberal arts requirements. He would eliminate all teaching credential work before the end of the fourth year. Particularly he stressed the importance of languages (German, French, and Italian), history, the other arts, and philosophy.

To sum up such a varied group of faculty points of view is not easy. Noteworthy in it is a great range of conceptions of liberal or general education—from a panacea for all ills to a form of unemployment insurance. As the relations between the liberal arts faculty and the music department faculty are quite close and friendly, the group shows a high "index of favorable attitude" on the Dressel survey. Actually, though, there is probably more extreme favorableness and more extreme unfavorableness toward liberal education, as understood for purposes of this study, within this group than in most.

No one, for example, squared off and said, "The music student was, is, and will be primarily a human being rather than an animated unit within a profession. He has dimensions as an individual—spiritual, civic, domestic, etc.—which make his purely musical activities not exactly his main reason for being." The faculty member interviewed who said that the student should take some liberal arts courses to fall back on if he could not make it as a musician represented an extreme form of the antiliberal viewpoint not encountered in such bluntness in any of the other interviews, here or elsewhere. A really liberal emphasis in a professional school program requires some agreement on ends, quite over and above the mere acceptance of a certain set of required courses. Within this particular faculty there is obviously a wide range of attitudes toward liberal education.

The interviews with students yielded a similarly wide range of reactions. As a hypothesis, the idea might be entertained that the older and more mature students—particularly those in their thirties and forties—would be more interested in liberal arts and more impatient of requirements in the professional area where they were repeating things they already knew. This is somewhat analogous to the point made in the Dressel survey that the older faculty members tend to be more favorable to liberal studies.

One of the youngest of the students interviewed was a freshman who hoped eventually to become a college teacher. Apparently he was an able student, for he had placed highly on the departmental examination and was taking a good deal of advanced work. He favored liberal arts—as a matter of fact, had come here rather than to a conservatory for this very reason. He felt that liberal arts were good because they helped one enjoy life to its fullest, made one's own specialty more enjoyable, and supplied a kind of breadth necessary for college teaching. His family, he said, also favored liberal arts. He had no objection to any liberal arts courses, but was particularly interested in humanities, languages, social sciences, philosophy, and anything dealing with human relations. The faculty, he said, were in favor of liberal arts and were people of some breadth. One faculty member, whom two or three students mentioned favorably, had suggested that this student round out his program by taking other branches of the humanities and avoid the sciences because of the time factor. Like all the other students, however, he seemed not to have been seriously consulted on what he himself wished to do with the liberal arts part of his program.

The rest of the students were junior, senior, or graduate students. Of course, a certain amount of student dissatisfaction becomes inevitable as students advance, and betokens maturity and unwillingness to accept the *status quo*. In a professional school few faculty members wish to cultivate the kind of sentimentality over memories of student days that some of the ivy-league colleges of a generation ago encouraged. Among the older students interviewed, there were some who obviously lacked enthusiasm for the carefully devised program which has just been given detailed consideration and who felt that both they and other students were taking liberal arts only to meet requirements.

One senior, for example, a man in his late thirties intending to teach public school music, had had an extensive music performance background and considerable experience in a variety of other fields as well. He very much favored liberal arts work outside of music; he said he was interested in all arts broadly and in life as a whole. One needs, he believed, a world view and a wide understanding of society; it is improper to live life within a single specialty. Moreover, the student cannot know music without breadth of education. He thought that students as a whole shared this wide interest. He was dissatisfied with the present prescription both in the liberal arts area and in the music field. He was rather bitter about the fact that he had never been consulted about his wishes or desires on the matter of the liberal arts, or any other matter, and he was rather bitter about the lack of individual contact in the school as a whole. He said that if he had an opportunity for further liberal arts work he would like to throw out the university language requirement, and take courses in the theater arts, psychology, studio art, and English literature. He believed the curriculum was excessively academic and departmentalized, and that the instrumental teaching lacked contact with aspects broader than simply learning the instrument. It was his view that the performance people in the faculty were cut off from the remainder of the department and did not have any substantial influence on the curriculum.

Another upperclassman, a woman in her forties, had returned to finish out a Bachelor's degree after having had conservatory training, some academic work, and years of experience in performance, particularly choral. She was entered as a junior. She very much favored liberal arts, and wanted to take courses to develop her general knowledge, more English, more foreign language (especially French, where she already had a background), and was considering sociology or history as a minor in case she might be called on to teach social studies in her public school work. She said that she would like further work in classical literature, French literature, philosophy, and mathematics—all for their own sake. She had experienced a certain feeling of frustration at having to repeat work in which she was already competent, especially in performance. She believed that the students in general were not highly motivated with respect to liberal arts, but were merely filling requirements to get a degree. Like other students interviewed, she felt that there was not sufficient advisement: The student was simply told to meet the requirements, and the lack of flexibility here, she said, was undesirable. No consideration had been given to what she would like to do in liberal arts. The history and theory courses were academic and dull, narrowly conceived, and not related to life. The composition courses were very much alive. The performance courses, especially those in choral work, were on too low a level for her background.

A great part of the interviews with students filled out the range between the two extremes, though perhaps tending more to the critical attitude toward the liberal arts portion of their work so forcibly expressed by the two upperclassmen than to the freshman's enthusiastic approval. It would be unfair to suggest that, in terms of sheer number of hours of liberal arts work included in the curriculum, the nonprofessional side of the curriculum was being neglected, or that the professional curriculum was highly technical or excessively demanding in character. Yet mature students felt shortchanged with respect to liberal arts. The real problem seemed to be the vitality of the relationship between students and faculty. There were some dynamic personalities among the performance leaders in the school, but they did not have much influence on the over-all character of the program. There were no evidences of studies made locally of students' attitudes toward the curriculum, or of consultation with graduates or other citizens. An excellent model for this sort of thing, incidentally, was discovered by the present writer on one of his visits, "A Follow-Up Study of the Graduates of the School of Music of the University of Illinois"—a doctoral dissertation which had helped direct some of the current thinking at the University of Illinois on the improvement of their curriculum.[8]

Actually, as a program the one just examined represents a very wholesome compromise between the liberal arts college and the conservatory approach. The even division between professional and liberal arts work is not so usual in music as it is in some of the other professions. With a vital approach, this school—at the time of the interviews scarcely out of its teens—would have great potential for development and leadership. Some marvelous things are being done there—for example, with foundation backing an institute of ethnomusicology has come into existence along with the reorganization of the college; in these days of global thinking, this represents a genuinely new and internationally significant development, and in terms of the geographical location of this institution is most logical and praiseworthy. Reviewing the history of the institution as a whole, one notes that the immediately surrounding institutional framework in which the department has operated has undergone a reorganization about every twenty years. At the time of the visit it was on the verge of one of these transformations. One would like to see it retain this general structure at least until it again reaches twenty-one and passes on into adulthood.

The purpose here, however, is less to analyze individual institutions as

---

[8] A. W. Humphreys, "A Follow-Up Study of the Graduates of the School of Music of the University of Illinois" (unpublished Ed.D. dissertation, University of Illinois, 1955).

such and more to understand typical situations and the actualities behind data selected from the Dressel survey. Let us therefore proceed to the other extreme in terms of its "index of favorable attitudes toward the liberal arts." At the institution now to be considered, the "index" stood as far below as in the one previously considered it stood above the median. Ostensibly, this music faculty is, comparatively, as hostile to the liberal arts as the previous one had been favorable. Whereas at the previous institution the majority of the music faculty consider something over 36 per cent allotment of time to the liberal arts appropriate, at this one the majority would hold it under 35 per cent, and more than a third even under 25 per cent.

The organizational structure here is that of a separate school within a university, under its own dean. Thus there seems to be a predisposing factor toward separateness of the music faculty that was not present in the previous music department situation. Also this music school is one of the older ones in the North Central area, and has had more time to develop its definite patterns of thought and feeling.

The charter for the university in which this music school has developed was granted in the mid-nineteenth century to a group of private citizens, including three Methodist ministers—a detail which suggests that it germinated from the same yeasty body of ideas that we have examined earlier in connection with the founding of Boston University and the New England Conservatory. Far enough away from the neighboring big city for safety, it early admitted women, much as did its contemporary institutions in Boston. By the 1870's a "college for ladies," with its music department, was absorbed by this university; and by the 1890's a department of music, with a full professorship and a relationship to the university like that of all the rest of its regular departments, was established. As outlined in the catalogue for 1892–93, the Bachelor of Music curriculum included acoustics, harmonization up to six parts, counterpoint (single and double) up to five parts, advanced canon, fugue, free composition, music history, analysis, and instrumentation, and required the composition of a work for chorus and orchestra, introducing five parts and contrapuntal treatment. This is an impressive set of requirements, similar to what today would be considered suitable for a Doctor's rather than a Bachelor's degree. It is somewhat comparable to Boston University's Bachelor of Music degree of the time, but without the preposterously high liberal arts requirement that was promulgated just before its demise.

That some liberal arts work was here envisaged appears from the catalogue of 1894–95, in which the candidate is required to prove his knowledge of English literature, mathematics, and his choice of Greek, Latin, German, or French—a requirement which might embarrass many B.M. candidates today and is now thought of more in terms of the Doctor's degree. Also at this time a Normal or Teacher's Course was introduced. In 1895 the Department was organized into a School, with its own dean and faculty, on the same basis as the other professional schools of the university (Law, Medicine, Pharmacy); for, as its first dean stated, "the lack of general culture among musicians is frequently a matter of reproach, and it would seem that the function of the University School of Music is precisely to correct this lack." In 1907 the Bachelor of Music—as at Oberlin—had only to prove his ability to matriculate in the College of Liberal Arts (plus one year of general physics) before he received his degree. In 1908 he had to have taken "one fourth of the total number of credits in the College of Liberal Arts necessary for the degree of Bachelor of Arts, one subject of which must be General Physics."

One may at first think the early history of such an institution irrelevant to an understanding of its present problems, but some interesting sidelights appeared in interviews. Some of the present applied music faculty, for instance, lamented the fact that it was difficult for their students who needed acoustics to work it into their programs because it does not count as fulfilling the general education requirement of the university for a science. The early faculty of the Music School, however, had, of their own volition, required General Physics, which would have included acoustics within its own natural-science framework. For some reason (perhaps worthy of reflection), this quite intelligent appreciation of the value of what they called "general culture" (or what we call liberal education) has been frustrated; this may have something to do with the present low "index" of this school on the Dressel survey. Also—and this is not a criticism of this particular school or of any individual, but of academic people generally who are usually so involved in the day-to-day problems of their particular institution that they never go back and see where it began, where it is now, and where it is headed—there is a general unawareness on the part of the faculty members at this institution of the precise nature of their past.

One man, who had been there for thirty years and who obviously had the welfare of the school deeply at heart, was under the impression that the B.M. had not come in until around 1910 and had then been purely professional, no college study being required. Of course, what he probably meant was that there had not been *many* of these B.M.'s before 1910; and in terms of the thousands graduating today with that degree from music schools all over the country the nineteenth-century B.M. seems like nothing much. But he should have known better. When another, in charge of composition and theory, was asked whether he thought any of the B.M. candidates today could write a composition for chorus and orchestra introducing five parts and contrapuntal treatment, he first said, "They have better things to do." Not knowing quite how this was meant, the interviewer persisted; and the reply was that, of course, such a Bachelor of

Music would be extremely rare today. In fact, the majority of them do not take any counterpoint at all. As the study of grammar is in the experience of most A.B.'s, so is the study of counterpoint in that of most B.M.'s today— no more, no less.

But obviously there was not much concern here with the school's realization of itself as a unique phenomenon in history—something that had never existed before and would perhaps never recur precisely in the same way again. While not a matter of life and death in the day-to-day conduct of a school, details like these are an important part of the faculty's liberal education in its own sphere. Somewhere around the institution, there should be available to one who has some real reason for studying it a clear picture of exactly what has happened in its history and a constant attempt should be made to discover the implications of these events for the present. Consequently, one recommendation that will be made at the end of this monograph is that wherever such an account does not exist a graduate student be asked to work on such a project.[9]

At this particular institution, the liberal arts component of the curriculum was increasing during the first decade of the present century. Obviously, the technical emphasis had to be lightened to make room. In 1913, instead of writing this five-part contrapuntal composition for chorus and orchestra, the Bachelor of Music had simply to score for full orchestra a movement of a Beethoven piano sonata. During the first World War, this Bachelor of Music composition requirement made a graceful exit from the curriculum, as in 1917 it was explained that the Bachelor of Music degree was now for performers as well as theorists and that the Master of Music degree was now offered to students "possessing distinct talent for composition." In the 1920's the Bachelor of Music degree—in accordance with NASM standards—became more or less the music school's equivalent of the college's Bachelor of Arts, the kind of specialization involved in the nineteenth-century Bachelor of Music degree having now passed into the realm of the Master of Music.

By the late 1920's, the academic requirement was set up at this school somewhat as it is now (roughly a fourth of the degree curriculum)—in harmony with a concurrent pattern in all the professional schools of this university which was at that time headed by a rather colorful president. The system was a quite free elective one: One-fourth of the program had to be in "College Electives" with freshman English the only specification, the advisers and other members of the faculty apparently not caring too much *what* the students took. In the music school there were some special needs: Voice majors needed language, and in the 1930's, reflecting the

[9] A good example is a master's thesis in music education by P. F. Lester, "The Development of Music at the University of Illinois and a History of the School of Music" (1943), which is in the School of Music library.

certification trend, the music education faculty set up an "academic minor" requirement—because the music teacher would be better off with a second string to his bow. But these restrictions are of the prudential kind that hardly need to be formalized.

Toward the mid-century there occurred, on the university level, a drastic revision of this somewhat easygoing situation, wiping out the "academic minor," making voice students apprehensive lest they not be able to get in enough language work, relegating acoustics to an inaccessible position, and so on—the full consequences of which could be only partially observed through the interviews as the students were in a state of transition from the "old" to the "new catalogue." Doubtless, this state of things had something to do with the low "index" of the school on the Dressel survey.

Moves toward trying to bring some order into the situation started with the introduction of some extensive interdepartmental courses in the humanities, social sciences, and sciences—with foundation backing. But in 1949 more definite action began to be taken: An administrator and professor of government from Harvard, where at the time a particular version of the general education idea was being formulated, came in as vice-president and dean of faculties—the president's deputy in any academic matters. One of his early steps in office was to make a study of duplications and overlapping in the curricula. In an interview with the present writer, he said that there had been considerable dissatisfaction—"in *this* office," he put it—over the haphazard way in which requirements outside the fields of specialization throughout the university were being fulfilled and a lack of cohesiveness on the campus or identification with the university as such. At a meeting of undergraduate deans in 1952, a common concern was expressed; and he appointed a committee of seven representatives—one from each of the schools, and headed by a professor in the school of education. Again with foundation backing, the chairman of this committee was enabled to give adequate time to the project and travel expenses and cost of literature were covered. In this way a very searching examination of the curricular offerings in terms of their relevance to the general education idea was carried out. The implication was that among the multifarious courses in existence those could be singled out that were suitable for all. The question asked was, "Is the approach and type of material such as to be beneficial to the non-specialist, or is it for the person going ahead in the field?" A "grass-roots approach," as the vice-president termed it, was used when results began to take shape: Instead of referring them to the university senate, each dean and school representative on the general education committee submitted the portions in question to the faculty of each school and whatever differences arose were ironed out.

In 1955 the committee on general education of the university issued a printed report, summarizing the background and results of their extensive activities. The intentions, as formulated by the vice-president, had been that general education should extend over the four undergraduate years and "should not be thought of as 'something to be got over with'," that existing courses be used ("in general, we are much more interested in stimulating faculty members to inject general education into their existing courses and in spreading the philosophy of general education among those now engaged in teaching"), and that "flexibility should be the rule and that there should be considerable room for student choice within a general framework. We do not believe in herding all undergraduates into a single ironclad curriculum which would not allow for individual abilities or tastes."

According to this printed committee report, all undergraduate students were to be required to take courses in each of the following five areas: reading, writing, and speaking; natural science; social science; fine arts, literature, and music; and history, philosophy, and religion. In addition, they were to take another course in an area that was not their major. Each of these required courses would have to amount to a full academic year's work in that subject and be taken from the list of 230 courses named in the booklet, with certain additional restrictions (A, B, and C level) to make sure that the subjects would be entered into deeply enough. Each student would take at least one of these general education courses each year. Thus about a third of his total college work would be devoted to general education—not too vastly different in hour-allotment from what had existed before, but quite sharply structured in terms of distribution. The committee, according to the booklet, believed that

> the integration of knowledge depends not only on the structure of the curriculum and the nature of the course but even more upon the student's own thinking.
> The problem is, of course, how to introduce the student adequately to the rich variety of men's experience and knowledge and at the same time to develop his ability to deal with facts critically and independently. The Committee's proposed answer to the problem is essentially a distribution requirement which must be fulfilled by elections from among courses whose primary aim is not to train specialists in a given field, but to contribute to the liberal education of the student.

From the vantage point of a couple of years in the operation of this general education program, the vice-president, who seemed to have been most responsible for it and to whom the printed committee report was addressed, felt that it had been a success, improving the educational base and stimulating faculty thinking. "It's a lever," he said; he believed that the students felt broadened, and had been awakened to the various areas—their significance and meaning to the rest of their lives. As for objective evaluation of its results, he said that so far the instructor and department had done a sort of self-evaluation; and the student government, which wanted student evaluation, had helped in the development of questionnaires. General education, he felt, had proved a springboard for a further step—a "total evaluation of the offering."

What he wished to open up now in the curriculum, he said, was the whole question of improved programs for superior students, particularly those in the graduate school. The superior student must have the opportunity to advance on his own. This development would, of course, involve the music school, which has about half as many graduate as undergraduate students, and is indicative of the general tendencies in the university to "firm up" the curriculum.

The music school representative on the general education committee, a musicologist, had been brought to the university under its present vice-president and dean of faculties; previously, this musicologist explained in interview, there had been really no department of music history (apparently he meant no department that, according to present-day musicological standards, would be so regarded). Here again we note the connection between musicology and the addition of a certain academic dimension to the music school curriculum. Also the present dean of the school had been elevated from the faculty to his administrative position under the present regime. Unquestionably a strong chain of influence in favor of the humanities has manifested itself from the president on through the dean of the school. In terms of interschool dynamics, it may be possible to see in this situation some aspects of the problem discussed by McGrath in *The Graduate School and the Decline of Liberal Education:* The recent changes here represent a strengthening of the role of the college of liberal arts, as it is the center for the humanistic disciplines, and of the graduate school, which is rather a paper school, consisting largely of the professorial faculties of all the separate schools.

In characterizing the survey that had been carried on by the general education committee, this faculty member said that it had required all of the two years that it had taken. The committee based its decisions on facts and opinions, though there was a tendency to accept the statement of the departments giving courses as to whether they felt a course was intended for the general or special student; there were a number of series of hearings before the list was finally printed.

During the brief operation of the new plan, he said, there had been some rather odd changes in some of the courses themselves, and some anomalous situations. As an inheritance from the previous interdepartmental committee of the humanities—headed, strangely enough, by a physicist—there was a course in the curriculum entitled "Music, Art, Philosophy, and Psychology of Art," of which one term was devoted to music, one to art, and one to philosophy and psychology. Each department had been handling its part of the course on its own and, at least for the music term, the result was what it would be in any introductory course (especially as the student might take one term without the other). This course was included by the committee on general education in its list. Another course provided from the music school is a music appreciation course, entitled "Music in Modern Life," and given by the same man as the course previously described, and really about the same content. Also, there is a "Comparative Arts" course, formerly given for graduate students by the man who is now dean of the school. It has now become an undergraduate general education course and has attracted a group of students with quite differing degrees of musical literacy and maturity; this has considerably changed the character of the course. In commenting on the problems posed, the musicologist on the general education committee said that more staff was needed. "More than we're doing," he said, "is what's wanted."

Another member of the faculty, teacher of theory and currently chairman of the school's curriculum committee, said that when the general education requirement was set up each school adjusted to it: The voice major, for instance, needed two foreign languages, which had to be counted as general education credit despite the fact that mathematics and foreign languages do not appear on the list of general education courses. In the music school, moreover, only four—instead of the five—areas had to be presented in the distribution of courses; and there had to be minor adjustments. He said he thought the idea was good, but that it had produced no real change in the music school, for the total *number* of hours had not been much affected—only the distribution. The general feeling, as he sensed it, was that the school had been doing as much as could be done without jeopardizing professional training. Right now, he said, they were working on an honors program for the juniors and seniors, which presents many problems because there is no common denominator for the seven schools on the campus and no accepted idea of how honors work should be set up in a music school. There are models for honors programs in the liberal arts areas: for example, a history major does more history. But in the music school, there is already so much specialization. Personally, he said, he would like to see superior students come out with a wider background rather than a narrower. The matter had been turned over to each school to work out and, at the time of the interview, a committee had been working on it since the previous fall. (Subsequent inquiry does not reveal that any real progress has been made despite the fact that at the time of the visit there was a prominent notice in the catalogue of the school about the honors program, specific information regarding which was "available from the Assistant Dean.")

This particular faculty member felt that liberal arts were essential to the musician who needs to see his art in relation to the larger social setting and to think beyond the immediate and practical application. Many of the students will be teachers in the public schools, and should exert a kind of leadership beyond just conducting orchestras. It is part of the indigenous character of a music school—as distinct from a conservatory, which he was inclined to see as individual and narrow—to provide a larger framework in which the musician's role can be seen. The trend at this school, as he had observed it during his eleven years there, was to try to incorporate a broader background and to realize the advantages that the school has within the university. Some of the developments in music education of the past quarter-century were discussed. It was his considered opinion that when the students came there to school they should be started in the traditional point of view; they had to be presented with an ordered body of content.

In discussing the theory and composition program with another teacher in the school, the interviewer told of a remark that one of the students had made about his courses: The applied courses, this student had said, were pretty professional, with really only an opportunity to work on technique, and the theory courses were almost as professional—"Theory—well, Theory is Theory." "Is there an attempt," the interviewer asked this faculty member, "to stress background in this type of work?" "Personally," this theory teacher said, "I feel that it needs to be straight. Scientists always have to have some 'higher value' in the background; but the student does have to have the first two years of theory, just as one needs to know what verb forms are. It is like grammar—a matter of being one of the tribe—like reading and writing and arithmetic." His attitude toward liberal studies, he stated, was "not negative." Graduate work, he said, had been revolutionized by musicology: "but we do not use the word 'musicology'—say 'music, history, and literature'."

A member of the music education faculty pointed out that, although not everyone on the staff accepted the idea of general education, the committee revised the requirements annually, and there was ample opportunity for reconsideration of various aspects. The program as it had begun to operate, he said, was better than it had been, but not as good as it should be. As an individual educator, he said he would like to see it move more in the direction of the humanities; as a member of the faculty, he saw the difficulties, for the institution attracts a high type of musician, and too drastic an increase in general education would result in weakening its professional aspects. He would like to see the program extended to five years, but realizes the dangers in this and thinks that a better job should be done with the four years. The music education Master's degree, he pointed out, requires a sizable block of hours on the principal instrument; some come in as finished artists, and yet have to fulfill this requirement. And in general cultural subjects, there is not enough attempt to measure attainments

—just a flat requirement of credit hours. Some move has been made in the direction of alleviating this situation: The applied faculty, for instance, has made it possible for an able student, on the basis of a syllabus, to be excused from certain requirements in piano, and thus to have some hours on his program freed. One proposal for the honors program which he mentioned was that the senior year be free of stated requirements.

This particular member of the faculty, originally an A.B., believed in breadth and depth of education for the musician—in other words, he considered cultural background important. Many professional skills, he thought, could be picked up on the job. Speaking of the attitude of many educators toward their students, he said that we tend to assume too much responsibility. As officer in charge of music education placement, he had formed the opinion that the largest single reason for graduates staying only one year in positions is their inability to get along with colleagues—rather than any purely musical deficiencies. As for the counseling program, there was enough so that there was some personal contact, but perhaps not enough—possibly too much was left to the student. No counselor, he said, should be responsible for more than thirty students, and most of the consultation should take place before registration. In general, this faculty member's attitude toward liberal arts seemed not atypical of music educators generally; in conversation he expressed himself as being quite favorable to the idea of the liberal component of the music student's program, yet was so close to the actualities and complexities of music education placement as not to be entirely free from occasional inconsistency of detail in his attitude.

The applied faculty, here as elsewhere, was inclined to be less favorable to the patterns of general education that have been put into operation during the past several years. This opposition is more than a matter of insensitivity or intellectual indolence: At its best, it arises from a thoughtful and considered approach to the nature of education, and from acute observation of how the mind of the learner works, in that very close and personal relationship fostered by individual instruction in music. Because music schools showed such a low "index" on the Dressel survey, and this institution was low among the music schools, and because the applied faculty seemed to be the focal point of this attitude, the interviews immediately following are extremely important—not so much because of the fine individuals who took time to make their opinions articulate, but because of the general type of attitude involved.

One teacher, who considers himself more a practicing church musician but who is professor of organ and church music at the school, said that he regarded himself as a victim of the general education idea. Largely at the insistence of his father, who was a physician, he took two years of liberal arts work at the University of Chicago, and found them a waste of time. In general, he said, he was not in sympathy with too broad a program: We ought not to frustrate a student's ability or talent. Music is a complex language, he remarked, one of the humanities itself. He was skeptical of getting culture through courses, particularly through liberal arts courses. "They say they will broaden the student; I'm not sure they will. A technique can be taught: This we can do. But liberal education goes on throughout life, and does not involve taking courses, necessarily." Although he was talking from a highly personal and individual viewpoint, it was entirely real. Certainly he was not, himself, an example of an anti-intellectual approach to life. So far as the source of this intellectual interest was concerned, he was inclined to attribute it to the high school, where he felt more emphasis should be placed. In Europe, where he had done advanced work in his specialty, "they expect students to be more mature." He was skeptical, he said, of Harvard—"you may by accident acquire something along the way."

So far as the immediate situation at his school was concerned, he felt that liberal arts courses should be channeled through the adviser. He was doubtful "of the value of remote areas." For his students he would like to see science included, but in the form of acoustics. What is taken, he believed, should be related more or less to the field, and should be carefully considered in terms of what is of greatest value to the particular student at that particular time.

Another faculty member in the church music department saw some value in the standardization of requirements thoughout the university, but would not like to see more general education. "It's largely a requirement," he said, "to get off." The student's real objective is to study music. The aim of the requirement is that the student become acquainted with other areas, but there should be "a pulling together rather than a spreading out."

The head of the voice department, who took his A.B. and B.M. back in the more gracious days of higher education without feeling too much pressure in doing so, said that the voice is indefinite and can't be evaluated week by week, and that it is difficult to keep tabs on what practicing the student is doing, except as it shows up over a longer period of time. Academic pressure, on the other hand, is more immediate and persistent, and the voice is neglected.

> We don't get the time for the student to practice his music because of the tendency to overload. Most of the students come because they want to develop a talent which they feel they have and that gives them some hope. Sometimes we take some of that enthusiasm out by placing too many other requirements upon them. It can be disheartening to a student to come and find he has little time for what he came here to study. We have to keep the spark alive. If it can be kept alive the first two years, they could have a heavier academic program later. Better later than earlier. The thing that draws people to a given profession has to be kept alive—can be, if in a place of prominence. The emotional experience is more important in

music than elsewhere. If dampened by what *they* [by which he meant the general educationists] deem important, that's bad.

Freshman composition, incidentally, he found not particularly helpful in his students' professional development. "They may study it," he said, "but they get no help in pronunciation—for example, breathing. I try to teach it in relation to the punctuation of the sentence." Students, he said, find freshman English "a trial." So far as their breadth of awareness is concerned, he felt that so much is happening that reading current news-papers and magazines is sufficient, and that students should be encouraged to read. Their program of studies, he believed, should be less diversified while they are learning the tools of their trade.

In reflecting on this interview, and on some of the other interviews at this school, one must realize that they were carried on in a rather free-flowing, improvisatory style. There are obviously overstatements which give a very different effect when set down in cold print as a passage of written rather than of spoken communication. Here, for instance, one might well wonder whether this music teacher seriously believed that students could use the English language precisely without special instruction in it—whether just reading newspapers and magazines would be enough. Obviously, he would doubtless not wish to go quite that far: He merely felt that what he considered first things should be placed first. The usual liberal arts college curriculum places English composition first to help the student write acceptable papers and examination answers in his more advanced courses. This is a need more real in liberal arts colleges than in music schools. Perhaps it scarcely needs to be pointed out that the placing of liberal studies in the music student's program later rather than earlier is not without its dubious aspects. However, we are here concerned more with attitudes than with whether we agree with them. This particular music teacher—like most of the teachers of actual musical performance—adopted an approach to the problem no doubt very close to the subjective world of the individual music student.

The chairman of the piano department, who had received his training in Europe and who had been here for ten years, felt that specialization should start when the student enters college: In France, he pointed out, after the student takes the baccalaureate at eighteen he enters the conservatory. But in America, he said, we have something that is half conservatory, half university. As for liberal education, he belived that the students *need* it—it is concerned with fundamentals. But it should take place in high school. "The high school teachers are better paid than college teachers," he stated, "and should know more." If the students could have got more there, he said, we could teach them more at the university. He himself, in his teaching, is in favor of instruction in small groups of three or four students—

one sits at the piano, the others listen and often learn more than the one who, on the piano bench, is perhaps a little frightened—a system that is common in Europe. It occurred to the interviewer that perhaps this is the very tradition that Tourjée encountered when, in the mid-nineteenth century, he went to Europe to investigate group music teaching, in preparation for opening what proved to be the first university-sponsored music school in this country. As head of the department of piano instruction, however, he did not insist that other members of the department use this system: "I like to let people stay personal," he said, "not be too eager to please—let them do what they want with students." Actually, there seems to be a great deal of professional working-together of the applied faculty: Every week, students perform; there are staff meetings; grades are given according to the jury system; upperclassmen take examinations before the whole faculty; and so on. What goes on here in the way of musical training is, without doubt, exacting, orderly, and responsible.

Of course, in this talk with the head of the piano faculty one must realize that some of his remarks were prompted by sheer vivacity, a sort of French *esprit*. As was mentioned before, we are concerned primarily with attitudes and only secondarily with facts or with the reasoning from which those attitudes might have arisen. Whether, for instance, high school teachers really are better paid than college teachers, or whether there is any point in wishing that the American high school were something it is not and probably never will become—these are not matters that can be discussed here. No doubt we have to take the American high school, with its aims and with all its strengths and weaknesses, as a point of departure.

The head of the stringed instruments department, a Latin American of considerable vigor and incisiveness of thinking, said that education will remain tailor-made, and the more versatile it is the better. "The more we make requirements rather than try to find areas where the student needs most help," he said, "the more we are suppressing individual expression—more so now than ever." Like the head of the piano department, he was in favor of general education, but unhappy that it must come at the university level. He would like to see students better prepared when they come to college. "The student arrives," he said; "and he meets with a complex situation: we ask him to be master of all trades in four years. He is so far behind the standard in which we believe." Chopping the enrollment in half or lengthening the program to five years would help, he thought; but the student needs musicianship, he needs theory, etc. "We keep pushing students into higher levels and neglecting fundamentals. There are tremendous psychological casualties," he said; "many haven't gone into any field in depth. They become restless, insecure. The world today offers so many tangents and parallels; the boundaries of one subject overlap those of another; there is so much more today to do—vast horizons in every field—and we have to touch on more fields; but what happens to study in depth? Are we sure that the mind develops through contact with so much—or is the mind more likely to mature through deeper concentration in depth?" He said that he believed in a common core, no matter how developed; but he felt that one develops it through intake in the area where one is most receptive. "Music is abstract—one has to soak in music to grow." He told of a student who two years ago needed acoustics, but ended up—through the operations of the distribution requirement—with chemistry. "In good faith," he said, "this gives a balanced diet—like vitamins. But the mind is not fed this way. This boy needed *acoustics.*" His students also, he felt, needed counterpoint, and the majority of them do not get it—that is, it is not on the applied string program, nor the music ed program, nor the applied voice program.

"The attitude of the music student," he said, "is often that we are the members of an extinct race. Often they are apologetic for being music students. In the first place, they have a love of something they consider will never allow them security or great earning power; in the second, they have not reached a mature point at which they know what it's all about, and they are subjected to the teasing and humor of other students." He did not know how the tendency toward general education could go further, and thought that it may have gone too far, as in any historical trend. The problem today, he believed, is with the parents of the present generation: More and more the parents of America have turned children over to teachers; under the older system, the father watched for aptitude in his children, "but this is now left to strangers (for the parents fear to be put to shame)." The most promising area in the present situation, he felt, is the Preparatory Department, which has been recently opened there.

The interviewer arrived for the visit to this school of music a day early, and had the pleasure of hearing several members of the applied faculty in a Sunday afternoon chamber-music program. From their playing, before a packed hall, it was obvious that this was a group of unusually thoughtful and responsible musicians. From the interviews it was clear that they were extremely aware of each of their students as human beings, rather than as abstractions, statistics, trends, or concepts. There is high tradition for this aspect of teaching: Even the original Academy of Plato set up as its model the highly personal kind of teaching that Socrates had practiced. Unquestionably they are an able, intelligent, and articulate faculty. It is interesting that Dressel on his visit to the school of journalism of this same university was similarly struck by the unusual ability of that faculty who, he wrote, "apparently have thought long and deeply about matters of liberal arts and liberal education, and · . . talk readily about these issues." The music faculty, similarly, is by no means unsophisticated.

The problem, as considered in these five interviews, is not merely one of applied vs. nonapplied teachers, nor one of Europeans vs. Americans. The majority of these last five musicians were educated within the regular channels of education in this country. Fundamental to the problem is the difference in the conception of the way human education is achieved: Should it be from the inside out, or from the outside in? Which, or who, is getting the education, the curriculum or the student?

The students interviewed here were not of as wide a range of age or maturity as those at the institution previously considered. All were between nineteen and twenty-two, and were juniors and seniors. They had entered just before the general education distribution requirement had gone into effect; consequently they were more or less "under the old catalogue" (as one of them put it), which allowed a rather free choice of liberal arts subjects. In their programs, however, there had been some influence from the mid-century trends toward regimentation, and they were, of course, aware of the reactions of their sophomore friends to the new scheme. As one student said, "they were not jumping with joy about the new general education system."

This student, a church music senior, said that the liberal arts work he had taken was "strictly a hodge-podge": he had "proficiencied" out of freshman English, and had been under the impression that he should take another English course, but maybe he did not have to; anyway, he had taken a term of French and found that he had had it in high school; a term of college algebra which proved relatively easy but of uncertain value; a term of astronomy which was presented as rote memorization; etc. When asked whether he wished he had taken more or other liberal arts courses, he said, "Not really. I wouldn't say 'liberal arts' was a waste of time, but it interferes." He felt that he had a pretty good background in high school, had always liked to read, and really wanted more professional courses. Although obviously his program would have been more orderly under the general education plan, and it is easy to see from his remarks what need has prompted the revision of the curriculum, the question arises of whether a boy like this—obviously somewhat individualistic, resentful of restrictions (he was not, for instance, in favor of fraternities, which are strong here, because he did not like the way "they order you around")—would suddenly find his liberal arts experience more meaningful if he were no longer allowed to drift here and there at will. Some expectation, some framework of anticipation, some motivation needs to be aroused.

Another student, a piano major in the music ed course, differed somewhat in that he wished he had more of a liberal education for purposes of wider social communication. In his first year he took general biology, which purported to be a survey of the whole animal kingdom: One term was on a field pig ("we scraped at it"), another was on botany ("absolutely no good at all—just fact on fact on fact"). He had taken a term of psychology, but found it poor, with "no chance for discussion, three hundred in the class, the room dark, the speaker spoke fast—I can't remember anything from this, just a person up on the stage." In freshman composition and literature, the class studied F. Scott Fitzgerald, reading some other novels too. "There was some connection between the books, I guess, but it was kind of vague to me. Once in a while we were supposed to tell something in 'narrative style', as in high school, and there were six themes a term." Except for a few courses under unusual professors, this student had found his educational experience depressing; he now felt, he said, that he was "just dragging himself along." He thought that more of a historical framework would have helped, and toward that end he had taken a survey course in English literature. He could have taken Western civilization instead, he said, but he was "afraid of courses *too* general, spending a whole year on big broad ideas." If you study a course in Dickens, he felt, you would be more likely to come out of it knowing more about the period than if you took a survey of English literature. When asked about the faculty attitude toward liberal arts courses, he said that he had had to get down on his knees to take French because they said a piano major did not need French, "but if they had seen that the catalogue said French was required they would have said it was required. My adviser," he said, "couldn't care less if I took anything outside of the music school; he only checks course cards."

A girl—a junior in violin, hoping to go into concert work, or, if that proves not feasible, to fall back on college teaching—felt that freshman English was "most unvaluable and very hard. The course is mostly taught by graduate students in their first or second year of teaching. Meeting four times a week, it called for a written theme each time." She did not think it improved her writing, ". . . with all those themes." She said that she had disliked the course before she had taken it, simply because it was required. She did not feel that there was much interchange with other students: "About the only place we get it is at The Gate of Horn—a sort of night club where there are folk-singers, or The Weaver . . . about fifteen of us will go in." There are a great many cliques among the students, she said—the organists form one, the singers are "in a world of their own," and so on. She thought that the school should be professional in everything, that there was too poor a quality in what goes on to the graduate school. "If we had more perfection, all the time!" she exclaimed. She thought she should concentrate more on her instrument—that liberal arts were "all right, *but . . .*" To the interviewer, she represented a type of student not uncommon in schools devoted to the arts: An A and B student in practically all her courses, she obviously had aspirations that would be difficult of complete fulfillment in college.

One music education student who wants to be a band director, preferably on the college level, believed that general education should be part of a music student's education, and that this was the unique feature of this school as distinct from a conservatory. Personally, he preferred the elective system rather than the new program. The education courses, he said, were "the biggest beef. Some of them are not too worthwhile." As far as the liberal arts go, he could see no reasons for the courses being specified.

Another student, a pianist who had played with the Boston Pops and Chicago Symphony, thought that liberal studies were important but was glad he had not had any more of them than he did. He considered that freshman English was valuable. History and psychology he found most valuable. But in most courses, he said, he felt lost in a class of a few hundred. What he was really concerned with was the possibility of trying out for Juilliard; he would try, he said, for the Chopin Prize, and the Leventritt Awards next year in New York, and so on.

Another piano student, a senior, who hoped to teach and play privately or in a conservatory, did not think he could have had more liberal arts in his program; he regretted that he could not have taken a course in philosophy (he wished he had had time to read Nietzsche) and would have preferred something like that instead of science. His only science course had been one quarter of "Outlines of Astronomy"; when asked why he had taken it, he answered "because it was offered at the right hour." He would have enjoyed later history instead of a quarter he took in "History of the United States" which, he discovered, never got to Roosevelt. He wanted the twentieth century, and was at the time taking "20th-Century British and American Literature." He thought that the school of music students kept too much to themselves; one could associate with musicians later, and college was not the time to be that one-sided. "The school of music students," he said, "are rather narrow, as a whole—but it's a matter of what you wish to emphasize."

A voice student, a girl in her junior year, thought that there were not enough liberal arts courses in the program. In her opinion, the main value of them was to enable one to converse with people about philosophy, literature, etc.—but "What I want to do," she said, "is sing." She hoped to go to Germany to study *lieder*. But she was now trying to find out whether she had talent, and for what—opera? concert? oratorio? "How would you know this?" she was asked, and replied, "From how people react to my singing." A member of a sorority, she believed that the "firesides," at which interesting guests led the discussions, were very valuable; and, in general, the experience of fraternity and sorority life, quite extensive at this particular university, seemed to her to embody meaningful educational experience.

Necessarily, there is a great deal of repetitiousness about the interviews with students, but perhaps the bits of conversation—and these really should be given in even more detail to catch the expressive nuance, which on this campus seemed to be significant—will suffice to reveal a quite widespread point of view.

It must be recognized that in all the data presented in this chapter, primarily the attitudes rather than the actual situations have been stressed. Favorableness to the liberal arts in the obvious sense was not widespread at this school, as the Dressel survey had led us to expect. As the first student interviewed said, "No one shouts on a stump that it's the greatest thing that ever happened." Active and positive enthusiasm for the liberal arts, in the institutional sense of the term, operates here from the top down rather than from the bottom up.

Perhaps some light might be shed on the situation in this institution by a comparison with an observation made by Dressel as a result of his visit to the school of journalism. With regard to the liberal arts courses taken by journalism students, he felt that there was "no ready channel of communication between the College of Liberal Arts faculties and the School of Journalism faculty." In other words, although formal institutional channels may exist, he felt that there was a lack of effectual communication. "There are several points at which problems arise which indicate that this lack of ready means for joint discussion is a handicap to developing the best possible program of courses." He noted

> . . . occasional dissatisfaction with some of the first courses in the liberal arts departments. This problem seems to be complicated by the fact that, from time to time, individuals in the various liberal arts departments who gain control of the first courses develop particular points of view about what this first course should be and usually do so in relationship to a particular set of concerns for majors in the department. This problem is not one that is of sole concern to the School of Journalism, and it would appear that there ought to be some means whereby the planning and offering of first courses in the various liberal arts departments could be maintained in terms of the obligation to contribute to the general education of all students. Professionalism in viewpoint is as rampant in some liberal arts departments as it is in the professional schools, and perhaps even more so.[10]

In general, Dressel found the attitude toward the liberal arts in the school of journalism more favorable than the present interviewer found it in the music school—no doubt the result of a great number of factors, such as the more verbalistic nature of journalism, the stronger backing of the liberal arts portion of the curriculum by the accrediting agency, and the comparatively recent establishment of the journalism school. There are evidences of developing separateness here, too: When the school of journalism was established in 1921, the students actually spent their first three

---

[10] This quotation and the ensuing one are from the unpublished first report written by Dressel on the basis of his visit to the journalism school of this same university and preserved in the files of the Institute of Higher Education.

years in the college of liberal arts, but "this pattern lasted only until the first group of students transferred to the School of Journalism, at which point the faculty was dismayed to find that the breadth of training which they desired was not present." He characterized the college of liberal arts as "a sprawling, anarchical kind of structure involving so many students that it is difficult to provide the minimum of personal contact." Dressel found the journalism faculty *pro*-liberal but not exactly *pro*–College-of-liberal-arts-courses; similarly, in the music school, there was a generally civilized, cultivated, and even sophisticated attitude toward cultural values, but not an active favorableness to the particular institutional means that were being employed ostensibly to achieve these ends. Dressel felt that the journalism faculty was quite eager for the students to achieve a liberally educated outlook, and in his report he raised the question of why the journalism school did not have more effect on the thinking elsewhere in the university. Among the possible answers, he suggested the small size of this professional school (actually the journalism and music schools have about the same number enrolled):

> . . . in contrast to the large size of the College of Liberal Arts and of the University as a whole. . . . Furthermore, no professional school is likely to have the prestige which would be necessary for it to become a model for thinking about the liberal arts. The School of Journalism faculty has been inclined to take a hands-off view with regard to liberal arts offerings, as perhaps they should. The result has been, however, that certain courses suggested or prescribed in liberal arts may be relatively unsuitable for journalism students or for any student who is not proposing to specialize in that particular field.
>
> From another point of view, the lack of impact might be seen as resulting from the very specialized point of view found in many liberal arts college departments. . . .
>
> Still another aspect of this matter is that the liberal arts colleges, again particularly in the large universities, have lost a good bit of the personal element; they have become content- rather than student-oriented. Advisers take a minimum of responsibility for contact with students, and the association between students and staff is primarily limited to the formal classroom situation.

Quite apart from questions of cause, there seemed to be—except among individuals high in the administrative ranks—little active favorableness toward the means currently being used to promote the liberal education of the students in the music school. A somewhat more passive favorableness is to be found among the ranks of the musicologists (though not here called by that name) and music educators. A still more hostile attitude is found among the thoroughly conscientious musicians concerned directly with musical performance—an unfavorableness that must be characterized as ideological. No doubt, as the Dressel survey suggests, it is fundamental in music—one of the professions that is itself one of the liberal arts. It goes almost as deep as religious, ethnic, and political differences, which may be proved absurd, but, as Camus maintained, the absurd is the very essence of the condition of man.

More toward the mid-point in the range of indices on the Dressel survey of attitudes toward the liberal arts were two other music schools in the same general North Central area. Though some of the extreme individual attitudes already expressed were encountered there, the views of both faculty and students were inclined to be less positive and the resulting impression was one more of homogeneity within the institution as a whole.

In one instance, the relationship between the institution and the state which supported it seemed to have acted as a cohesive factor. Because it is one of the older music schools of the Middle West, and exemplifies the liberalizing role of the music school that has grown up within a state university, its origin and early phases might well be stressed here as part of the historical framework underlying this monograph.

With the federal aid of the Morrill Land Grant Act of 1862, this particular state in 1868 opened what it called an Industrial University. For nearly the first quarter-century of its existence, its chief concern was industrial and agricultural, with little attention to music. In 1885 it became a University, and in 1894 it established a College of Literature and Arts. In 1897 the trustees voted that "first-class courses in musical instruction should be arranged, to be taken in connection with other University work," for which diplomas and appropriate degrees should be awarded, and that "the School of Music should be conducted on the same basis as the School of Law, Medicine, etc." This provision was carried out quite literally, in that students in the music school do not pay for private lessons in instrument or voice, any more than the law or medical student would pay separately for individual conferences with his instructor—an enviable arrangement, as private fees are the source of a great deal of many music schools' troubles.

The first curriculum leading to the Bachelor of Music degree was announced in 1897. It had a reasonable balance between professional and nonprofessional courses: 80 semester hours in prescribed music courses, 50 in nonmusic courses (20 in foreign languages, 2 in plane geometry, 5 in general physics, 6 in rhetoric, 5 in military or physical training, 12 in electives from the College of Literature and Arts). The rationale behind such a curriculum is set forth in the 1903–04 catalogue:

> The successful pursuit of music as a profession requires not only special aptitude and talent but a cultivated general intelligence as well. This fact has been too often overlooked and the results have been one-sided and incomplete. A school of music in connection with a great university offers

ample opportunity for supplying the elements frequently lacking in the education of musicians.

During the succeeding decades the number of prescribed music courses crept up into the 90's and the number of prescribed nonmusic courses and general electives dwindled: for example, by the 1950's some B.M. curricula had only 8 hours of foreign languages. There were many considerations that might explain this, such as the conversion of an 1897 B.M. degree (which was more like an LL.B., in its way) to the B.M. of the 1920's (which was more like an A.B.), as well as actual changes within the field of music education itself.

In the course of the extensive interviews with members of the administration, faculty, and students of this state university and its school of music, the author of this monograph was struck by the comparatively orderly and self-aware way in which the many developments in the curriculum of the university and school had been carried out. There was a fine sense of responsibility toward the citizens of the state, and a high degree of integration—and yet variety—within the institution.

Another institution visited, the index of which on the Dressel survey was around the mid-point for music schools, is a conservatory which forms part of a small liberal arts college. The college itself arrived at its present form in 1913 through the coalition of two pre-existing Methodist institutions. One of the guiding figures in shaping the conservatory was also quite active in the NASM and was a Bach specialist, establishing a tradition there of an annual festival of works by that composer. The relationship between liberal and professional studies at this institution seemed to be quite favorable, partly as a result of its small size. Some of the fiercer aspects of the conflict between liberal and professional education appear only at larger institutions. So long as the institution stays small enough, it is usually spared some of the more crushing phenomena of power politics.

This is not to suggest that at an institution like this one there is not a good deal of soul-searching with respect to whether the individual faculty member or the school is doing the right thing. But, oddly enough, an awareness of the problem and a sense of the possibility of one's own shortcomings are in themselves a first step toward its solution.

In 1957, for instance, there was issued to the president and board of trustees of this college a survey report prepared by an outside group of visitors under the auspices of the University Senate of the Board of Education of the Methodist Church. The whole question was thus raised: What direction should the institution take? A recommendation was made that it hold more firmly than it had been doing to its role as a liberal arts college. Other institutions in the state, the survey said, were fulfilling more professional roles. The report criticized the curriculum of the conservatory as being too professional, implying that its liberal arts requirements did not even meet the NASM standards. This was, of course, a thrust in a very sensitive spot, as the conservatory had long assumed that it was doing so. The matter here involved hinges on how music history courses are counted, and other such points. Unfortunately, the NASM requirements are ambiguous on this point: In all sincerity, the survey report committee could cite the avowed purpose of the "General Culture" requirements, the Conservatory the stated "examples," and both feel that they were justified in maintaining they were correct in their quite different statements of what the NASM standards were. The survey committee seemed to think that the conservatory should be made a part of the humanities division of the college and thus be brought under the core curriculum—a move which would not be feasible, however, in terms of other requirements of the NASM and of state teacher certification. The details of the issues here are not necessary for our present purposes: The fact is that there has been considerable concern on this campus over the liberal component of the professional curriculum; the president and the dean of the college actively favor liberal arts work in the conservatory, and to the ultimate question of what kind of enterprise should be pursued by the institution as a whole there is high administrative sanction for the possible answer—"a small liberal-arts college." Under the influence of this study there has been an intensification of the core curriculum. The director of the conservatory was of the opinion that a great deal of the thinking of the survey committee had been influenced by the Harvard Report.

The general attitude of the conservatory faculty was favorable to the liberal arts. They thought them important, and they liked to teach there because what they were doing was a part of the liberal arts tradition. The question in their minds, however, was, If the liberal arts requirements were increased, what would be cut out in music?

Many of the teachers, particularly of instruments, showed the same kind of thoughtful and questioning approach as did some of the applied faculty in the institution with the low index number on the Dressel survey —but here the attitude was a little more tentative, more speculative. One teacher of the double reeds and of theory (a fairly young man though a sometime symphony player) said that most of the conservatory faculty recognized the need for a more liberal curriculum achieved in some way, perhaps by enlarging the course content in music history and literature. Musicians start off specialized and get broader, he said, whereas other subjects start off broad and become specialized. "Music is a perfect art. You have to develop your skills young. It's not true that in it you become keener in your ability to discern and relate facts." He said that all the faculty viewed liberal education as desirable, and recognized shortcomings in this respect. "We are trying to be as broad in the history and literature courses as possible. But do we give the liberal arts person a course that is general enough? Aren't we as guilty as they?" Perhaps this is enough to suggest a prevailingly more temperate version of some of the attitudes we had encountered earlier.

The interviews with the students also revealed an attitude toward both their professional and nonprofessional work that was, on the whole, free from the bitterness noted at some other places.

The Southwestern institution presented an even more gracious attitude. It is of comparatively recent foundation; the university—like the previous one, Methodist—held its first classes in 1915, and up to recent years was rather small. The music faculty forms a separate school of the university, with its own dean. In general, there is enthusiastic support for the liberal education of all students. The dean of the college of arts and sciences has apparently exercised a humanizing influence, and the dean of the school of music has "steadfastly resisted the 'artist's programs' except when they included liberal or general education. Liberal arts and music," he said, "are a two-way street: There is a considerable number of courses that belong in the Arts and Sciences philosophy, and several of ours are getting recognition. Arts and Sciences students should be taking music."

The university has something of a rotating system for committee assignments, and eventually all regular faculty members serve on school as well as all-university committees. Since there is a general requirement of arts and sciences courses, any committee assignment is likely to bring the faculty member in contact with some aspect of liberal education.

Among the issues before the faculty are some connected with teacher training, as teaching certificates in the state are granted through the degree-conferring institutions. Another educational issue focuses around a curriculum that is being developed in music and theology, in which the requirements in the two fields are about equally balanced.

Among the faculty members interviewed, all but one had an interested or enthusiastic attitude toward liberal arts. With rare exceptions, they are satisfied with the present allocation among the various subject fields required of music majors. From the inception of the university, the various schools have been completely autonomous in curricular matters—a fact which makes the harmonious relationship almost amazing. Good working relationships between music and liberal arts faculties have apparently been fostered by careful appointments, deliberate focus on "all-university" feeling, social possibilities in and around school, and high status of music at the university. Doubtless many individuals have contributed to making this possible—for example, the music school dean and the musicology professor. In the not too remote past, an extensive self-evaluation and self-study had been voluntarily undertaken by the music school—with beneficial results. How the spirit of a school comes into being is often a rather mysterious thing: It is notable at this particular branch of this university because when McGrath visited the school of business administration there he found a less favorable attitude toward the general education or liberal arts courses among both faculty and students than the present interviewer did among the musicians. At the business school, apparently, the dean had been more concerned with hiring specialists and then encouraging them to stress strictly professional attitudes. The curricular autonomy of the various schools of this university can, on occasion, foster this kind of difference.

All the students interviewed were in their early twenties, and the majority of them had come from rather small high schools (of five hundred students or less). Their attitude toward liberal arts was generally favorable. One had not had nearly enough, and had definitely planned to come back for an A.B. Another had found the philosophy courses best. Another would have liked more liberal arts—if necessary, in place of some of the theory and instrumental techniques. Still another liked a comparative literature course because of the fine teacher: "I still remember specific things he said although it was two years ago—he propped statements with so many analogies."

Although, as in any human situation, there were some differences of attitude, the interviewer's intuitive reaction to the atmosphere of the school was that many of the aims and purposes of general education were here being achieved, without any fanfare and without the presence of any general college. Two of the regular departments of the college of arts and sciences—those of economics and history—seemed to have brought about, mostly through sectioning and inspiring class discussions, some "illumination of principles."

Finally, mention should be made of one more institution that was visited—rather in the central part of the country. There were not enough replies on the Dressel survey from the teachers here to give a very significant index of attitudes. But the interviews showed a quite favorable one, particularly as, at the time, the music work at this university was simply integrated into that of the college of arts and sciences as a whole. As one of the music professors said, "We are an integral part of the Arts and Sciences. We are supposed to act and respond that way. But civic pressure almost dictates that we operate as a separate school."

This university is a dynamic representative of a somewhat different type of institution from the ones so far considered, and was visited at an interesting moment in its development. It had been chartered in 1929 and, after a city-wide drive for funds, began classes in 1933. It expanded rapidly in a number of directions, the student body—soon numbering in the thousands—coming mostly from the city whose name the institution bears.

At the time of the visit made for purposes of this study, however, not many students were majoring in music—actually only about forty. Most students were concentrating in other fields and, if they studied music, did so privately. Interviews with students who were majoring in music at the university showed an attitude favorable to their nonprofessional studies. But further development in the direction of increasing work in music and combining it significantly with a broad educational background seemed blocked by the accessibility of a strong independent conservatory which had been in existence since 1907. Although what seemed at the time to the interviewer the only solution to the problem—the merging of the two institutions—was said to be unlikely, this development did occur, only a few months later, and the conservatory became a school of the university.

In the resulting curriculum there are general requirements for all degrees, involving choices from certain groups of subjects. The Bachelor of Music Education candidate, for instance, during his four years will have taken the following: (1st year) a physical science and a course in world history; (2nd year) American history, general psychology, and world literature or foreign language; (3rd year) education courses and music in western civilization; and (4th year) human development, philosophy or biology, and an elective.

Perhaps the main significance for the present study of the interviews at this school is to suggest that problems of the relationship between professional and nonprofessional studies are being worked out at institutions that have been rapidly changing within the past few years and decades. The development of institutions for higher education in music, particularly under university auspices, is not something that has taken place solely in the remote past or become fixed and unalterable. It is going on around us, and—as Thoreau concluded *Walden*—"There is more light to dawn. The sun is but a morning star."

Chapter 5

CRITICAL ISSUES AND RECENT DEVELOPMENTS

ENOUGH OF THIS DETAILED CONSIDERATION OF ACTUAL PROGRAMS, IN A world where academic organization, leadership, and curricula sometimes change with the rapidity of styles in automobiles or women's hats! What discussions—particularly in the publications of the music associations—lie behind these changes? And if the reader would like to find fuller information on some of the issues involved, where might he go to find it?

The role of the university-sponsored music school has been, in general, a liberalizing one in the development of the professional curriculum. At least, that was a prominent feature of its original reason for being. Back in 1906, the head of the Nebraska University School of Music, Willard Kimball, told the MTNA that anyone choosing a place to study music should consider the greater opportunities for general education and the extracurricular advantages of a university. The crying need, he said, is for "educated musicians" who would combine with their general training "an acquaintance with modern languages and a knowledge of the relations between music and other subjects (such as psychology, physiology, other fine arts, etc.)." A university is the place to do this, he said, for there

> are found students of the natural sciences, of mechanical arts, of literature and language, and association with them has the effect of widening the horizon of the student of music, teaches him sympathy with others' occupations, and gives him that mental perception called tact, "that fine sense of how to avoid giving offense," without which he can never achieve the best success.[1]

The brilliant vision of a university-conservatory combination which Tourjée had glimpsed but had been unable to carry out on a lasting basis—a truly American undertaking—was given as solid a material basis as possible in the state universities.

[1] Willard Kimball, "The School of Music as a Place for Study," *PMTNA*, Vol. 1 (1906), p. 38.

CAN CONSERVATORY AND UNIVERSITY MATE?

Whether this combination has really been achieved in a genuinely fruitful manner—or whether it ought to be or even *can* be—is one of the persistent questions that keep cropping up in discussions of music in higher education. Frank Damrosch, for example, expressed an old-line, vigorously conservatory point of view in 1927:

> It is true that many colleges combine a musical together with an academic course, but I doubt if they lead to any great artistic results. The academic atmosphere which of necessity reigns in an academic institution rarely permits the creation of the artistic atmosphere required for the generation and cultivation of the imagination without which no work of art, no matter how correctly performed, can be properly interpreted.[2]

In allusion to this remark, Howard Hanson, in 1948, said, "There are a number of distinguished musical scholars today who take an opposite opinion."[3] Otto Kinkeldey of Cornell, who (though a native American) taught at the University of Breslau in the early years of the present century and who became one of the patriarchal figures in the annals of American musicology, told the MTNA that he personally favored the European separation of the music school and the university; but, he added, perhaps we may be branching out on a new road in American higher musical education which should not be expected to lead to entirely satisfactory or mature results for a few centuries—at least to results comparable to those attained by European conservatories during a corresponding period of development.[4]

Whether segregation or integration of the two types of school is desirable, the attempt to answer the question should be deferred, at least until further developments in the present century have been considered. One of these is the expansion of the music curriculum—down into the elementary and high schools, and on up into the area of the master's and doctor's degrees. The latter developments have had the effect on the undergraduate curriculum of providing at first a place where some of the professionalism that was involved in the nineteenth-century conception of the Bachelor of Music degree could go, and then—through the inevitable collision there with the graduate schools of arts and sciences—of increasing the liberal arts content of higher musical study, exerting a kind of back-influence on the undergraduate music curriculum. Another development of the present century (actually, of the second quarter of it) is the great stimulus given to musicology in the United States by the emigration to our shores of

[2] Frank Damrosch, "A College Degree in the Education of the Musician," *PMTNA*, Vol. 21 (1927), p. 82.

[3] Howard Hanson, "The Scope of the Music Education Program," *Music Educators Journal*, Vol. 34, No. 6 (June–July, 1948), p. 7.

[4] Otto Kinkeldey, "American Higher Musical Education Compared with That in Europe," *PMTNA*, Vol. 29 (1935), p. 27.

world-famous scholars in this field because of the activities of Hitler—a historical event as stimulating to American musical life as were the migrations that followed upon the French Revolution and the mid-nineteenth-century German uprisings. Other twentieth-century events have had their effect. Perhaps after considering them, we can return to the question—trying to see it, however, not so much through our own eyes (with their inevitably subjective bias) as through those of some foreign observers.

MATTERS OF DEGREE: BACHELOR'S

The NASM, having been organized to save the B.M., was at first opposed to students taking an A.B. with music major as the regular approach to teaching school music. From the point of view of the liberal arts college, however, this was an inevitable concomitant to the shift from non-professional to *de facto* professional training on its part.[5] In many institutions the A.B. was the only degree offered. Where both the A.B. and B.M. were offered, the question arose as to which course the student should follow. From the point of view of the music school, backed by the NASM, there was considerable danger that students might graduate from a university with something vaguely known as a "bachelor's degree in music" although they had taken very little actual music work. Possible employers are often not very clear on academic distinctions, and the reputation of the university in the music field was endangered by the granting of the bachelor's degree "in music" on two different bases.

Defining and explaining the difference between the two degrees has been a persistent source of concern ever since they were set up on approximately corresponding bases. In 1935, Glen Haydon of the University of North Carolina pointed out the difference as mainly a matter of intention: the A.B. with music major was, historically, more allied with cultural education and emanated from the college; the B.M. was more allied with professional education and the conservatory ("conservatory," that is, in the Oberlin, not the Peabody, sense). The difference, he concluded, is more in the realm of intangibles. The A.B.-with-music-major usually spends two-thirds of his time in general and one-third in musical study; the B.M. student, two-fifths and three-fifths. Obviously, this difference between a 5 : 10 and a 6 : 9 ratio of general to special study is rather slight, from the actual and practical point of view, although, of course, a medieval bachelor of music, still warmed up from his lecture on Boethius, would have taken great delight in pointing out the presence of the harmonic proportion

[5] Earl J. McGrath and Charles H. Russell, *Are Liberal Arts Colleges Becoming Professional Schools?* (New York: Bureau of Publications, Teachers College, Columbia University, 1958).

in one and not in the other. The presence of the word "liberal" in conjunction with the one, and "professional" in conjunction with the other, helps to orient each. On graduation from the liberal arts–music program, the student may follow music vocationally or avocationally, go into graduate work, teach, enter journalism, marriage, and so on. The aim of the music school or conservatory course, on the other hand, is ostensibly more professional than generally cultural. Haydon felt that each of the two approaches to music education was quite justified; however,

> in a very considerable number of instances the difference between the B.M. and B.A. courses is only nominal. In fact, many institutions offer both degrees and oftentimes a student may get a B.M. degree after four years of work and a B.A. in one more year, or the reverse may happen. . . . The fundamental objectives are similar, in many instances identical. The differences, in so far as there are differences, are matters of degree—where the emphasis is placed on the conception and execution of the whole program.[6]

In short, the difference between the A.B. and the B.M. is mainly one of degree. There is a difference in their history. But in their actual twentieth-century state, according to Haydon, it is not perfectly simple and easy to see wherein the difference lies. At least, this is true on the ideal level—in terms of the announced standards of the associations.

When one moves from this theoretical level down to the actual level, however, variation appears in the curricula of different institutions, even within the same general category. In 1940, Archie N. Jones, then at the University of Idaho, pointed out the great variety that existed, using data assembled in master's theses that had been prepared under his direction:

> One of the most startling indications of haphazard growth in music curricula and courses is the large variation among music schools in credits, course titles, degrees, and administrative practices. . . . Wilson, for example, found a range of from 0–60 credits required for graduation (liberal arts degree) in applied music in 43 state universities; from 20–62 credits in theory of music; from 0–18 credits in ensemble; from 4–58 credits in academic courses; from 0–52 credits in electives; and from 0–8 credits in physical education and military science. . . . That the situation described does not represent an isolated case is shown by a study of music curricula in 126 state teachers colleges and normal schools by Moe in which she found a range of music credits required for graduation of 67, even more than in state universities. The author's comment in this connection is interesting: "It seems strange that an institution requiring only 8 credits in music should offer the same degree as does the school requiring 75 credits for the degree." These same variations persist throughout the various requirements for the several degrees offered for musical training, and while the writer does not presume to set up a suggested formula, it is quite obvious

[6] Glen Haydon, "Aims and Objectives of the College and Conservatory Curricula in Music," *YMENC,* Vol. 28 (1935), p. 386.

from such tremendous discrepancies that much is wrong with the present system.[7]

The formation of the National Commission on Accrediting in 1949, mentioned in Chapter 3, was a step in the direction of doing something about this problem. But it is not one that will be solved overnight, especially in view of the fact that about fifty kinds of bachelor's degrees in music are being awarded each year to several thousand people.[8]

When one examines only the central type among these degrees, the B.M.—according to E. W. Doty, who says that he has had occasion frequently to do so in advising applicants for advanced degrees in music education—one gets the impression that

> The present Bachelor of Music degree program in music education as recommended and as found in leading universities resembles nothing so much as an omnibus in trying to do four separate and distinct jobs. The graduate in this curriculum is expected to have a thorough training in education, music education, and methods, including practice teaching. In the second place, he must have at least one-quarter of his work in theory and music literature. Third, he must have at least one-quarter of his work in applied music. And finally, one-sixth to one-fifth of the work may be taken in non-music or non-education courses, with the option of perhaps six hours of electives in which he may splurge himself.
>
> In contrast to this degree program which attempts to do at least four things, compare the degree program of any other subject matter in the universities or of the training of any teacher of any other subject matter graduated by a university or college. Such an investigation reveals that not more than two jobs or possibly at the most three are attempted, namely, the training in the specific subject-matter field, giving of a general education, and specific training in education and teaching methods in the major subjects, or minor subjects, perhaps. Wherein does the greater difficulty lie with training in music?[9]

The difference, of course, lies in the problem of applied music, or actual practice in music making, which is not such an item in other fields.

Cutting down on this creates its problems when the student goes out to teach. Doty's suggestion is that certain overspecialized areas of the curriculum be liberalized:

> The solution seems to me to lie in two directions. First, the Bachelor of Music curriculum should be given in such a way that the student receives not only fine training in music, but knowledge of and growth in the

[7] Archie N. Jones, "The Problem of Standardization," *PMTNA,* Vol. 34 (1940), pp. 188–189.

[8] Walter Crosby Eells and Harold A. Haswell, *Academic Degrees,* United States Department of Health, Education, and Welfare, Bulletin No. 28 (Washington, D.C.: Government Printing Office, 1960), pp. 177–180; cf. Virginia Ruth Mountney, "The History of the Bachelor's Degree in the Field of Music in the United States" (unpublished D.M.A. dissertation, Boston University, 1961), pp. 307–311.

[9] E. W. Doty, "The Training of Music Teachers," *YMENC,* Vol. 30 (1940), pp. 425–426.

recognized fruits of higher education. The professional courses in education and in music must be reoriented in many cases, however, if the Bachelor of Music degree program in music is to give the students a good
general education, special subject mastery, and professional training in
teaching.[10]

Concretely, he suggests that courses in musical literature and theory "be
presented with a general cultural emphasis" and that the education courses
"turn over to the primary and secondary system the responsibility for some
of the skills and training."

In understanding the issues here involved, one must realize that the
conservatories and professional music schools, largely under NASM influence, had set their houses in reasonable order by the 1940's (beginning
with the "music ed" people and working out). The source of confusion
over the music degree now largely came from the colleges of liberal arts
and the teachers colleges: Some wished to place less emphasis on semester
hours and class attendance and more on demonstration of ability to handle
a subject or field of knowledge in a comprehensive examination, thus following the lead of the older conservatories which granted diplomas more
on the attainment of certain standards of performance; others wished to
emphasize semester hours and electives, and bring the B.M. and the A.B.
still closer together. It even became possible, in extreme cases, that an
A.B. might be allowed more music credits toward graduation than a B.M.:
One such instance of a teachers college permitting 57 per cent of an A.B.
program to be in music is cited in a report by the MTNA Committee on
Colleges and Universities.[11] In some colleges, incipient general education
programs made it difficult for music to be fitted into the first two years.

In 1942, through a joint meeting at Clear Lake Camp of committees
from the American Association of Teachers Colleges and the NASM, an
"Outline of the Course Leading to the Degree, Bachelor of Music Education" was established. This "Outline" assigned 40 semester hours to its
first category, "Preparation to Insure a Broad General Culture." This
schedule, however, proved to have neither enough music history and
literature for the music people, nor enough general culture for the
liberal arts people. Accordingly, at Chicago, in 1952, a new set of "Standards," jointly sponsored by NASM, MENC, AACTE, and MTNA, was
drawn up in which there are still the 40 hours (under the heading "General
Culture"), but some Music History and Literature are counted as part of
it. Also, the "Professional Education" part of the course was raised from
18 to 24 hours. This was interpreted by the liberal arts people as a further
move to neglect content in favor of methods. Obviously, the Chicago
"Standards" were even less applicable to the A.B. teacher training program

---

[10] *Ibid.,* p. 426.
[11] Karl Eschman, "College Degrees in Music," *PMTNA,* Vol. 39 (1945), p. 98.

which was definitely on the rise. In commenting on this move from the liberal arts side, Henry Leland Clark of UCLA said:

> The philosophies of the Professional Schools and the liberal arts Music Departments are distinct, and the standards of one cannot be used to measure the programs of the other.
>
> On the one hand, the NASM states bluntly in its *By-laws and Regulations,* "The Association deplores and accepts only with great reluctance the use of the Bachelor of Arts degree in connection with the professional preparation of teachers of school music" (p. 32). On the other hand, the liberal arts Music Departments throughout the country are unanimous in finding the Chicago *Standards* incompatible with the aims of the Bachelor of Art in Music. A fair sample of this opinion is contained, I believe, in the following quotation from chairmen of liberal arts Music Departments in colleges and universities, private and state, in the West, East, and South:
> 1. This program "would seem to be typical of a B.S. degree in Education. . . . My general criticism of this program is that it is neither a liberal arts program nor a B.M. program."
> 2. "I consider the recommended program very bad because I think it turns out students with a college background far too narrow and specialized to become good teachers."
> 3. "The whole program . . . has no particular connection whatever with any sound program of education."
> 4. "The NASM recommendations . . . are very short on the liberal arts and I feel it is necessary to call attention of our administrators to the problem which, if solved along NASM lines, would mean that liberal arts colleges are not qualified to train teachers—certainly a contradiction in terms, if there ever was one."
> 5. "The *Standards* in their present form will tend to bring undue pressure upon institutions to force them to conform to a particular undergraduate curriculum set-up which may be alien to their basic collegiate philosophy."[12]

The positive suggestion made by Clark was that the liberal arts music departments get together and work out *their* requirements, as the professional schools had done: A beginning had been made, he felt, in the three campuses of the University of California. The implication is that there be an approximate balance between music and nonmusic courses. He also suggested that the length of the college training for the school music teacher would have to go to five years—as it had already done at some institutions.

Desirable as some sort of united front among liberal arts institutions comparable to the NASM unquestionably would be, there are difficulties in the way of its coming into existence. The suggested solution to the problem of teacher training, for instance, of simply prolonging the course to five years in order to "get everything in," is perhaps easier for a public than a private institution to carry out in actuality. Oberlin and many other institutions have long had five- and six-year programs in the catalogue, just

---

[12] Henry Leland Clark, "Music Is a Liberal Art," *NASM Bulletin,* No. 40 (1955), pp. 26–27.

as Boston University had what amounted to a very impressive six-year
B.M. program under Tourjée (although, as Boston University boasted in
1892, only five had completed it in nineteen years).

The relationship between the B.A. and the B.M. was, accordingly, an
area of some tension and controversy, not because the two programs were
so different but because they were so similar. It is a little like the problem of disarmament in international affairs: It would be wonderful if all
countries would disarm, and at the same instant; but will they? A report on
the existing situation among NASM member institutions was made at the
MTNA convention in 1944 by the Committee on Colleges and Universities,
headed by Karl Eschman, director of the Conservatory at Denison University. Eschman found that there had been a drop-off in the granting of
the A.B. with Music Major where the two degrees, B.M. and B.A., existed
within the one institution. He compared the numbers involved in 1930
and in 1945: In the former year, this degree had been awarded by 47 of
the NASM institutions, and only 35 awarded it in 1945—and then, with
but few exceptions, there were only three or four candidates at each institution granting the Music Major A.B.[13]

Although progress was apparently being made in NASM institutions
where both degrees existed, the more extensive aspects of the problem still
remained at institutions with no music schools. At the 1955 NASM meeting a panel discussion was held on the place of the A.B. with music major.
Thomas Williams, of Knox College, opened with the contention that while
the A.B. with concentration in music might not be quite as good in terms
of musical performance as the B.M., it was the natural degree for musicology, composition, and research:

> History reveals clearly that great changes are not uncommon in the
> pattern of music curricula, and today after more than a decade of strong
> emphasis on specialization, perhaps the pendulum is swinging back toward
> the pattern of earlier times. The call for teachers who have a high level
> of performance, and whose training imbues them with human understand-
> ing is never ending. To merit the demands of today's musically literate
> and ever increasing population is a charge we must all face. By virtue of
> its merit, the Bachelor of Arts Music Major graduate finds himself ac-
> cepted by graduate schools and the faculties of our institutions of higher
> learning.[14]

The real crux of the matter, though, is the suitability of the A.B. Music
Major as a preparation for school music teaching. Williams suggested that
the NASM reverse its earlier stand against this possibility:

> Music as taught in our schools, colleges, and universities today is in large
> part a professional subject. The development of the various musical skills

[13] Eschman, *op. cit.,* pp. 98–99.
[14] Thomas Williams, "The Place of the Bachelor of Arts Degree in Music,"
NASM Bulletin, No. 41 (1956), p. 14.

so essential for a good teacher is being well cared for. But, on a broader plane, I sometimes wonder if in our plan for the development of these skills, we have neglected another facet so essential in our society of today —the development of personal judgment and a true sense of values. If the bachelor of arts degree with its academic background attains this objective, might it not be well to consider the potential of the degree as a desirable tool in teacher training?[15]

Williams also suggested that a five-year course might be necessary, but he considered the basic question to be whether the A.B. with music major might not be acknowledged by the NASM as suitable for many branches of musical training.

Speaking more from the music schools' point of view, Raymond Kendall of the University of Michigan, in this same discussion, maintained that the B.M. had a real excuse for being when the administration of the school kept a sharp eye on the possibilities of employment within the various musical fields, and where it prepared students in terms of existing and anticipated needs. Talented students, adequate facilities, and realistic appraisal of existing professional outlets he considered absolutely necessary for the justification of the professional school, with its distinctive degree.[16]

In a special report of the A.B. Committee presented to the NASM in 1957, A. Kunrad Kvam formulated some of the areas of agreement between the bachelor's program as administered by professional music schools and by departments of music in liberal arts colleges:

> We all realize that on the one hand the professional schools have been moving in the direction of broader cultural training, whereas on the other hand the liberal arts curriculum has been expanded to include considerable professional training. These tendencies on the part of diverse kinds of training institutions, moving toward one another, have brought to our attention the fact that our common areas of agreement are large. This point is made somewhat humorously by John Mason Brown as he compares educational changes in MIT and Harvard. Mr. Brown describes the MIT process of change as "humanizing the scientist," and the Harvard process of change as that of "simonizing the humanist." Perhaps what Mr. Brown describes as occurring in the Boston area, is also prevalent on other educational fronts, particularly in music, and more especially in the training of music teachers. There is little doubt in my mind that there exists today a growing demand for a broader education of all teachers, irrespective of their special fields. It seems evident at this time that this has been recognized by the officers and members of NASM in regard to music teaching.[17]

The full report is too important for our present study to be excerpted, and should be read in full by anyone especially interested in the A.B. with

[15] *Ibid.,* p. 14.
[16] Raymond Kendall, "At What Point Is the Professional Degree Justified?" *NASM Bulletin,* No. 41 (1956), pp. 14–17.
[17] A. Kunrad Kvam, "Report of the A.B. Committee," *NASM Bulletin,* No. 42 (1957), p. 9.

music major. However, the conclusion of this report sums up the concept of a liberally educated musician thus:

> The music major who is graduated with an A.B. degree should have behind him a solid and systematic knowledge of training in the theory, history, literature, and performance of music, all of these resting upon and nourished by an understanding of our common heritage in the sister arts, social and political history, philosophy, languages, literature, and the social and natural sciences. Such a student need not, indeed should not be a "walking encyclopedia," but he should be an intelligent, well-rounded musician with a depth as well as a spread of understanding, with the means of leading a rich life, while enriching the lives of others, regardless of his eventual, specific calling in the field of music.[18]

Thus, although the NASM was called into being to save the B.M., it has clearly passed beyond the stage of mere special pleading for one particular degree or institutional form. The B.M. was saved, and standards were set up. Wisely the NASM realized that there was no need to continue fighting a battle after it had been won. Rather, it has gone on, as the accrediting body of higher education in music—since the mid-century with the backing of the National Commission on Accrediting—to adjust to the actualities of the situation and to recognize shifts of focus as they occur. The A.B. with music major is at once a new development and a reversion to an older norm in which music was one of the liberal arts, and in which the B.M. coexisted with it.

ELEMENTARY AND HIGH SCHOOL PROGRAMS

The implications of the establishment of the Bachelor of Music curriculum in the 1920's, essentially on its present-day basis, cannot be fully understood without realizing that it is part of a much larger pattern which extends from the elementary school program to the doctorate. When the committee of the MSNC in 1921 made the proposal that has more or less stabilized the B.M. degree as it exists today in American institutions of higher learning, it included also the high school prerequisites, projecting the college pattern out onto it: four years, two grades of piano (MTNA), sight singing, dictation, and the like. In discussing the music supervisor that was envisaged by this program, Karl Gehrkens explained that at Oberlin a not entirely satisfactory type of training had come into existence, according to which the would-be supervisor either went to the College of Liberal Arts for five years, taking three-fifths of his work in academic subjects, or else went to the Conservatory for three years, took his school music work with no academic work to speak of, and received his certificate without any degree. A six-year curriculum would be ideal, Gehrkens said, but that

[18] *Ibid.*, p. 12.

"would probably mean that no one would elect it." He accordingly suggested as a compromise:

> Let the prospective supervisor of music go to high school for four years, spending three-fourths of his time studying languages, science, history, and other academic subjects, and the other fourth in studying music for credit: then let him come to college or conservatory and study four years longer, spending approximately three-fourths of his time in musical work of various sorts, including the principles of teaching music, and the other fourth in studying additional carefully selected academic subjects which will have a tendency to broaden his mind with respect to other fields of knowledge, to enlarge his sympathies for people of all classes, and in general to give him what is termed a social outlook upon life.[19]

In other words, the "music ed" problem was really too big to handle within the four years of college; if the claims of professional and liberal training could not be perfectly reconciled at the college level, a way out could be found by bringing the high school preparation into consideration. The same general principle (as enunciated at the 1915 MSNC convention) was here involved in both areas: ". . . added joy . . . refinement . . ." with emphasis on "social consciousness."

The involvement of the high school in the over-all plan for higher musical education had been attempted earlier. As early as 1905 delegates from a group of Eastern colleges in which there were music departments had proposed that the College Entrance Examinations Board give entrance examinations in music; accordingly, examinations were prepared in music appreciation, harmony, counterpoint, piano, voice, and violin. As with the American College of Musicians back in the '80's, the attempt was not successful: The appreciation examination was too difficult; the counterpoint examination had no applicants. By 1920 the CEEB examinations in music were discontinued, and all colleges granting entrance credits had to prepare and handle their own music examinations; but in 1922, with MTNA backing, the proposal was made again and carried through. The whole matter of recognizing what the high schools—many of which have developed musical facilities and arrays of courses that would put not a few conservatories to shame—are doing in the preparation of musicians would ease the pressure on higher education in music. Slow as recognition of the high school's work has been in coming,[20] it does offer a possibility of the B.M.'s being devoted not so much to elementary work, but instead to genuinely higher education—thus perhaps moving back into its original position of a more advanced degree than the B.A.

---

[19] Karl W. Gehrkens, "The Music Supervisor of the Future," *PMTNA*, Vol. 14 (1921), pp. 41–42.

[20] Karl H. Eschman, "A Survey of College Entrance Credits in Music," *PMTNA*, Vol. 18 (1924), pp. 149–161; Paul J. Weaver, "The Crediting of Music in the High Schools and Colleges," *PMENC*, Vol. 20 (1927), pp. 327–333.

One definite and dramatic step in the direction of a high school's undertaking some responsibility for the professional education of the gifted child is the High School of Music and Art in New York City. Twice a year application blanks are sent to elementary school principals, and from the applicants—as explained by Alexander Richter, of the school, to the MTNA in 1939—some four hundred are selected to take examinations, on the basis of which 125 are chosen in music and a similar number in art. This high school in the public school system of the city is not conceived of as a vocational school; its purpose is not to offer specilized courses leading directly to employment on graduation. Rather, the emphasis is on a well-rounded academic education:

> Academic studies at the High School of Music and Art, especially English and the natural and social sciences, are integrated with the courses in music. The English department endeavors to present the students with appropriate critical, historical, and biographical literature; the science department emphasizes the study of acoustics and the properties and development of musical instruments; the history department correlates its work especially with the fourth year course in the history of musical development by intensive readings pertaining to important musical periods, and to the social, industrial, and political backgrounds of the development of music through the ages. Thus, four periods in the day are devoted to academic subjects, three to music, one to physical education, and one for lunch.[21]

Not only is the high school involved in this twentieth-century conception of the Bachelor of Music, but also the roots of the program extend on down into the elementary grades. As part of the 1921 committee report that contained the Bachelor of Music program that has since become standard, there is a recommended Standard Course in Music for eight years of elementary and secondary schooling, in terms of Aims, Material, Procedure, and Attainments. The underlying purpose is the coordinating of music with the other fundamental school subjects—reading, writing, and arithmetic. The principle is that

> Music must be given a reasonable and fair amount of the time of the school day, not only as an art subject both beautiful and useful, but as a subject broadly educational. In a daily schedule of 300 or more minutes, music as such should be allowed not less than 15 minutes daily in primary grades, not less than 20 minutes daily in intermediate grades, and not less than the equivalent of 25 minutes daily in grammar, junior high and high school grades.[22]

The terrible concentration of requirements that had rendered the Bachelor of Music degree ineffectual in the late nineteenth century was alleviated by

[21] Alexander Richter, "The High School of Music and Art: A Program of Education for the Gifted Child," *PMTNA,* Vol. 33 (1939), p. 254.
[22] Karl W. Gehrkens, "Report of the Committee on Training Courses for Supervisors," *PMENC,* Vol. 14 (1921), p. 221.

a conception that would spread the required courses over a long continuum, beginning in the elementary grades, and stressing its social aspects.

There is, however, an issue involved here that perhaps can be only suggested. Is this—as the late Manfred Bukofzer, who came to this country as a refugee in the 1940's, asked—education *for* music or education *in* music? That is, anyone would grant that if you subject a child first to 15 minutes of music, then to 20, then to 25, etc., you condition him to tolerate greater and greater quantities of music. But is this *really* musical education or just social conditioning? "For a long time," Bukofzer wrote,

> the slogan has been to bring music to the people, the more the better. I believe that the time has come to switch from the extensive and quantitative approach to the intensive and qualitative approach. Music is not a commodity that is brought to the people like a cake of soap. The number of recordings sold in any one year is not necessarily the true barometer of the musical climate. Our slogan should be to bring the people to music. This is not a job of promotion and advertising but a task of education. It is the true goal of music education to which music itself has set the standards. Let us squarely meet this challenge.[23]

This has relevancy to our problem of professional vs. liberal values. "One is forced to admit," Kendall says, "that in America, with rare exceptions, a full-time concert career probably does not exist any more for most of those who are taking their professional training in music."[24] With us, the school and community constitute a much more active realm of professional musical activity. Does our problem of professional vs. liberal values focus now on the problem of "music ed" vs. "music," rather than on the old problem of "technique" vs. "meaning"? In other words, when we say professional vs. liberal, do we need to think of the pedagogue, rather than the concert artist, as the "professional" and stop beating the dead horse of "virtuosity," which has long ago passed out of the picture?

MASTER'S AND DOCTOR'S DEGREES

Under the aegis of the MSNC and NASM, not only was the terrible concentration of the nineteenth-century Bachelor of Music degree alleviated by spreading its requirements over the elementary and secondary school system, but also certain of its features were simply shoved along into a rapidly developing realm of graduate education. Without the development of master's and doctor's programs, it would doubtless have been impossible to lay the ghost of the old bachelor's degree. With the existence of the advanced degrees, however, the faculty could say, "We are not really lowering our standards

---

[23] Manfred F. Bukofzer, "Changing Standards in Music Education," *PMTNA*, Vol. 43 (1951), p. 7.

[24] Raymond Kendall, "Professional Training in Music," *NASM Bulletin*, No. 40 (1955), p. 18.

or neglecting the exceptional student; we are simply making more explicit provision for him." Also, the development of these programs has had a rather unexpected feature of liberalizing still further the undergraduate program, for several reasons: Many would-be masters and doctors have found themselves in the position of having to make up prerequisites for courses specified in the graduate programs; the granting of advanced degrees has inevitably brought musicians into closer relationship with other members of the graduate faculty, as these degrees are usually administered through the graduate school rather than the music school; musicology has played an increasingly important role in graduate education and has begun to exert a liberalizing back-influence on undergraduate education; and, as with undergraduate curricula, the active impulse for developing graduate curricula has proceeded from a basically "music ed" center, with inevitable emphasis on social adjustment and broad human awareness rather than on a narrow ideal of virtuosity or research.

As with the bachelor's degree, some conception of the early history of the master's degree helps one understand the peculiar changes it has undergone in America—especially in music.[25] Back in the Middle Ages, there was no very great difference between the use of such words as *magister* (master, or teacher), *doctor,* and *professor;* a *maestro* was not an orchestral conductor necessarily, but a teacher. All these words simply meant that the person so called had a bachelor's degree, had had it for a while, had been exercising the functions that it implied, and intended to continue to do so. Consequently, after a student received the B.A., he merely paid certain fees regularly to keep his name on the college rolls, normally lived in a college building, and—without necessarily taking another course or passing another examination—received his M.A. automatically after the lapse of a few years (usually three). This is the normal British conception of the master's degree, and there is also a long-standing conception that the doctor's degree is somehow more honorific than the master's. These ideas go back to Renaissance times and before. The early Tudor composer Thomas Tallis, for example, took his B.A. in 1528 and his M.A. in 1531; Christopher Tye, his B.Mus. at Cambridge in 1536 and his Dr.Mus. at Oxford in 1548.

It is interesting that when the Master of Music degree was standardized by the NASM in 1933, it was required that two years elapse between the Bachelor of Music degree and the Master of Music degree—in contrast to the practice that had developed in American universities of a student's taking the A.B. and the A.M. in successive years—and the result was a slight inequality in the ease of securing an A.M. or an M.M., which perhaps kept

[25] A full account of the history and present state of this degree is given in Wilbur Dale Fulbright, "The History and Development of the Master's Degree in Music in the United States" (unpublished Ph.D. dissertation, Boston University, 1960).

some students away from the latter degree. The NASM, however, has held to the desirability of this provision of at least two years between the B.M. and M.M., so that the candidate has time really to decide whether he wishes to go on teaching and so that his professional capacities may be observed in the actual teaching situation. Obviously, there is some sense to the traditional British conception of the M.A., though with the passing of the religious-community aspects of the "college" and the teaching-certificate aspects of the A.B., the British degree—obtained in the course of time by the mere "aging" of the bachelor's degree as if it were old wine or cheese —seems to an American rather odd.

At first, naturally, the British idea of the master's degree was maintained in America, with slight variations. The Harvard Laws of 1655 require that the person wishing a master's degree must submit ". . . a written Synopsis, or Compendium of Logicke, Naturall Philosophy, morall philosophy, Arithmeticke, Geometry, or Astronomy"[26] and waives the residence requirement, merely stating that the candidate must be of good reputation. Fundamentally, though, this is still the British idea of a master's degree "in course."

When Charles William Eliot became president of Harvard in 1869, one of the first things he did was to abolish this type of master's degree: The Class of 1869 was the last to receive their M.A.'s thus automatically. At some other institutions, however, master's degrees "in course" were awarded until well into the first quarter of the present century. But, in the nineteenth century, America had responded strongly to the "gospel of work" as it was being preached by men like Carlyle; also, from Germany had come the idea that the higher degree should emphasize research. The sheer vigor and will that appeared in the founding of the Peabody Institute, of Johns Hopkins, of the New England Conservatory, of Boston University, gave a dynamic course-content to the master's degree. This spread like wildfire throughout the country: In 1900 over a thousand were awarded, in 1910 over two thousand, in 1920 over three thousand, in 1930 over fourteen thousand, and in 1950 over sixty thousand.[27]

From the beginning of the present century there were occasional M.A.'s and Ph.D.'s whose work happened to be largely in some field connected with music. In 1905, for example, Harvard awarded an earned doctorate on a dissertation relating to music, and in 1906 several master's degrees.[28] It was not until the World War I period, however, that the Master of Music degree began to appear in any very definite form.

[26] Samuel Eliot Morison, *Harvard College in the Seventeenth Century* (Cambridge: Harvard University Press, 1936), p. 148.
[27] Edgar W. Knight, *Fifty Years of American Education, 1900–1950* (New York: The Ronald Press Co., 1952), p. 187.
[28] Rose Yont, *The Value of Music in Education* (Boston: Richard G. Badger, 1916), p. 97.

Northwestern University was one of the pioneers in this, and its handling of the B.M. and the M.M. degrees shows clearly the historical relationship between them. As originally set up in the 1890's, the B.M. at Northwestern included what would today be regarded as a formidable array of technical skills and literary, linguistic, and other academic requirements for a bachelor's degree. Gradually these were whittled down. Of course, as actually administered, these early degree requirements may possibly have been softened, and the published requirements in the later days may represent only a realistic statement of what had actually sometimes been accepted; on the other hand, things may well have operated at one time the other way around, and stated requirements may have been administered with extreme strictness. It would be very interesting to try to find out through talking with old graduates their recollections of actual procedure in their day and to see some of their work. Certainly they are members of a vanishing race. Among the recommendations made at the end of this study, along with the one for graduate research into the history of each school, is that some effort be made to learn from early students at the school how the work was carried on then, and what the relationship between the professional and liberal part of the training was at that time. At all events, the only real evidence that we have today is "what the catalogue says," and in the light of that evidence the degree was obviously heading in the general direction we have observed: a watering-down of the B.M. Inevitably the question must have arisen: What is being done now for the superior student? The answer was the M.M., which began to make its appearance around the time of World War I. Thus, within a quarter of a century, one degree had actually become two (B.M. and M.M.) and was shortly to put forth a shoot in still another direction (the B.M.E.). In about another quarter of a century the new addition to the academic family would, in turn, have become two—with the introduction of the Doctor of Musical Arts degree.

As with additions to a human family, the coming of a new member to the group usually involves unexpected complications, encroachments on privacy, and, eventually, the reorganization of everything on a more liberal and human basis. The problem of liberal education in the professional undergraduate curriculum can no more be separated from the developments in the graduate curriculum than the parents of a new baby can avoid hearing its cries.

At Northwestern, for instance, there had been a certain inner bifurcation between what was called in the 1895 catalogue the Theoretical School and the Practical School within the Music Department, the one leading toward the B.M., the other toward a mere graduation certificate. In 1906 a one-year Public School Methods program was introduced; by 1910 it had become a two-year program (now called Public and High School Music

Methods); by 1916 it was three years, and by 1923 it was four years, with its own special type of bachelor's degree, B.M.E. In more graphic form, here were the curricula open to the student, according to the 1923 Catalogue:

1. Applied Music→Graduate in Music
2. Applied Music→B.M.
3. Theory and Composition→B.M. and M.M.
4. Public School and Community Music→Graduate in Music
5. Public School and Community Music→B.M.E.

The two types of musical baccalaureate were somewhat similar and not too far from the MSNC concept of the bachelor's degree: an approximately equal distribution of academic, general music, applied music, and professional or education courses. The M.M. degree, however, had originally proceeded from the B.M., and was a natural continuation into a realm of further specialization for the student of theory and composition. But the student who had received the B.M.E. and then wanted a master's degree had first to "return to the bachelor status and include all of the items of the Bachelor of Music degree which were omitted from his Bachelor of Music Education degree."[29]

The opposite situation was to be found at this time at Indiana, where it was the "music ed" degree rather than the "music" degree that had pushed on into the graduate realm: There the master's degree was a Master of Public School Music. One would, consequently, study for four years and receive either the Bachelor of Music or the Bachelor of Public School Music degree; or one could study for six years and receive both. With *either* bachelor's degree and thirty more hours of graduate work one could obtain the Master of Public School Music degree. But, obviously, if one had come to the music school hoping to become "a pianist," and then after four years had decided to "switch over" from this highly competitive field, or had been made aware of what really professional performance at the piano involved, then one was in for a little back-tracking before he could take the bachelor's and master's "music ed" degrees.

Of course, in the process one would have his approach to music and to life somewhat broadened, and there would be an inevitable liberalization of the professional course in the sense of greater knowledge and a general widening of outlook. In some instances it might work the other way, and the student might be forced to make a choice between the two roads before he really knew what he was choosing; and, having embarked on the one, he might feel that he had to go on with it. In practice, however, it has perhaps more often worked out in the former way.

[29] Peter W. Dykema, "Higher Degrees in Music Education," *PMTNA*, Vol. 20 (1926), p. 70.

Highly significant in this matter of the two forms of the bachelor's degree and the master of music degree is the fact that in actual practice more students have probably had to take more courses as a result of it, rather than fewer. Also highly significant is the underlying cleavage between "music" and "music ed." In discussing the problem which the Northwestern M.M. posed for the B.M.E., Peter W. Dykema, who for many years was Professor of Music Education at Teachers College, Columbia University, made this remark about the would-be master's degree student which unconsciously reveals how definite this cleavage had become: In order to achieve "a higher state of expertness in the field of teaching music, he must have the qualifications of the student who is preparing to become not a teacher but a performer of music." Some musicians do not recognize the legitimacy of such a split. They would maintain that the performer teaches by performing, and that the person who thinks he is teaching while not performing is fooling himself: He is really teaching nonperformance. At all events, the introduction of the M.M. degree was not a mere place for the specialization in the old B.M. to go, nor was it merely a way of accommodating the superior student. It soon became much more, and encountered and created situations in which its existence caused many students to take more courses than their streamlined professional program seemed to require. To be sure, these "more courses" were doubtless applied theory courses, or education courses, usually considered "professional." But first steps toward liberalization of the curriculum must be taken first: The first step was to get the musician out of the rut of his single specialty into an awareness of other "branches" of music; the next step was to make him aware of other "branches" of human activity in general.

Other pioneering institutions in the master of music degree—besides Northwestern, Indiana, and Oberlin—were Iowa and Wisconsin. Like the MSNC itself, this development came out of the Middle West and flourished in the post–World-War-I period. The NASM also addressed itself to the problem of standardizing the M.M. degree, and in 1933 recommended certain features that have become a definite part of it: the two-year lapse of time between the B.M. and the M.M., the one-year residence requirement, and the possibility of its being taken with an applied major as well as with a composition major. By joint action of the MTNA and NASM, a committee was set up for further study of the problems involved in graduate study in music, with Howard Hanson as chairman; and after careful consideration of the situation, recommendations were made in 1934 which were adopted and which continue in effect with negligible changes today.

In terms of actual provisions, the M.M. requirements are largely a matter of courses usually considered professional. The concepts "professional" and "liberal," however, are somewhat relative; and anything that tends to shift the student's attention from sheer physical, mechanical how-to-do-it is, in a way, liberal, and is bound to influence the undergraduate program if there is any thought of the student's ultimately applying for graduate work. Thus the ensuing summary of the implications of the NASM requirements is not intended as a complete catalogue of all of them, but rather as an interpretation of them in terms of their liberal and professional implications. When one thinks of what has normally been considered a master's program in, for example, English literature—it may be simply a group of specialized courses in this field, perhaps differentiated according to historical periods, and usually with a course like Anglo-Saxon or Chaucer to bring home to the student the fact that the language has changed in the course of its development—or in chemistry, or in zoology, the conscious distribution of emphasis and effort at real broadening of the M.M. student's concept of the world of music is amazing. It is not so much a matter of sharpening the student to a point as it is of spreading him out and filling up the gaps.

All entering graduate students—whether they wish to go on in an instrument, voice, composition, or music education—are given a very searching examination in the theory and history of music. There are also special entrance requirements for those wishing to do graduate work in the different fields. The musicology major, for instance, should have passed the usual courses in English composition and literature, should have facility in the organization and expression of ideas in English, and should have a reading knowledge of at least one foreign language. The "music ed" major must be able to play Bach inventions and Haydn and Mozart piano sonatas if he wishes to become a general supervisor, and easy accompaniments, folk songs, and chorales if he wishes to become an instrumental supervisor; thus the worst features of the dichotomy between being "a teacher" and "a performer" are ameliorated. The applied voice major must also be able to play Bach inventions and Haydn and Mozart piano sonatas; the old idea of a singer being a sheer vocal acrobat must yield to a broader concern with music. This is certainly, in a sense, "liberalization" of the curriculum. In other words, the Master of Music is definitely not a research-type degree, in which the student may end up knowing "more and more about less and less." Right from the start, in the admission requirements, he is obliged to show that he has widened his area of concern with music to something much more than a mere technical approach to one particular skill.

These admission requirements are quite exacting. Competency in piano is required of prospective majors in musicology, composition, music education, and voice. The musicology major should be able to sight-read at the piano the simpler Haydn string quartets or the Bach chorales in the original clefs. Majors in composition and music education should have studied representative instruments of the string, woodwind, and brass sections of the orchestra; and the would-be supervisor in music education should have a working knowledge of all orchestral instruments.

As for the master's degree programs themselves, the NASM requirements make a distinction between M.A. and M.M. curricula. The M.A. involves a slightly broader background of general study than the M.M., which is more concentratedly professional. A musicology student, for instance, might well take an M.A.; a composition student, an M.M. The musicology major might well take two-thirds of the total credit hours in musicology, culminating in the thesis, and the remaining one-third in the humanities or sciences. This is externally like the conventional M.A. program, except for the definite provision that a third of the program be spent on avowedly liberal education. A composition student, on the other hand, might take half of his program in composition courses, submit an original work in one of the larger forms in lieu of a thesis, and take the rest of his course work in advanced theory (including canon, fugue, and orchestration). In other words, the M.A. and M.M. are here somewhat parallel, except for the more liberal cast of the M.A.

By no means do the actual programs specified for the different majors consist *entirely* of courses in the major field; in fact, none of them do. The NASM recommends that in addition to the major area of concentration, the student should have at least one minor area of study. An applied voice major, for example, may take not more than one-third of the M.M. course work in voice; one-third must be in piano, and one-third in theory, musicology, or modern foreign language. Reading knowledge of two modern foreign languages and diction in a third are recommended. A public recital is, of course, also specified. An applied instrumental major may take not more than two-thirds of his course work in applied music (which also culminates in a public recital); in addition he must have one or two minors, of which the first would be in theory and musicology, and the second would be in any field in which the student is interested and in which he is prepared by his undergraduate study. This latter offers the possibility that the student extend his work in any direction he wishes—fine arts, aesthetics, mathematics, etc.

Currently the master's degree in the field of music is offered at 185 institutions, more than half of which are accredited by the NASM. In most schools the degree takes the form of an M.A. and an M.M., somewhat as has been indicated. Some institutions have a Master of Fine Arts, Master of Music Education, Master of Sacred Music, or Master of Science. There are, of course, many local variations; but the general effect of the development in this field during the past half-century has been to broaden rather than narrow music study.

One possibility of future development in the music curriculum that would permit a better balance between professional and liberal studies is the combining of the bachelor's and master's or the bachelor of music and of arts programs into a six-year curriculum. Oberlin and other conservatory-college combinations have long had such programs in their catalogues, but the development of the master's degree has given the possibility still greater cogency. In 1940 the composer Quincy Porter, then Dean of the New England Conservatory, began a one-year study for the MTNA Committee on Colleges and Universities on the reactions to the proposal of a six-year course. The suggestion was made quite tentatively as merely a supplementary curriculum, to interfere in no way with existing separate bachelor's or master's curricula; and the intention was more to sound out a number of institutions for their reactions to the idea. Porter suggested that a six-year plan would allow a more "well-balanced opportunity of supplementary musical and strictly academic subjects"; and in commenting on the 72 questionnaire responses that he had received, he elaborated on the idea that a six-year plan would allow a more harmonious development of the student's special abilities and would

> at the same time provide the broadening benefits of an all-around education—both musical and cultural. We have so often seen students who have remarkable attainments in certain directions, but seem to come up against barriers to further progress, and we sometimes wonder whether, if they had had the advantage of a broader point of view toward their art and toward life in general, they might not have been able to overcome some of these obstacles. Education is not always at fault, of course, but our only interest as educators is to see that it is *not* our fault.[30]

Particularly in the school music field, Porter thought, a six-year curriculum would be helpful—where the student has to take academic work, methods courses, become a "musical Jack-of-all-trades," and sometimes also fit himself to teach subjects in addition to music. One question asked of the respondents was what distribution of hours, out of the 180-hour total, they would give to each of the three major types of courses; and the answers were as follows:

	LEAST ALLOWED	MOST ALLOWED	AVERAGE
Major subject or instrument	36 hours	108 hours	57.4 hours
Supplementary musical subjects	35	96	61.4
Strictly academic subjects	36	90	60.8

The balance here is remarkable, with actual technical training in the specialty slightly in last place among the three major components of a music curriculum.

Porter also quoted some of the personal reactions to the suggestion,

---

[30] Quincy Porter, "A Six-Year Curriculum for Post High School Musical Education," *PMTNA*, Vol. 36 (1942), p. 274.

all of which show a desire for more academic courses if the opportunity could be created:

> R. E. Stuart says: "Teachers of music, church organists, and other musicians who come in daily contact with the so-called 'better educated people' need a broad general education in addition to their work in music. A six-year curriculum would, of course, make it possible to include more academic work and should enable the students to become much better performers."

> F. B. Stiven writes: "I believe that our present undergraduate curricula in music are too professional, and that our students ought to have a more general education, in addition to the professional subjects studied. . . . Because I believe that in applied music in particular the element of time is so vital, I should like to see a curriculum established which would involve more studies in the Liberal Arts and at the same time allow the student to pursue his subject in music (especially in his major applied music subject) for the entire six years, probably on a somewhat reduced schedule of credit. It might be that such a course would lead to both the degrees of Bachelor of Music and Bachelor of Arts, but it seems to me that it ought to be essentially undergraduate in every respect."

> Price Doyle says: "In general I approve of the idea. It seems to me that the background for the entire problem consists of this fact: that in four years time it is impossible for us to train students sufficiently well in music, and at the same time to have time for them to absorb enough in the way of cultural academic work so that they are prepared socially to live with people outside of their own profession."

> To quote from D. M. Swarthout: "Speaking from the state universities' standpoint, I am leaning more and more, year after year, to a feeling that with a musician going out into society as a more or less intelligent citizen, who will have to deal with considerable other matters probably than music, a six-year set-up might possibly be best, combining the four-year B.A. and the Mus.B."[31]

Although the phrase "six-year course" has a rather forbidding sound, there is evidence that lengthening of the time involved in the curriculum is widely desired by many who are responsible for higher education in music. The growth of the master's degree has actually extended the educational process for one who seriously intends to go into music teaching, and has shown that a very great number of the students can somehow achieve the six-year span of university study. Perhaps the day will come when the six years there involved will be planned more as a whole and thought of as a unit. Judging from the personal comments, one would say that a six-year A.B.–B.M. combination seems more natural than a six-year bachelor's–master's combination; and, in the light of the history of the B.M. degree, one might observe that such a development would bring things around a little closer to what Tourjée originally envisaged.

More recent and even more significant is the development of the doc-

[31] *Ibid.,* p. 279.

toral program, which exhibits some of the same features as have been observed in the master's.[32] Some forty institutions currently sponsor doctoral degrees in music, more often than not through the graduate school rather than the music school. As with the master's degree, the basic pattern is a remarkably broad curriculum, tending more to the "general education" idea than to the idea of specialized research. There are, for example, extensive prerequisite requirements in liberal arts courses. At Boston University the doctorate in music may be taken as either a Doctor of Philosophy or a Doctor of Musical Arts degree; in the former, the student entering on the program must have taken 50 semester hours of "liberal arts courses distributed among the humanities, natural and social sciences," and in the latter, 32 to 35 semester hours similarly distributed. At Indiana University, 30 semester hours of similar sort are required; at Northwestern, 75 quarter hours; at Chicago University, an Arts degree is preferred; at Columbia, an A.B. is required. Where there are deficiencies in these liberal arts admissions requirements, they must be made up without credit toward the degree. Obviously, a student with a narrowly professional previous training who wishes to enter on one of these programs will have to make up these prerequisites. Particularly where the doctoral degree is administered by the graduate school, there is always an extensive liberal arts prerequisite. Also, over and above the particular student's problem, the presence of a terminal curriculum to the whole enterprise of musical study that places as heavy an emphasis on a well-rounded education as the doctorate in music at present does inevitably influences the undergraduate curriculum structure.

The doctorate in music is, of course, quite old; but in European universities it became more an honorary degree as the basis of university education shifted from an ecclesiastical to a secular foundation. As the degree came over to America, it was largely an honorary degree, right on through the mid-nineteenth century; in 1849, for instance, Georgetown University granted a doctorate in music to Henry Dielman; in 1855, New York University granted one to Lowell Mason, and in 1858, to Thomas Hastings, etc.[33] Rather few and far between (perhaps fifty in the last half of the nineteenth century), they were primarily honorary.

In the 1870's, however, there was a strong tendency in this country to stress research, course work, and the German idea of higher education— with devastating effect on the liberal-education tradition that had begun to show signs of stiffening into rigidity by this time.[34] We have seen how the

[32] For a fuller treatment of the whole matter, see Arthur Ward Kennedy, "The Doctoral Degree in Music in Universities and Colleges in the United States" (unpublished Ph.D. dissertation, Northwestern University, 1955).

[33] For a full list *see* Grove's *Dictionary,* fourth edition, 1940, p. 185.

[34] See Earl J. McGrath, *The Graduate School and the Decline of Liberal Education* (New York: Bureau of Publications, Teachers College, Columbia University, 1959), pp. 14 ff.

master's degree underwent a profound change. The presence of the unearned doctorate in the academic scheme was even more of an anomaly in
the eyes of late-nineteenth-century educators than was that of the unearned
master's degree. The giving of a positive research-type content to the doctorate had proved fruitful: The mere numerical increase in awarded doc-
torates, of the "earned" type, indicates its vitality: in 1890, 164; in 1900,
342; in 1910, 409; in 1920, 532; in 1930, 2,078; in 1940, 3,086; and in
1950, 6,510.[35]

Inevitably, basic questions have arisen of whether the fundamental
purpose here involved is (1) recognition of merit, actual or potential; (2)
research, for the sheer increase of human knowledge; (3) training in some
special field for the service of society by the practice of this specialty; or
(4) training of teachers. While these four purposes overlap, each has its
distinct focus, and conflicts over academic precedence inevitably arise
where two or more aims are pursued simultaneously. Some professions,
such as that of medicine, have been able to eliminate the easygoing old
idea of the doctorate's being a recognition of outstanding work done (or
hoped for) on the part of the recipient, and at the same time resist the
strong late-nineteenth-century pressure to turn the doctorate into a sheer
research degree. The humanistic professions, on the other hand, veered
strongly in the latter direction: The research Ph.D. became, as William
James called it, an "octopus."

Protests against the rather unreal turn taken by the degree that is the
very capstone of the academic arch have been lodged at various times—
comparable, in their way, to the protest of men like Gilman, Eliot, and
Harper against the narrow confines of the earlier classical curriculum which
had been pushed to absurd extremes by the same late-eighteenth- and early-
nineteenth-century tendencies as had also produced the quasi-Roman
statues of the Founders of the Republic and the Greek Revival architecture
of both the North and the South. Early in the nineteenth century this
classical pattern had been the source of great strength, but the Civil War
had been at once its great moment of fulfillment and of self-destruction.
As the fragments in the post–Civil War world began to be pieced together,
the *hybris* of the Classicists had begun to attract its retaliation from the
jealous gods of the here-and-now as they had somehow crept into the academic pantheon. The Doctor of Education degree was a protest on the
part of the colleges of education against the narrow confines of the Ph.D.
program. Slow in being accepted, the Doctor of Education degree was
granted by only six institutions of higher learning in 1930, but by 31 in
1945;[36] in general, it has flourished within the past two decades. In some

[35] Mary Irwin, Editor, *American Universities and Colleges* (Washington, D.C.:
American Council on Education, 1952), p. 60.
[36] Kennedy, *op. cit.,* p. 37.

institutions it has represented a more liberal trend; in others it has exemplified a more unadulterated move in the direction of sheer, myopic, factual-detail "research." At all events, it does represent a move intended to relate more definitely the work done for the doctorate to something really existing and verifiable within the teaching profession.

The admission of music into the realm of doctoral study, in the present-day sense of the term, occurred rather unexpectedly and from several directions. At various times, Ph.D. dissertations have involved the candidate in matters with musical implications. Early in the present century, departments of psychology and sociology showed particular boldness in stepping into this area of musical research. Carl Seashore, at the State University of Iowa, pioneered in the scientific approach to musical phenomena, and under his direction several students completed dissertations and obtained Ph.D. degrees on the basis of research in restricted aspects of pitch discrimination during the opening decades of the present century. This is a perfect example of doctoral work according to the German research pattern—a group of scholars working on a common area, to some extent forgetting themselves in it, and their combined efforts over a number of years resulting in an impressive synthesis of the objective truths discovered in that field—in this instance, primarily pitch in the singing voice.[37] Seashore himself explained how graduate work in music came into the academic picture at Iowa, thus:

> The first impetus to the recognition of graduate work in music in our institution came through the establishment of the Child Welfare Research Station, the mother institution of its kind, devoted to scientific study of the normal child. One of the seven areas approved by the Legislature in the charter of the Station was the study of fine arts in the training of children.
>
> About this time the demand for instruction in music was fully recognized by the public schools, in the face of the absence of adequately prepared teachers. This brought a challenge to the University for the advanced training of teachers of music, and led to the organization of the School of Fine Arts. This, in turn, led to an extensive building program, which resulted in specialized music halls in which provision was made for research in advanced workshops, libraries, collections, superior facilities for performance, and the developing art center.[38]

Obviously, advanced research work in music just grew—like Topsy. It had always grown, in one form or another: Bach called his artful treatment of a musical theme given him by Frederick the Great *ricercare,* or "research," in *The Musical Offering;* A. W. Thayer undertook definitive

---

[37] A detailed account of psychological research in music early in the present century is given in Yont, *op. cit.,* pp. 229–238. The synthesis of the sector of it under the direction of Carl Seashore is his *Psychology of Music* (New York: McGraw-Hill Book Company, Inc., 1938).

[38] Carl E. Seashore, "Advanced Degrees in Music," *Music Educators Journal* (April 1945), p. 34.

research into Beethoven's life—but these were all individualistic matters. The distinctive phenomenon of twentieth-century musical research is its sponsorship by the university and its connection with degrees—a phenomenon also shared by musical composition. One way in which music got into the doctoral realm was via the social sciences: In the sociology department of Columbia University in 1913, for example, Alma Webster Powell wrote a doctor's thesis on "Music Is a Human Need, Increasing and Decreasing with Social Pressure."

What strikes one most forcibly about this particular development in higher education in music is the variety of approaches brought together. After all, the conservatory idea, as exemplified in Peabody—and in more recent foundations like Juilliard and Curtis—is the basic form for higher education in music, coming straight from Europe. The Ph.D. idea came from a totally different European realm and, as it made its way into American higher education in the late nineteenth century, was more suitable for scientific than for humanistic study. Music *as music* scarcely lends itself to this kind of objective, piecemeal research. Music as human behavior, or as social pattern, or as historical data perhaps does; but *as an art* it cannot very well be split up into tiny areas with each one attacked by an individual doctoral student. In so far as the subject of music appeared in the early twentieth-century doctoral work devoted to it, there were many points of view brought to bear on it—some of them not, at first sight, what one would think of as particularly musical. Seashore has thus characterized this feature of the early graduate work in music:

> The crowning feature in this groundwork for the recognition of music in the Graduate College was the faculty's provision for the breaking down of departmental barriers and the broadening of training through the cooperation of related departments in this new field of research. To illustrate, in music it provided that the candidate for the doctorate shall take his acoustics under a physicist, his psychology under a psychologist, his education under an educationist, his anatomy under an anatomist—in addition to the basic courses in composition, history of music, the development of musical skills, and the research or creative work leading to a thesis or a dissertation. This not only gave music a graduate academic status but enlarged the research interests in these various departments for the sharing of approaches to the science of music. For example, the departments of physics, anatomy, psychology, and child welfare have for more than twenty years given highly specialized courses for advanced students in music and speech.[39]

One senses here something of the excitement that was to appear on the undergraduate level during the mid-century general education movement. The experience at Iowa was, of course, somewhat exceptional because of the initial impulse given by the establishment of the Child Welfare Research

[39] *Ibid.,* p. 34.

Station—an interesting example of the "whole child" approach which we have seen as influential on music education from the beginning of the present century.

By and large, the doctoral dissertations on musical subjects listed by the MTNA and the AMS (American Musicological Society) for the years from 1918 on, favor historical pursuits—especially as musicology became a more and more prominent feature of the higher education in music in America during the 1930's and '40's. Whatever the emphasis in particular dissertations, music was removed from its "art for art's sake" status to become the subject of doctoral studies. To one unsympathetic to this development, it might seem as if music had been removed from its status "as music," and that something similar to what Bach did in his *Musical Offering* would seem more to the point. With the ultimate opening of the doctorate, at the mid-century, to applied music as well as to composition— that is, to performance as well as to creative work—the theoretical ground for objections to this development was removed.

As the doctorate in music has developed, there are seven fields in which it may be pursued today: theory, composition, musicology, music history and literature, music education, church music, and applied music. All actual programs of doctoral study in music include more than one field, and, as Kennedy has characterized the situation, "Commonly, the general frameworks permit, if not require, the student to investigate at least one area outside of music, in addition to two fields within the area of music."[40] It is particularly in the Doctor of Education and Doctor of Musical Arts degrees that this breadth of conception (in place of the late nineteenth-century ideal of narrow specialization) appears.

Various associations have been influential in setting standards for this degree. The NASM requires that three years elapse between the bachelor's and doctor's degrees, with at least one year of residence beyond the master's. It approves the fields of musicology, composition, theory, and music education for the Ph.D. Two modern foreign languages are required; and, for musicology students, a third modern foreign language and Latin are "strongly recommended." In general, there is a congruence between the NASM approach to doctoral and to master's degrees, the Doctor of Musical Arts being a special concern of the NASM, as it constitutes a terminal degree normally under the direct administrative control of the music school itself. There is also a general congruence between the NASM approach to the two forms of the musical doctorate and the two forms of the musical bachelor's degree. Other accrediting agencies, such as the American Association of Colleges for Teacher Education, have also helped to structure the doctoral programs in music as they are given at some institutions.

Hanson, who—perhaps more than any other one person—has had

[40] Kennedy, *op. cit.*, p. 160.

most to do with the NASM's work in standardizing curricula, recently summed up the situation thus:

> It is an example of basic and wise conservatism of the Association that the proposal of a professional doctorate in music waited almost fifteen years for approval. Now, at long last, this has been accomplished and we have the Doctor of Philosophy degree in music for the research scholar, and the Doctor of Musical Arts degree for the musical practitioner. And so music education has in a little more than a quarter of a century integrated itself as a member of the academic family, changing from the European conservatory pattern to the American university pattern, with results which will, I believe, prove beneficial both to music and to education.[41]

A significant development in the doctorate in music, particularly with the inauguration of the Doctor of Musical Arts degree, has been the greater possibilities for creative work instead of merely historical research. In commenting on this development, Hanson said:

> Dichotomy between scholarly research on the one hand and creation and participation and performance on the other, which is characteristic of the European and British universities, no longer exists in a large number of American universities. Here the student of music history and theory works shoulder to shoulder with his companions in the fields of composition and performance. The faculty of the departments of history and theory collaborates with the faculties of applied music and composition and, indeed, frequently an individual teacher may be a member of more than one department. Under these conditions, which involve the practicalities of appointment, rank, and tenure, the doctorate frequently assumes an importance which it perhaps has not deserved and the teacher who is barred from acquiring the doctorate simply because of the branch of the art in which he is concentrating may be placed under a severe and inequitable handicap. The professional doctorate in music, fortunately, obviates this handicap and, I might add, parenthetically, that an increasing number of university and college presidents seeking candidates holding a "doctor's degree" frequently specify *either* the Doctor of Philosophy or the Doctor of Musical Arts degree.[42]

When this was written in 1958, there were ten institutions offering the Doctor of Musical Arts. Hanson saw great possibilities in its still further development as it might be organized in additional institutions:

> If I have any criticism it would be that we have in some cases been, perhaps, over-cautious, patterning the new degree too carefully after the curriculum of the Doctor of Philosophy degree; that the professional doctorate still needs more daring, more imaginative experimentation if it is to fulfill its optimal possibilities. We must, I believe, try to overcome the long established academic prejudice against the performing arts. We must, in my opinion, realize—and teach others to realize—that the successful per-

[41] Howard Hanson, "Professional Music Education in the United States," *Musical Courier,* Vol. 151, No. 3 (February 1955), p. 64.
[42] Howard Hanson, "The Doctorate in Music," *NASM Bulletin,* No. 46 (February 1958), p. 5.

formance of a Bartók piano concerto not only with technical facility but with an understanding of its historic, theoretical, and aesthetic implications, is not merely a feat of digital dexterity but an accomplishment which deserves our respect, even as academicians.

Nor are we being so radical as we might think in assuming this attitude. The recent meeting of the Association of Graduate Deans was enlivened by a number of heartening diatribes by some of its members against the atrophy which at times seems to be afflicting much graduate work in the humanities; by objections against the practice of jamming square pegs into round holes; and by pleas that each discipline be considered in terms of its own characteristics. There were criticisms of the lack of creativity in many doctoral programs in the humanities. There were complaints against the freezing of academic patterns into hard, icy molds, and protests against bureaucratic regulations which seemed to consider everything important but the needs of the student. These criticisms came, not from a group of educational radicals, but from experienced graduate deans, leading some of us who have ventured into experimental fields to believe that we are not, like the famous left footed soldier, "all out of step but Jim."[43]

Dr. Hanson expressed the hope that the development of this degree would help rejuvenate graduate study generally:

> Under these conditions it is my hope that the member schools of the NASM which are now offering this degree will strike out with boldness and imagination in the creation of a philosophy toward professional graduate study in music which will emancipate it from unnecessary academic restrictions and will move in the direction of a full realization of the oneness, the indivisibility, of the total art of music. It is my hope that we may work against all philosophies which would frustrate the potency of a great art by creating an artificial dichotomy between scholarship and creation or recreative performance.[44]

Looking speculatively toward the distant future, it is not impossible that this doctorate might eventually render obsolete the welter of diplomas and certificates, of bachelor's and master's degrees, that have come into being within the past century. A hopeful precedent for such a development is the way in which, in the field of medicine, the old Bachelor of Medicine and Bachelor of Surgery degrees, as well as the florid diplomas of the proprietary medical schools, have ultimately given place to one comprehensive doctorate which somehow combines practice with research.

The introduction of the doctor's degree in musical performance in the 1950's represented a bold step in this direction. The presence of many concert artists on college faculties has increased the feasibility of this development. The pianist Edward Kilenyi has formulated a widely held conception behind this move:

> In my opinion, even understanding the performance requirements of the profound classics would not in itself justify the doctoral degree. We ap-

[43] *Ibid.*, p. 6.
[44] *Ibid.*

proach the desired characteristic more closely, however, when the pianist's background knowledge enables him to answer authoritatively questions raised by the various schools of thought about interpretation.[45]

Attainments needed for the doctoral degree, he believes, would include teaching knowledge, performing ability, knowledge of theory and music history, ability to impart knowledge, ability to lecture on music, ability to do independent research, and broad cultural background; "since the doctoral candidate, whether primarily a performer or a researcher, is bound to be a teacher, the pedagogic art both as a science and as intuition must not be neglected. The human touch must be cultivated at least as thoroughly as the pianistic." This suggests that, on a higher level, the dichotomies which manifested themselves on the undergraduate level cease to exist, and it is possible that a certain influence toward unification of music study may, in the course of time, work its way down from the doctoral level —as it has already, in many ways, begun to do.

A performing artist who has also served as professor of music at Indiana University, Sidney Foster, has expressed his belief in the deep significance of this close connection between the academic music departments and the concert world—a really new development of the past few decades:

> The artistic playing of a musical instrument represents much more than a skill. It is a highly complex art, requiring a broad background and wide experience. The student, realizing that a musician's education consists of infinitely more than practice and knowledge of theoretical subjects, is drawn more and more to the college where he gets not only these but a good general education, a well-organized day, the stimulation of association with his fellows, sufficient recreation, *and* a teacher who is *also* an outstanding performer.
>
> In a word, music has come into its own in the colleges. And perhaps the most telling evidence of this is the introduction during the past two or three years of the Doctor's degree in music performance. While it is still not unanimously agreed that the highest level of scholarship and intellectual achievement goes into the making of an accomplished musical artist, those institutions where no doubt exists are now offering the Doctor of Music degree, not as an honorary award, but on the same academic level as the Ph.D. And as more institutions offer this degree, the need for expert performing artists to administer it will become greater, and we may look forward to more and more of our professional performers becoming college professors.[46]

Perhaps it may be felt that the foregoing discussion of graduate work in music is a little outside the scope of this monograph, which was mainly intended to deal with liberal arts work in undergraduate music programs.

[45] Edward Kilenyi, "Doctoral Degrees for Applied Music," *Music Journal,* Vol. 14, No. 2 (February 1956), p. 22.

[46] Sidney Foster, "The Concert Artist as College Teacher," *Music Journal,* Vol. 14, No. 2 (February 1956), p. 21.

But it is in the nature of the way one learns music that he starts out fairly specifically and begins to concern himself with wider and more general matters only after he has reached a certain stage in his development as a musician. One learns journalism or business administration or law or medicine in the opposite sequence: One does not begin practicing surgery on people and then, later on, begin to reflect on what he has been doing; whereas one does, normally, begin practicing music and only later reflects on it theoretically. The place where liberal tendencies in the educational structure can most naturally manifest themselves—in music—are at the doctoral level. And this they have done.

On one of the visits, some uncertainty was encountered as to just what honors work in music would be like. Obviously, there are undesirable aspects to letting the superior student just do "more music," in the way that a superior student might be allowed to take honors in a liberal arts department. Does not the pattern of graduate work developed by the music schools themselves offer an idea of what undergraduate honors work in music might be like? Normally, when a student does honors work as an undergraduate, he is simply permitted to do more advanced work; in English, for example, he would usually take some advanced courses or write an essay somewhat like a doctoral dissertation. This pattern would hardly fit the music school, nor would the abolition of all stated requirements in the senior year and reversion to the *laissez-faire* free elective system which has just been eliminated from the program with such difficulty. This latter possibility seems a frank admission on the part of the faculty that they do not have any idea what honors work in music should be. Undergraduate honors in music would seem logically to be something patterned after the programs just discussed that have been developed in the music schools' own graduate realm.

MUSICOLOGY

If there have been some misgivings over the scholarly appropriateness of linking the academic with the concert or performance world, there can scarcely be any over the development of musicology in America, particularly during the past quarter century. Musicology has come onto the American scene with the full sanction of the Continental universities. It is obviously the other half of a polar relationship within musical studies which, by virtue of the separation of conservatories from universities on the Continent, could enjoy uninhibited development, particularly in Central Europe; and the prestige of German scholarship, from the 1870's on, has been very great in America. In the matter of musicology, the Continental universities were far in advance of the British universities; and as a result of the extensive emigration of musicologists from Central Europe during the 1940's, America actually moved into a position of world leadership in this field.

So far as America is concerned, however, musicology is only one part of higher education in music. As Raymond Kendall of the University of Michigan wrote in 1955,

> There are at least two aspects of professional training in music—manipulation and verbalization. In the former are the composers, singers, instrumentalists and conductors. In the latter, the historian and critic. These need to exist and to work together side by side and to be given appropriate emphasis in the curricula of American colleges and universities. In a strictly professional program, there will be time and place for more emphasis upon music itself; less in a non-professional program. But no program of music education worthy of the name dares to verbalize about music without providing its students a chance to manipulate the materials of music. Conversely, no professional program dares to emphasize the manipulative aspects of music-making to the exclusion of studies concerning the history and aesthetics of the art.[47]

Obvious as this point seems, it has not been always possible to realize this interrelation between the performing and the scholarly aspects of music under the European system of sharp separation between conservatories and universities. Of course, in connection with musicological work in the European universities, there is usually a *collegium musicum* in which works are at once studied and performed, and there is quite a bit of extracurricular music making. From Otto Kinkeldey's description of a "seminar" at the University of Breslau where he had taught,[48] it is clear that matters of general and collateral education (languages, history, philosophy, and the like) were either simply dealt with as they arose or were just generally anticipated by the students, according to the educational traditions of the country. To America, however, musicology came as a fully developed, mature, academic discipline, suddenly yanked out of its native habitat, and —like a fish flopping on the bank and gasping for breath—it unexpectedly found new waters in which to swim on this side of the Atlantic.

More or less as the developments in nuclear physics had been on the way since the beginning of the present century but were suddenly precipitated into actuality by World War II, so there had been in America an awareness of musicology since the beginning of the century but without much really being done about it.

The United States Section of the International Society of Music *(Internationale Musik Gesellschaft,* or *IMG)* was organized early in the century, and from 1907 to 1916 a group of some two dozen members met each year

---

[47] Raymond Kendall, "Professional Training in Music," *NASM Bulletin,* No. 40 (April 1955), p. 19.

[48] Otto Kinkeldey, "Music in the Universities of Europe and America," *PMTNA,* Vol. 10 (1916), pp. 79–91.

in connection with the MTNA. The *IMG* was a World War I casualty. In the United States, however, a scholarly magazine, *The Musical Quarterly,* was begun in 1915, largely under the impetus of O. G. Sonneck, Director of the Publications Department at G. Schirmer, Inc., in New York. The opening article in this quarterly was an essay, "On Behalf of Musicology," by the president of the moribund American section of the *IMG,* Waldo S. Pratt, of Hartford Theological Seminary and past-president of the MTNA. Today *The Musical Quarterly* continues to be—so far as its many commitments will allow—an organ for the communication of research that is of general interest to musicians. Pratt's article is mainly about the propriety of the word "musicology," which at the time he did not find listed in any English dictionary but which had been "creeping in as a twentieth-century innovation." "Musicology" is, of course, a rendering of the German word *Musikwissenschaft* (music knowledge, or musical science)—music approached from the objective rather than the subjective point of view. The implication here is that abroad the conservatories mainly approached music from the subjective and intuitive, the universities from the more objective and methodical point of view. As explained later in an article in *The Musical Quarterly* by Sonneck, musicology : music :: philology : literature.[49] Pratt's article closes with an interesting prophecy (which was to come true only fifteen years later with the establishment of a department of musicology at Cornell under Kinkeldey):

> It may even be that sometime there will be in the faculties of certain large institutions a professorship of "musicology", whose function shall be to unfold the broad outlines of the science and to demonstrate not only its intellectual dignity among other sciences, but its practical utility on a large scale to hosts of musicians and music lovers.[50]

In 1927, on the occasion of the Beethoven Centennial, a musicological congress met in Vienna, and a new international organization was formed, the International Society of Musicology, with its center in Basel. The editor of *The Musical Quarterly* and the head of the music division of the Library of Congress, Carl Engel, were responsible for a musicological festival at the Library of Congress, at which a project connected with the Library was proposed. The strongly Continental character of the whole operation is noteworthy: Both Sonneck and Engel had been educated in Germany, Engel being a Parisian by birth. Also noteworthy is the fact that all this activity directed toward serious scholarship in music had only a peripheral relationship to the world of higher musical education in America during the first quarter of the present century: A music publishing firm and a library, rather than a university, kept alive the enterprise of research in musical

[49] O. G. Sonneck, "The Future of Musicology in America," *MQ,* Vol. 15 (1929), p. 318.
[50] Waldo S. Pratt, "On Behalf of Musicology," *MQ,* Vol. 1 (1915), p. 16.

science, or musical scholarship in an objective sense of the term. The colleges and universities were more occupied with bringing music to the masses—school music, music appreciation, community service—than with bringing people to the inner precincts of music. The 1920's were the real coming-of-age of "music ed," and there was little time or energy left within the universities for really steady and serious concern over musical scholarship *as such*.

In 1934 the American Musicological Society was founded in New York as a direct outgrowth of the New York Musicological Society, which had held meetings for several years previously. Otto Kinkeldey was the first president, and the first annual meeting was held in connection with the MTNA. The activities of Hitler in Central Europe had begun by this time to send refugees to America, and it was clear that before the end of the '30's America would be called on to play a very different role in this branch of music from the one that it had played before. Luckily, many of the fundamental problems connected with the bachelor's degree and the music education program had been settled during the '20's, so attention could shift to the problem of sustaining genuine musical scholarship, as it was being ruthlessly discarded by Central Europe.

The Committee on Colleges and Universities reported at the 1933 MTNA convention that there was not, as yet, much actual musicological work going on in American institutions of higher learning:

> According to the report on "Musicology in the United States," resulting from a survey conducted under the auspices of the American Council of Learned Societies, musical research is not yet a serious function of American institutions. In fact, scarcely a beginning has been made in this important field. The colleges and universities, in the main, are ill-equipped for such work, and trained instructors would be hard to find. Besides, such energy as the colleges have to spare at this time is being directed—wisely, no doubt—towards attempting to provide a musical background for the general culture of the entire student body, to prepare future generations for the leisure which, we are warned, is soon to be thrust upon us,—that is, all of us who are not college music teachers![51]

The AMS, however, grew rather rapidly, with chapters being formed throughout the country. At the time of the outbreak of World War II, in 1939, an International Congress of Musicology was held in New York, with delegates from many countries; and with the assistance of the Carnegie Corporation of New York and the ACLS, and in cooperation with the MENC, the papers read at the Congress were published. Its own magazine, the *Journal* of the AMS, was begun; bibliographies have been published; notable scholarly projects interrupted by the war have been resumed and sponsored by the Society; meetings of local chapters and of the na-

[51] John Lawrence Erb, "Report of the Committee on Colleges and Universities," *PMTNA,* Vol. 28 (1934), p. 202.

tional body have been held. Summarizing and interpreting all these musicological developments of the decade from 1934 to 1944, Carl Engel wrote:

> Small comfort may lie in the thought that the death-laden storm which has swept the world in recent years is not so ill a wind as to have profited nobody; yet the gain, in one line, is clear and indisputable. Refugees of distinction in every calling have fled to our shores and been made welcome. Especially welcome, because they filled a gap not equalled in any other professional group, have been those European scholars who have brought added strength and luster, in America, to musicology.[52]

Commenting on the developments in American musicology by 1947, Glen Haydon, of the University of North Carolina, concludes his excellent survey thus:

> During the war years from 1939–45, the increasing independence of American musicological scholarship has gradually become more apparent. Since the early 1930's, American musicologists have, in a sense, been taking serious stock of themselves in an effort to improve scholarly standards in both teaching and research with the result that American musicology has come of age. And, although in recent years the arrival of so many refugee scholars has greatly strengthened the field, independence from Europe has been achieved and probably would have been without the refugees. . . . The American musician is primarily and properly most interested in the practical and creative aspects of the art, and when and as this interest rests upon a solid scholarly basis, there results a combination which augurs well for the future of both musicology and music in the United States.[53]

The crucial question for our present purposes, however, is whether the effect of all this musicological activity has been one of professionalizing or liberalizing the undergraduate music school curriculum. At first thought, it might seem a move in the direction of specialization. Its initial impetus was from the kind of German scientism which played such havoc with the liberal arts curriculum toward the end of the nineteenth century. To some people, any suggestion that music should be approached from the point of view of the sciences is "dangerous or nihilistic"; Cecil Smith, for example, declared:

> If such arts as music and literature are studied through approaches which are primarily appropriate to the physical sciences, . . . the methods employed in the study of these arts automatically remove them from the area of the humanities. . . . An art is to be understood artistically; the exactness of scientific method proves to be exceedingly inexact when imposed upon an artistic problem.[54]

In advocating that music should be approached "humanistically" rather than "scientifically," he no doubt would approve of Welch's contention that

[52] Carl Engel, "Views and Reviews," *MQ,* Vol. 20 (1944), p. 234.
[53] Glen Haydon, "Musicology in the United States: A Survey of Recent Trends," *PMTNA,* Vol. 41 (1947), p. 340.
[54] Cecil Michener Smith, "Music and the Humanities," *Modern Music,* Vol. 22 (1945), pp. 99–101.

music appreciation is the proper sphere for college music: "It is professionalism that has made music study abortive and unintelligent even in the conservatories and private studios. . . . Under the time restrictions and division of interests of an academic program of study the cultural or
appreciative . . . study is the only proper focus for a department of music."[55]
For this rather sentimental approach to music study, Carl Engel had nothing
but contempt: "Imagine a university devising courses in law for non-
practicing, non-professional students of law! or holding a clinic for non-
practicing, non-professional physicians!!"[56] Of course, the music-apprecia-
tionists are against professionalism; well and good, said Engel: "It must be
kept out of college. What creeps in, instead, is profusionalism—a nibbling
at a lavish lot of things, with nowhere a bite that nourishes and sustains."[57]

The point is that liberal tendencies in the American undergraduate
musical curriculum during the 1930's could have gone in the direction of
emphasis on "music appreciation" and a kind of aestheticism that, sooner
or later, would have been self-defeating. Instead, musicology came in and
saved this tendency from gaining full sway. In a sense, musicology does
entail a greater emphasis on the objective and factual element in music,
less emphasis on sheer feeling. As Edward N. Waters of the Library of
Congress pointed out, it is not a branch of music:

> It may be an approach to music or a method for studying music or a key to
> the understanding of music, but it must not be looked upon as a part of
> music. As Otto Kinkeldey pointed out in *The International Cyclopedia of
> Music and Musicians* (ed. by Oscar Thompson, New York, 1939 and
> 1943), musicology embraces "the whole body of systematized knowledge
> about music, which results from the application of a scientific method of
> investigation or research, or of philosophical speculation and rational sys-
> tematization, to the facts, the processes and the development of musical
> art, and to the relation of man in general . . . to that art." Musicology is,
> therefore, a department of human learning rather than a branch of the art
> of music.[58]

In terms of a present-day concept of liberal education as essential
knowledge, intellectual skill, and desirable traits of personality and character, musicology can scarcely be ruled out of the liberal fold by invoking
some abstract distinction between music as an art and music as a science.

Active steps to establish rapport between music educators and musicologists have been taken by their respective associations. The MTNA has
long had a committee on Musicology and Music Education, and, as we

[55] Roy Dickinson Welch, *The Study of Music in the American College* (Northampton, Massachusetts: Smith College, 1925), pp. 29, 49.
[56] Carl Engel, "Views and Reviews," *MQ,* Vol. 11 (1925), p. 620.
[57] *Ibid.,* p. 623.
[58] Edward N. Waters, "Musicology and the Teacher," *PMTNA,* Vol. 38 (1944),
pp. 185–186.

have seen, was part of the matrix out of which the musicological movement in America grew. In the early '40's, the MENC appointed a Committee on Music Education and Musicology, to establish contacts with musicological societies and to sponsor meetings of common interest. At the December 1944 meeting of the AMS, moreover, a Committee on Musicology and Music Education was authorized. In 1945 a round-table discussion was held in New York under MENC auspices.[59] In summarizing and commenting on some of these moves toward rapprochement, Charles Seeger, of the Pan American Union, said of the music educators and the musicologists:

> Both are, as a matter of fact, now broadening their space and time vision and values. And in so doing they are coming closer together. From the nursery-school to the seminar is not two processes but one. Extent, concentration, and emphasis may vary. But new values and new achievement may as well originate in the school as in the learned society.[60]

Musicology, as it has been transplanted into America, has undertaken to show the relationship of music to history, to the rest of life, as well as the inner relationships of music among its various branches. In further commenting on what musicology can offer the potential music teacher, Waters has written:

> Perhaps the most important thing that musicology can teach to teachers is the necessity of viewing music and its infinite history as a whole, a phenomenon of humanity which is as essential to our health as it is normal to our life. We casually think of history in terms that are too circumscribed and limiting. Actually it can be broken down and systematized and analyzed endlessly, and when the facts and evidences are assembled again, the complex whole is greater than the sum of any or all of its parts. So it is with music, and it is through musicology that both the analysis and synthesis can best be accomplished. The musicologist dissects, examines and reconstructs. The teacher guides, illustrates and exemplifies. How different, yet how closely akin are their duties. Both now seem essential to the cultivation of musicians in the future, for they complement each other in fostering the comprehension of music as an integrated whole.[61]

During the '40's, musicology spread also into the conservatories, constituting a broadening of the curriculum there, in the sense of diverting attention from an exclusive emphasis on performance. In 1941 Hans Rosenwald, of the Chicago Musical College, pointed out that though the conservatories had not done as much with musicology as the universities, he had for the past four years been chairman of a musicology department

[59] For the summarizing speech, see Curt Sachs, "The Music Historian," *Music Educators Journal,* Vol. 31, No. 6 (May–June 1945), pp. 78–79.

[60] Charles Seeger, "Music Education and Musicology," *Music Educators Journal,* Vol. 31, No. 6 (May–June 1945), p. 78.

[61] Waters, *op. cit.,* pp. 188–189.

in a conservatory.[62] During the past quarter century, moreover, outstanding research work in musicology has been carried on at Peabody.

For the large proportion of undergraduate students in music schools, however, the coming of musicology onto the American scene has meant the appearance of an integrative element which potentially can bring the *membra disjecta* of the curriculum into relationship with each other. Donald J. Grout, of Cornell, has characterized the significance of musicology for the undergraduate thus:

> Musicology . . . is the general name for all that study of music which has as its aim not performance, not composition, not pedagogy, but the understanding of music. Musicology regards the understanding—the "appreciation", if you will—of music as an end, not as a means. It is therefore an attitude, a point of view, rather than a separate course of study.[63]

He then goes on to discuss the various aspects of music that the undergraduate may encounter: first, actual physical laws of sound, which are scientific and absolute; second, regulative principles or norms, which are relative, though often presented as if they were universally true; and he continues:

> There is a third kind of musical knowledge which has for its object not the establishment of laws or norms but the contemplation of the finished musical composition as a work of art, a unique phenomenon having greater or less aesthetic value. It is this kind of knowledge which is the peculiar and special province of musicology. It regards the study of music as a branch of the humanities, to be undertaken in the same spirit and with the same ideals as the study of literature or the fine arts. Like these, it makes use of certain preliminary techniques to establish the object of its investigation with the utmost possible fullness and accuracy.[64]

Probably it is not too important to point out here that this is a different sort of enterprise from what Pratt and Sonneck were talking about when they said "musicology"—just as it is no indictment of Tourjée that when he said "conservatory" he meant "class system of instruction." One takes from the past or from a foreign body of ideas what one needs. The point is that even musicology has undergone certain changes in the course of its adaptation to an American environment, and it has also changed that environment.

Grout thus characterizes the implications of musicology for the undergraduate student:

> The prosecution of such work has nothing whatever to do with the practical requirements of performers and composers of music, but is directed solely to the enrichment of our knowledge about the inexhaustible subject of the human spirit itself, as manifested in the whole history of its development

[62] Hans Rosenwald, "Musicology and the Conservatory," *PMTNA*, Vol. 35 (1941), pp. 265–268.

[63] Donald J. Grout, "Musicology and the Undergraduate Student," *PMTNA*, Vol. 38 (1944), p. 190.

[64] *Ibid.*, p. 193.

. . . musicology is directed primarily not at making better musicians, but at contributing to human knowledge and thereby increasing our understanding of ourselves.[65]

The present undergraduate curriculum, Grout feels, is too chopped up:

> The chief fault of the musical education of our undergraduates is not so much that it is superficial, but that it is too compartmentalized. Not only does it tend to divorce music from the rest of our intellectual interests, but even within the domain of music itself we have a rift between knowing and doing, theory and practice, thought and feeling. If the separated parts of our music education could be brought together again, and if the whole realm of music could be brought into closer relation with the rest of our educational system, it would be better for all of us. We need composers, performers, and scholars, but above all we need—especially in a democracy—a public educated to the knowledge of music not simply as a craft or a technique, but as an art in living contact with the whole of our cultural life.[66]

To musicology he looks for the means of achieving integration, and one even observes an element of "social consciousness" creeping into the expectations he entertains for this type of music study. To the extent that such a content can be poured into the word "musicology," it certainly acts as a liberalizing force in the curriculum, providing essential knowledge and cultivating intellectual skills and traits of personality and character.

EFFECT OF MAJOR EVENTS OF THE TWENTIETH CENTURY

Reviewing the development of liberal and professional study in higher education in music during the present century, one is struck by the steady and purposeful development that has occurred, largely under the leadership of the various associations. The first comprehensive survey of the situation made under governmental auspices appeared in 1908. It concludes:

> It is clear that the present status of formal music education is one of transition. With many independent schools of music, colleges, and universities offering well-conceived music courses of high standard, there is still lacking the unity and complete coordination of effort that should characterize a well-grounded scheme of education. . . . Each school is a law unto itself; hence when a student presents credits from one to another there is no basis of agreement as to the value of such credits. Secondary schools, which in general education take care to have their courses closely articulated with those of institutions of higher education, attempt the same grade of musical instruction as the best equipped conservatory or college. There are no secondary music schools. A well-defined, properly regulated development of music education from its most elementary to its highest grades does not yet exist.

[65] *Ibid.*, p. 194.
[66] *Ibid.*, p. 199.

> Music needs the college atmosphere, its spirit of culture, and its well-directed effort. It needs the application to its methods of the system and orderliness that characterize college work. . . . That such a consummation will be reached present conditions give basis for belief.[67]

It is remarkable how much has been accomplished in this direction during but little more than half a century.

World War I brought with it great activity in the field of community music. A certain kind of "art-for-art's-sake" perfectionism suddenly became obsolete. "Before the war," commented Charles D. Isaacson, "the number of people in attendance at concert-halls and operas constituted a little less than 2% of our total population. Since the war began the percentage mounted perhaps to 15%."[68] In the educational world, an element of social consciousness was never henceforth to be lost.

In the field of music education, the great development took place in the 1920's, resulting in the stabilization of the bachelor's degree and the establishment of the NASM. The Depression and the growth of mass media like radio and sound-film had consequences particularly felt by musicians. The effect on institutions of higher learning was to increase their sense of community responsibility: Instead of thinking of themselves as conservatories in the old sense, they thought of themselves more as music centers. Toward the end of the 1930's, musicology became much more of an actuality in the curriculum. The 1940's, with the full impact of World War II, were rather different from the World War I years: Musical matters were more organized.

At the 1940 MTNA meeting, the Committee on Colleges and Universities reported:

> The problem of attaining a reasonable balance between a broad education in the liberal arts and an intensive professional training in music is receiving more and more attention. In a number of instances serious attempts are being made at courses integrating music with art and literature. The faculties of several departments ordinarily collaborate in giving these courses. Some institutions are studying and experimenting with five- and six-year programs leading to combined A.B. and M.M. degrees. There is also evidence that senior comprehensive examinations are being more widely given.[69]

In 1945 the Committee reported:

> The importance of liberal arts courses in the training of the music student is welling up as a dominant issue. Illinois colleges have had this

[67] Arthur L. Manchester, *Music Education in the United States Schools and Departments of Music,* U.S. Bureau of Education, Bulletin, 1908, No. 4, Whole Number 387 (Washington, D.C.: 1908), pp. 82–83.

[68] Charles D. Isaacson, "A New Musical Outlook—and the War," *MQ,* Vol. 6 (1920), p. 1.

[69] Glen Haydon, "Report of the Committee on Colleges and Universities," *PMTNA,* Vol. 35 (1941), p. 441.

matter thrust upon them by a recent state law covering the certification of teachers which adds 24 semester hours of academic work beyond that formerly required. Added subjects include survey courses in Social Science, Humanities, and Natural Science. Indiana colleges face a similar prospect. At Iowa changes in the B.A. curriculum have been made which are favorable to the Fine Arts. Kentucky is seeking to give its music majors a broader cultural background in the Social Studies, the Humanities, and English. Knox has this year instituted a "program of integrated education" in which "general education" includes Fine Arts along with Science, Society, Mathematics, English, and Language. A tutorial system is part of the plan. . . .[70]

The general education movement—with its "core curriculum" which came to the fore around 1950—caused some difficulties for music students because of the necessity for applied music. The report of the Committee on Schools and Conservatories of Music, printed in 1950, stated:

> If the requirements in general education can be spaced throughout the four years of undergraduate study, or (provided they are located in the first two years), if their total demands still leave enough time for a minimum of five hours a semester for music in these years, a core-curriculum will not seriously affect specialization in music.[71]

Discussing the problem at length in 1951, Thomas W. Williams, of Knox College, wrote:

> Perhaps it may be that the ultimate answer of "curricula conflict" can be reached when the music teacher finds the proper degree to which general education can be incorporated into our existing music courses. This is not a new thought. Numerous studies have been made on this identical problem, and in many institutions we find courses which embody this principle. History and appreciation courses offer a vast field for the presentation of the very fundamentals of general education. Certainly the study of music history can achieve greater impact and vitality when it relates itself to larger aspects of the historical field.[72]

During the 1950's there was increasing recognition of the role that public junior colleges were coming to play, and the suggestion was made with greater frequency that they offered a possible solution to the problem of special vs. liberal education.[73] During the two years of the junior college the student could pursue a liberal education with certain basic music work,

[70] Leland A. Coon, "Report of the Committee on Colleges and Universities," *PMTNA,* Vol. 39 (1945), p. 163.

[71] Karl H. Eschman, "Report of the Committee on Schools and Conservatories of Music," *PMTNA,* Vol. 42 (1950), p. 355.

[72] Thomas W. Williams, "The Influence of General Education on Music Curricula," *PMTNA,* Vol. 43 (1951), p. 82.

[73] Muriel Reiss, "The Place of the Junior College in Training Musicians," *Music Educators Journal,* Vol. 36, No. 3 (January 1950), pp. 20–21; C. Burdette Wolfe, chairman, "Junior College Problems," *NASM Bulletin,* No. 40 (April 1955), pp. 27–28.

and then, if he wished, proceed to definite specialization in music. Also, throughout the whole music education world, there has been increased attention during the past several years to the international aspects of music: its implications for an understanding of America abroad, possibilities of projects of international cooperation, and so on. But perhaps most important in terms of our historical review of the university curriculum in music has been the achievement during the past decade of a specifically music doctorate.

This brief review of higher education in music during the twentieth century by no means covers all aspects of it, but does serve to recall the vast development which it has undergone in the course of but sixty years. In comparison with what has taken place so far in the present century, the efforts of the previous two and a half centuries seem quite sporadic and individual or local.

OBSERVERS FROM ABROAD

Many of the European musicologists who have come to the United States have brought a very incisive type of criticism to bear on the relationship between professional and liberal education that they have found here. In a book published posthumously in 1957, Manfred Bukofzer (who died in 1955 at the age of forty-five) presented a very sharp critique of the tendency on the part of university music schools to introduce liberal arts type courses into their curriculum:

> Given its essentially practical aim, a conservatory or School of Music cannot make it its business to supply a general education any more than can, say, a School of Mining or of Medicine. The special arts and techniques required in these fields call for high concentration and thorough training, which take up a great amount of time. This means that the conservatory must take the cultural values of music for granted. In other words, the student at a professional school should already possess a general education or should be in the process of acquiring one concurrently at institutions best suited to this purpose.[74]

Bukofzer was here advocating a sharp separation of functions, as between the conservatory and the university music school, the music school and the college of liberal arts. One senses immediately a sharpness of thinking, and a kind of neo-orthodoxy, that was absent from earlier twentieth-century discussions of this subject. In justifying the distinctions thus drawn, he added:

> A School of Music . . . operates within the normal four years of a college curriculum. Now, it is generally agreed among musicians that professional competence cannot possibly be developed within this period, not even with a graduate year added. Yet the Schools of Music claim to do

[74] Manfred Bukofzer, *The Place of Musicology in American Institutions of Higher Learning* (New York: The Liberal Arts Press, 1957), p. 13.

just this and even pretend to supply in addition some kind of general education, all within the same time. . . . Even under ideal conditions a School of Music can only make a pretense of carrying out its program; it envisages too many disparate activities over too short a period. There is an inner contradiction in its conception that makes it a permanent problem child of the university. In the conservatory, on the other hand, no such contradiction exists—at least, none need exist.[75]

Actually, with the operation of the graduate program and the existence of fairly highly developed high school courses in music, the four years of college undergraduate work are not the whole training of the school of music trained musician. Bukofzer was contrasting here, however, the *idea* of the undergraduate university music school with the *idea* of the conservatory—the school of music *principle* and the conservatory *principle.* For, as he wrote, "It is the choice of principle that matters. Bad teaching can be corrected, a bad principle cannot." As an actual matter of fact, the time that elapses between the student's entry and his graduation is about the same in a conservatory and in a music school—at least so far as any existing conservatories and music schools in the United States are concerned. Perhaps in the realm of ideas or ideals, however, there may be a distinction to which the rather pragmatic approach of most Americans has rendered them insensitive.

Obviously, the American situation in higher education in music has become very confusing to a person used to certain clear-cut distinctions in a neat quasi-feudal or hierarchical pattern of professional education:

> The gradual assimilation of curricula is a peculiarly American phenomenon, but a most questionable form of singularity. The mixing of aims makes it impossible to pursue a clear policy, and the result may be that neither a general musical education nor professional competence can be achieved. The idea of offering a little of everything, which obviously satisfies only the requirements of the lower levels of music education, is an attempt at organized mediocrity. It can be overcome only by the most talented and determined students working against the system. If there is any prevailing danger in our national music education today, it is what may be called the department-store conception of music instruction, in which the essentials of both curricula are reduced and offered at bargain prices.[76]

Bukofzer's criticism of the situation might be called radical, in the sense of going to the *radix,* or root, of the matter. He did not wish to accept its fundamental assumptions: The fact that a music school was patterned after a college seemed to him an aping of one thing by another—the college being the legitimate form, and the music school the caricature of it:

> The external imitation of the college has in effect supplanted honest certificates by specious degrees in an effort to profit from the prestige of genuinely academic institutions. The notorious "upgrading" that has taken

[75] *Ibid.,* p. 15.
[76] *Ibid.,* p. 18.

place at Music Schools has most frequently taken the form of interlarding professional courses with so-called "cultural" courses in languages, literature, and other fields. Those are frequently but the window-dressing of an essentially unchanged, though watered-down, professional curriculum. The substitute courses have generally proved to be poor because they are lacking a special faculty, proper library facilities, and, not infrequently, a congenial academic climate. On the other hand, they take away much needed time from the professional training, so that the door is opened to what can really be called amateurish standards. Unfortunately, even some conservatories have followed this trend and reorganized themselves after the pattern of the School of Music. Here again the new "collegiate department," which cannot compare with the genuine article, has been established at the expense of high professional standards.[77]

What Bukofzer was driving at in his book was that musicology should be a graduate study. The student should come to it with a genuine background in the liberal arts.

Time and again has it been observed that students holding the degree of Bachelor of Music are not adequately prepared for the graduate study of musicology. They lack languages, general history, and also the broad orientation in music and music history that a liberal arts college properly equipped for the purpose would normally offer. Lacking essential preliminary training, the student enters advanced studies with deficiencies that must be made up at an inordinate cost of time and at the price of personal disappointment and frustration.[78]

In other words, let there be a clear-cut distribution of duties and responsibilities, and let each one perform his duty properly; then there will be no difficulty. "Good fences," as the conservative farmer in Frost's poem says, "make good neighbors."

This is a point of view that can be urged with clarity and force; and doubtless some of Bukofzer's criticisms have had their provocation. It should be noted, however, that the purpose of his remarks was definitely hortatory rather than merely factual and reportorial; he called for repentance and return to the good old days when everyone knew his place. The fact of the matter is that the good old days no longer exist—and possibly they never did, really. To be sure, the university music school is based on an inner contradiction of principle, just as any living body has within it the seeds of its own death. Is the music school a conservatory or a college? Like any work of art, it is a harmony of two opposed elements. When the tension between them ceases to exist, the institution is dead. Historically, his conception of the music school as a cheap imitation of the college of liberal arts does not bear close examination: Both have claims to legitimacy. Originally they were one—the religious community. The Bachelor

[77] *Ibid.*, pp. 19–20.
[78] *Ibid.*, p. 32.

of Music degree and the Bachelor of Arts degree are both quite old: Their inner nature, of course, has been different at different times and places. The mistaken idea that the former is a grotesque imitation of the latter can easily be gained from a superficial acquaintance with merely the twentieth-century situation. Many of the criticisms of the program of the music schools that Bukofzer expressed have no doubt been in the minds of leaders responsible for the virtual lengthening of the period of study through the development of master's and doctor's programs, and the requirement of very many skills and, most significantly for our purposes, of liberal arts work on the part of those entering on these graduate programs.

True, when Tourjée invented the idea of a "college of music" within a university, perhaps he faltered in not calling it a "school." On the other hand, perhaps it would not have made much difference if he had. The only point is that a century of trial and error, of bitter experience and of profiting by that experience, has gone into making the situation in American higher education in music what it is; and it is not through ignorance of the European relationships or any unwillingness to try to reconstruct them on American soil that it is as it is.

Since Bukofzer's discussion was intended primarily for the stimulation of reflection and increased self-criticism on the part of his fellow music teachers in America, the purely factual aspects of his statements may well be discounted. More significant of the actual state of things in American higher education in music is the evidence of visiting observers who have written for their own fellow-countrymen abroad. They point to the fact that something really has developed on American soil—in the mating of the conservatory and the college—that is of genuine international significance, and that might well be emulated in Europe itself.

Lest it be thought that the purpose of ending this essay with the laudatory remarks of foreign observers writing for their own readers is merely to provide a happy ending for this account of the historical background of higher education in music and thereby to increase our sense of complacency, one set of rather grim and objective facts should be mentioned: The census figures for the period from 1850 to 1950 show that the actual number of musicians and music teachers in the country—or at least those who are willing to tell the census taker that that is what they think they are—is declining, as shown in the following tabulation.[79]

[79] Precise figures and interpretation can be obtained in Henry J. Harris, "The Occupation of Musician in the United States," *MQ*, Vol. 1 (1915), pp. 299–311; Robert A. Choate, "Music Education," in *Education for the Professions,* edited by Lloyd E. Blauch (Washington: U.S. Department of Health, Education, and Welfare, 1955), pp. 144–151; and the government reports (e.g. *Occupation Outlook Handbook,* Bulletin No. 1215, U.S. Department of Labor, and *1950 Census of Population,* Washington, 1953).

PROFESSED MUSICIANS AND MUSIC TEACHERS
IN THE UNITED STATES, 1850 TO 1950

1850	3,550	1910	139,310
1860	10,354	1920	130,265
1870	16,010	1930	165,128
1880	30,477	1940	161,536
1890	62,155	1950	161,307
1900	92,174		

One would expect the number of musicians to move in the same general direction as the total number of people: For example, between 1880 and 1910 the population doubled and the number of professed musicians increased fivefold. That is understandable. The United States changed from an agricultural to an industrial country around 1880–90, and higher education in music presupposes city conditions. Some of the fantastic aspects of the Peace Jubilees and the early days of the conservatories and the nineteenth-century Bachelor of Music degree make sense against this background. But—the population continues to rise, and what happens to the musicians? One can dismiss all this as unrelated to the question of professional and liberal curricula for the would-be musician; one can say that probably some of these early "musicians and teachers of music" were not worthy the name (a remark which they, perfectly well, might make of their mid-twentieth-century successors if they were, perhaps, not restrained by a Victorian sense of modulating their reactions); one can say that this phenomenon of the numerical decline in the members of a profession as against the numerical increase of the population is not peculiar to music, and that it even shows the glories of automation, modern efficiency, and so on. But, like the question in the Book of Job, it continues to crop up. And whatever our conclusions about the desirability of more professional or more liberal education may be, *this* is the framework within which we, at the mid-twentieth century, are operating.

Among foreign visitors who have observed the American system of higher education in music are Paul Nettl, a Central European, and Harry Lowery, an Englishman. Nettl, a musicologist, and formerly instructor in the German university in Prague and music director of a radio station in that city, discussed the musical situation in American universities, particularly in Indiana, in an article published in the German magazine, *Musica:*

> Among the many university institutes the "School of Music" plays a highly significant role. In contrast to the situation in Europe, music is in almost all the universities a matter of professional training. Europeans are accustomed to the idea that in universities only *musicology* is pursued, and that perhaps a university director of music may conduct a laymen's chorus and a corresponding amateur orchestra. In contrast to this stepmotherly

treatment of music on the part of European universities, the American university is the principal place where music is cultivated. The university music schools are the real conservatories of the country. To be sure, there is in addition a group of significant special music schools, among which I would like to mention the Juilliard School in New York, the Curtis Institute in Philadelphia, the Chicago Musical College, and the Cincinnati Conservatory of Music. These pure trade schools *(diese reinen Fachschulen)* stress the professional and technical aspects of music more than do the music schools at the universities whose students take, along with the purely musical courses, academic subjects.[80]

Nettl's observation that university music schools are, actually, the conservatories here *(die eigentlichen Konservatorien des Landes)* suggests that, in his opinion, Tourjée's vision of a university-linked conservatory has—perhaps not quite in the way anticipated—become an actuality. Nettl further observes that in the American situation music has been restored to a place among the seven liberal arts:

> One naturally wonders how it is possible that in these some eight hundred to a thousand universities there can be, each year, as many as fifteen or twenty thousand students graduated to go out into the field and find jobs. Music is, in America, not a matter of professional study alone, but a matter of general education. In this connection America—like England—continues the classical and medieval tradition according to which music was one of the liberal arts that was taught in an orderly way. . . . Continental rationalism of the late 18th and 19th centuries eliminated music as a genuine object of instruction from the curriculum of the secondary schools and left it only a modest little area. This is different in America, to the extent that all the high schools treat music as a major matter and that also at the universities music as a subject is more or less a required course for students in general.[81]

The important connection between music education and university music schools did not escape Nettl's observation.

An interesting report by Harry Lowery, Principal of the South-West Essex Technical College and School of Art, appeared in 1952 in *Music Book,* an annual British publication. Lowery points out that institutions like Juilliard have superseded European conservatories as international magnets for music study, and continues:

> Something must now be said regarding the course of study for university degrees in music. Here we must begin by renouncing all ideas of university work gained from our experience in English Universities, where a tradition has grown up that degrees are awarded in the main for theoretical studies leading to *composition.* The American position derives from the fact that a greater percentage of the population receives post-high-school education than with us (2.0 per cent as against 0.2 per cent), and in

---

[80] Paul Nettl, "Musik an amerikanischen Universitäten," *Musica,* Vol. 5 (October 1951), p. 406.

[81] *Ibid.,* p. 407.

consequence a greater proportion take music as a degree subject without professional objectives. This being so, we need not be surprised to find that some universities regard *musical appreciation* and *history* as suitable subjects in themselves for degree purposes. Moreover, musicology, covering many aspects of scholarship related to music, is frequently found as a degree subject.[82]

The calmness with which Lowery accepts this difference between the American and the British conception of university training in music contrasts with the anxiety felt by some representatives of the older New England colleges lest they depart from the British practice current at the time of their founding. Lowery simply recognizes that, with the differences in sheer numerical extent of higher education in the United States, there must inevitably be different matters covered by this education.

But most significant for our present study is his discussion of the curriculum in the music schools:

> A matter of great importance which I noted in all types of higher educational institution in the U.S.A. is the desire to ensure that advanced courses shall provide a *liberal* education, as distinct from a narrow technical training. In this it is possible that England has something to learn, for alarm has recently been expressed by eminent educationists that our university and college courses show a tendency to become too highly specialised, with the result that graduates and diploma candidates frequently pass out without possessing that broad culture which should characterize the truly educated person. Opinions may differ as to how this is to be achieved. At any rate, the danger is recognised in the American institutions, and courses in *general subjects* outside the field of the selected specialised study are required of the students. Quite frequently these extra courses are drawn from what are called "human studies", such as literature, citizenship, history, sociology, psychology, and foreign languages, and this is usually the case in the musical academies.[83]

The fact that a foreign observer, writing for his own people, could remark that they possibly had something to learn from the combination of liberal and professional studies that had come into being in American higher education in music suggests that the particular development which has been here traced historically has achieved genuine international significance and merits the detailed consideration which it has received in the foregoing pages.

[82] Harry Lowery, "Some Aspects of Musical Education in the United States of America," *Music Book, Vol. VII of Hinrichsen's Musical Year Book,* edited by Max Hinrichsen (London: Hinrichsen Ed., Ltd., 1952), p. 106.

[83] *Ibid.,* p. 107.

Chapter 6

RECOMMENDATIONS

WHAT A LONG WAY THIS STUDY HAS LED US—FROM THE GREEKS TO THE present, and across the country and back to England! The original purpose was more one of fact-finding and observation. The general problem of liberal education within the work of the professional schools was raised; current influences emanating from associations and state certification boards were reviewed, and some two dozen representative curricula were analyzed; then the attitudes toward the nonprofessional part of the work being done by students in music schools were examined, first in terms of the Dressel survey and then in terms of visits to half a dozen institutions of learning; finally, various critical issues and recent developments were considered, as they have been reflected in the professional literature of the field.

A few recommendations have been made along the way and will be brought together here. The first two are intended more for the individual faculty member and administrator in the music school itself, the third for the university administrator (who may not happen to have any personal knowledge of music teaching or music students), and the last two for the music associations—though, in a sense, everyone connected with higher education in music is involved in all five of these.

1. The first recommendation is that each school really make a study of the way it has moved into its own particular position in this matter of the relationship between professional and nonprofessional components in the work it is doing. Such a study should begin with a reconsideration of the very ideas explicit in its founding. The faculty should try to discover for itself what lines of direction have since been manifested, so that these may be reflected upon in all seriousness and may serve as the basis either for an intensification of what is happening or for a change of direction. Preparation of such a study might be a master's or doctor's project, though each faculty member might well, on his own and in a small way, do this sort of thing as a guide to his own thinking.

An attempt should be made, as soon as possible, to discover through interviews with old graduates and through other means of research, how well both the professional and nonprofessional part of their work prepared them for their occupations in the field of music and for the other activities of life. Higher education in music and the conditions of life generally change rapidly, and without a clear idea of how and how well it has been done in the past, the question of what it *should be* becomes unanswerable.

Within the growing field of graduate study in music—and, more particularly, in music education—there is a potential source that will help the undergraduate professional school faculty to realize more clearly where it stands and what it should do in the future. Individual graduate students may well be asked to work on problems that are of genuine concern both locally and generally. The field here is by no means exhausted. At the end of her dissertation on the B.M., Virginia Mountney makes the following suggestions for further study:

> 1.   There is need for a study of existing practices in the bachelor's degree in the field of music. Such a study would show practices, trends, strengths, and weaknesses of the various degrees, both as vocational preparation and as preparation for graduate study.
> 2.   There is need for a study of existing admission practices for the various degrees. Such a study should include the requirements which are prerequisite to enrollment for study in the numerous types of institutions.
> 3.   There is a need for a study to show the influence which professional music and educational organizations and accrediting agencies have had on bachelors' degrees in music.
> 4.   There is a need for a more intensive study of the history of particular kinds of music schools, such as the conservatories, professional music schools, and music programs in liberal arts colleges.
> 5.   There is a need for studies to determine whether students who have followed one type of degree program are more successful than students who have pursued another type of music curriculum in regard to their chosen profession.[1]

Reference has already been made to some excellent research of this type in terms of the local and actual situation at the University of Illinois. Of course, once studies of this kind have been made, the results should be made available and should be brought to the attention of those immediately concerned—as has been done at Illinois.

2.   Particularly students and faculty members should be encouraged to think about the over-all purpose of professional and liberal education so that they may have a considered awareness of what they are doing; they need to know, as one of the applied music faculty members said in inter-

---

[1] Virginia Ruth Mountney, "The History of the Bachelor's Degree in the Field of Music in the United States" (unpublished D.M.A. dissertation, Boston University, 1961), pp. 276–277.

view, "what it's all about." Some frame of expectation, some picture of what they *want,* should be consciously and overtly fostered. Some music educators of the 1920's, under the influence of behavioristic psychology, thought that students could be conditioned, like Pavlov's dogs, to enjoy music and could generally be well adjusted if they had fifteen minutes a day in the primary grades, twenty minutes a day in the secondary grades, twenty-five minutes a day . . . and so on. Unquestionably, this was an advance over the demon for solmization who in the late nineteenth century no doubt marched in with his pointer and frightened half the children within an inch of their lives and drove the other half to achieve prodigious feats of note reading. But, well intentioned and effective as this theory of gentle conditioning no doubt is with the majority of students, it is by no means the whole story. Now well into the latter half of the twentieth century, we need to re-think this whole matter. The mid-nineteenth century thought of music as moral improvement; the early twentieth thought of it as enjoyment—and neither conception, at least in its old formulation, seems to have the same force, the same sense of excitement about it, that it did in its prime. A new vision is needed.[2]

Obviously, a great deal needs to be done at the faculty level of the professional school in the way of thinking out the problem here involved. A solution imposed from the top down, or from the outside in, is not likely to improve the situation. Merely placing members of the professional school faculty on a committee that has been given responsibility for part of the revision does not solve the problem, as there are great variations of attitude within the professional school faculty.

3. Administrative officers, particularly those without direct personal experience of performing or teaching music, or of the way musicians feel and think, should avail themselves of the particular insights of the applied music faculty into the situation. The distinct character of each professional discipline should be considered in evaluating the role that liberal education should play. There are fundamental differences in the nature of learning as it transpires in the different professions—and, presumably as a re-

[2] In the professional school of which the present writer is a staff member, there will be definite study of the foregoing and related material (as there has already been of parts of it while they were yet in the formative stages) by both faculty members and advanced students concerned with matters of curriculum. It is the author's intention to mimeograph some of the material thus used, and to summarize the results. This will be available on request at the office of the Institute of Higher Education. Anyone interested in using the foregoing study as a means of focusing attention on this professional-liberal problem can see what has been done at one school and can adapt the approach there used to his own situation. *Vice versa,* the writer would be glad to assist in developing any such projects of study elsewhere and to hear of the results and possibly add some account of them to the available mimeographed material.

sult, on the part of those attracted to them. In its beginning stages, music is usually pursued very specifically. There is sheer concentration on the present few minutes taken to perform a piece, and on the immediate split second that binds together the performer and the listener. Later, the student of music begins to reflect on the larger questions of meaning. But the study of music itself proceeds from the part to the whole. The study of journalism, on the other hand, requires the larger aspects first and can leave the details of technique until later. That is why there are sometimes child-prodigy musicians, but never child-prodigy journalists, or nurses. Anyone attempting to initiate and encourage widespread curricular reform must take into account the fundamental difference in the operations of the normal human mind in and through the various symbol systems which it has devised—one of which is music. Usually the applied music faculty member has come closer to this than other members of the professional school faculty.

Also growing out of this investigation is a recommendation that anyone undertaking to help a music school develop a clearer sense of its mission in life realizes that there is a difference between a music school and most of the other professional schools. When anyone who has had the training involved in a school of music (no matter what the particular name happened to be) says "music school," he does not mean just any school where music figures in the curriculum; he means something rather definite by it. To use an analogy, it is like the phrase "short story," which does not mean just a story that happens to be short. There are short narratives that are essays, anecdotes, fables, ballads, and so on. When a person who has had any literary experience says "short story," he means a certain definite thing, with faint images of the work of Poe, DeMaupassant, Chekhov, somewhere in the back of his mind. A "music school" is something in the mind of one who has been through it in a way that a school of journalism or of nursing or of public relations and communications is not.

This is no disparagement of the other professional schools—in fact, many weaknesses of the music school, as such, have been felt more acutely by some great musicians like Berlioz and Debussy than by those who have spent less time in one or who have been less gifted musically. The greater age of the tradition of higher educational institutions in music makes the problem of achieving a right relationship between professional and liberal studies within them a more difficult matter than it is in some other professional schools.

From the data presented, however, a recommendation might be made —one which stands rather in the relationship of an amendment to the foregoing: It must be realized that there has developed and is developing on American soil a unique institution—one in which both the professional training and the nonprofessional education of the students are dealt with seriously by the faculty as a corporate body. This development has gone so far that a return can no longer be made to the relatively simpler forms of sheer professional training or sheer academic training; it cannot be made without involving a whole series of rather alarming regressive tendencies.

4. There is a tendency on the part of music schools to keep the non-music part of their curricula to the lowest possible limit permitted by their professional accrediting agency, and a tendency on the part of the music accrediting agency to set a lower standard in this respect than the accrediting agencies in the other professions. This is a matter that involves more than merely juggling numbers of hours of credit. The entire rationale of the presence of liberal studies in the music curriculum has, in the course of time, become obscured and misunderstood. The purpose of this study has been to provide material that might contribute to a clarification of the matter and to the possible liberalization of the music school program.

Everyone connected with higher education in music should participate, to the best of his ability, in the development of an adequate philosophy of undergraduate education in music that will be generally acceptable. Most of the arguments on either side of the issue of liberal studies have focused on means rather than ends. In sharp contrast to these latter-day leaders, some of the influential figures of the past have had genuine, forceful ideas of the ends they were pursuing. But as of the mid-twentieth century, higher education in music seems—like Dante in the early pages of *The Divine Comedy*—to have wandered off into the woods and become terrified by all sorts of external pressures rather than to have kept its eye on some clear-cut, shining goal.

The responsibility for this sort of clarification and illumination of aims, of course, becomes all the greater as one ascends in the professional hierarchy. The national music associations should have among their leadership persons who could undertake a restatement of the objectives of undergraduate music education with the cogency and persuasiveness of a Lowell Mason or Eben Tourjée or Karl Gehrkens. The whole philosophical and social substructure has, somehow, shifted from under these earlier ideas. There should be objectives of a character and quality as relevant to this latter part of the twentieth century as were these earlier ideas to their own day.

Perhaps a first step toward the development of such a really thorough-going examination of ends rather than means is an awareness that within less than a century the B.M. degree has considerably changed in America. Much of its content has been shifted to the newly developed master's and doctor's degrees. The profession of music also seems to have contracted. Both within the university community and the larger community of modern life—in both the microcosm and the macrocosm—there are signs of a strange isolation, a narrowing professionalism, on the part of musicians, which has gone on despite the wishes of all concerned and despite much public proclamation to the contrary. Which of these two considerations—education for the profession and the state of the profession itself—is cause and which effect, or whether (as is more probable) both are the effects of larger causes, can perhaps not be dwelt upon profitably at this point. The important thing is that, as soon as possible, something be done about whichever one is susceptible of having something done about it.

5.   Consequently, the final recommendation is that the national associations—and, more specifically, the NASM, since it finds itself in the 1960's occupying a position of hitherto unparalleled potential influence in this respect—require the accredited institutions to meet their minimum standards in spirit as well as in fact. The nonprofessional requirements in music schools are pitifully low. Of course, when an individual case comes up for criticism, there can easily be a long argument over how a particular course is to be counted: Is music history, for instance, liberal or professional? The answer adopted in this study is: for a music student, professional; for a law student, liberal. As of 1962, the NASM answer is: You can count it either way—as music history and theory, which is professional, or as "and/or history," which is supposed to be general or liberal. Precisely because of the ambiguity of individual details, both the spirit and the letter of the requirements should be clarified and stressed.

From the present study it seems fairly obvious that the standards promulgated by the accrediting association in music are timid, defensive, and ambiguous. They are not backed up by any positive concept of the music graduate with intellectual and spiritual dimensions far beyond, far more important, than the mere exercise of particular skills. A starting point in the improvement of the situation would be a move by the NASM to require full conformity with its standards in the nonprofessional area and an active campaign for the restoration of the ideal of a genuinely educated musician—a human being who has breadth of sheer subject-matter knowledge, who knows how to think, and who has positive and active values or ideals for which he is working.

The NASM should thoroughly revise its B.M. and B.M.E. requirements before they are reprinted in any kind of complete and up-to-date form. The obvious absurdity of proclaiming one conception of general culture for the music graduate in the stated aims and then proceeding immediately to nullify it by including music courses among the specific examples under that heading should not be allowed in the final printing.

All the music associations and agencies (but particularly the MENC) should do what they can—and even what they perhaps have never felt they could do before—to bring some order into the chaos of state certification of music teachers. Once this area has been set in order, music educators will be free to carry out ideals in which they really believe—with respect to balancing the music and nonmusic portions of the curriculum. Is it possible that too much of the energy of the associations has been expended in recent years on quite lofty but rather remote problems faced by musicians, such as accreditation (and the accreditation of accreditation), "revision of copyright law, international cultural exchange program of the Federal government, the development of the new national Cultural Center in Washington, the recruitment of talented young men and women for the music profession in an age of science"?[3] May we not let the Russians be the first to launch a musician into outer space if they want to do so? Are there not more pressing needs for vigorous action on the part of the associations in dealing with problems quite close to home: teacher certification, ambiguity of degree standards, firmness in enforcing standards once they have been clarified—in general, a clear-eyed re-examination of actual existing programs in music schools by those most deeply involved, and ultimately the adoption of changes to remedy weaknesses that fairly cry out for necessary change, particularly in the nonprofessional part of the work being carried on in these schools?

[3] Thomas Gorton, "President's Report," *NASM Bulletin*, No. 48 (February 1960), p. 16.

SUGGESTED READINGS

The works cited in the foregoing pages, plus those listed below, form a bibliography on liberal education in music schools. A mimeographed copy of a somewhat fuller bibliography, with annotations, may be had on request from the Institute of Higher Education, Teachers College, Columbia University.

BARNETT, DAVID. "The Comparison of the Amateur and the Professional Student," *Proceedings of the Music Teachers National Association for 1948,* 42:71–76, 1950.

COOLIDGE, ARLAN R. "College Degrees in Music: A Study of Opportunities for a Music Major within the A.B. Degree," *Proceedings of the Music Teachers National Association for 1946,* 40:191–209, 1946.

DICKINSON, EDWARD. *Music and the Higher Education.* New York: Charles Scribner's Sons, 1915.

ERB, JOHN LAWRENCE. "The Trend of Professional Education in Music," *Proceedings of the Music Teachers National Association for 1930,* 25:9–20, 1931.

HANSON, HOWARD. "The Eastman Plan and Other Matters," *The Bulletin of the National Association of Schools of Music,* 42:5–9, January 1957.

HINDEMITH, PAUL. *A Composer's World: Horizons and Limitations.* Cambridge: Harvard University Press, 1952.

HOOD, MARGUERITE V. "Teacher Training as Part of College Music Study," *The Bulletin of the National Association of Schools of Music,* 40:20–24, April 1955.

HORN, FRANCIS HENRY. "The Folk-Lore of Liberal Education," *Association of American Colleges Bulletin,* 41:114–120, March 1955.

KESTENBERG, LEO. "Music Education Goes Its Own Way," *The Musical Quarterly,* 25:442–454, October 1939.

McGRATH, EARL J., AND OTHERS. *Toward General Education.* New York: The Macmillan Company, 1948.

MURSELL, JAMES L. *Music Education Principles and Programs.* Morristown, N.J.: Silver Burdett Co., 1956.

SOMMERS, HOBART H. "General Education and the Music Teacher," *Music Educators Journal,* 39:19–21, 42, June–July 1953.

SQUIRE, RUSSEL N. *Introduction to Music Education.* New York: The Ronald Press Co., 1952.

VALENTINE, ALAN. "Music and Reconstruction in American Education," *Proceedings of the Music Teachers National Association for 1946,* 40:17–25, 1946.